THE STRONG AND THE WEAK

THE STRONG
AND
THE WEAK

PAUL TOURNIER

Translated by Edwin Hudson

THE WESTMINSTER PRESS
Philadelphia

First published in English by S C M Press Ltd. in 1963

Translation of *Les Forts et Les Faibles*. Delachaux &
Niestlé, Neuchâtel, Switzerland, 1948

Library of Congress Catalog Card No. 63–8898

TYPESET IN GREAT BRITAIN
Printed in the United States of America

9   8   7   6   5   4   3

To my colleagues and friends
who took part in the first International
Study-Week on the Medicine of the Person
at the Bossey Œcumenical Institute,
in August, 1947,
and especially to those who with me
shared the responsibility for it,
Drs Theo Bovet, Diederik Doyer,
Philippe Kressmann, Alphonse Maeder,
Henri Mentha, and Jean de Rougemont,
I dedicate this book.

If my neighbour is stronger than I, I fear him; if he is weaker, I despise him; if we are equal, I resort to subterfuge. What motive could I have for obeying him, what reason for loving him?

Dr Jean de Rougemont

CONTENTS

Part One

ON BEING HUMAN

Part Two

REACTIONS

Part Three

PSYCHOLOGY AND FAITH

PART ONE

ON BEING HUMAN

APPEARANCE AND REALITY

I HAVE JUST come into a restaurant in order to begin writing this book. While I am taking from my brief-case the plan which I have carefully drawn up, a little scene is being enacted before my eyes—a commonplace scene, but most instructive. The restaurant-keeper's wife is bending over her son, a child two or three years of age, who is stamping and screaming in a tearful tantrum. On the floor at his feet lie some torn scraps of paper. His mother shakes him and repeats over and over again: 'Are you going to pick up those bits of paper? Are you going to pick up those bits of paper?'

The diners all watch placidly. None of them, it seems, expects to see the child stop crying and docilely pick up the paper. Nor, of course, does the mother. The more she shakes him, the more he screams. She is extremely annoyed. Were it not for the spectators, it seems most likely that she would slap her son.

The father is talking to some customers at a table on the pavement outside. To be sure, nothing of what is going on inside escapes him, but he appears to be engrossed in the conversation in which he is taking part. In face of the conflict going on a few paces away from him he adopts an attitude of neutrality, just as many another father in similar circumstances pretends to be reading his newspaper or to be asleep in his armchair. The presence of the diners allows him to affect an air of inattention and to avoid taking sides. Could it be that he does not mind his wife suffering a little humiliation? Or does he presume that if he intervened he would be no more successful than his wife, and so wishes to spare himself a defeat in public? However that may be, the mother's irritation seems to be aggravated by this sort of abdication on the part of the father, and to be directed as much against him as against the child.

Tears are the weapon of the weak. Doubtless the child has already observed that in the restaurant his mother cannot dominate him by force as perhaps she would elsewhere; and that anyway she cannot keep up the struggle until he gives in. The longer the struggle goes on, in fact, the greater the embarrassment of the mother. Her son's resistance humiliates her doubly in public: in the first place, if he does not obey her, that is because she has brought him up badly; if, on the other hand, in spite of the disproportion in their respective strengths she does not succeed in imposing her will on her son, that is because she is weaker than she would like to appear. This feeling of embarrassment aggravates her annoyance with the child. But we are always ashamed of losing our tempers, especially with someone apparently weaker than ourselves. So the irritability of the mother, in its turn, increases her embarrassment; and her defeat will be the more ridiculous the longer the struggle lasts.

In fact, it is this fear of an even more stinging defeat that has brought about the failure of the mother.

Abruptly, therefore, she picks up the paper herself and drags her son out on to the terrace. The child is not strong enough to resist, but he is clearly the victor, since it was his mother who picked up the pieces of paper. So, interrupted by an occasional sob, his calm quickly returns; he takes the hand which his father absently offers him, while his mother disappears into the kitchen to resume her work.

One further remark, which raises an important question: an idealist moralist might maintain that the mother is the real victor, since she overcame her annoyance and obstinacy, and that she deserves credit for putting an end, by her self-sacrifice, to a hopeless struggle. The true moral victory, he might say, lies in the renunciation by the strong of the use of their strength, in their being generous enough to give way to the weak. True enough—and perhaps it is with some such flattering reflection that the mother is consoling herself in her kitchen. But this view does not correspond with the facts. None of the witnesses saw what the mother did as an act of generosity. It is one thing to renounce a victory which could certainly be won. It is quite another to give in because one is not strong enough to win. We are very prone thus to represent to ourselves our defeats as victories, and flight as an act of virtuous renunciation.

There are other considerations in which this mother may seek consolation. For instance, she may say to herself: 'That child is abominably stubborn; he has his father's evil character.' Such a thought makes it agreeably possible for a mother to avoid asking herself whether the obedience she claims is just, and in particular whether the tone of voice in which she demands it is just. Of course it as frequently happens that a father says to his child: 'You have your mother's evil character.' In doing so he is taking a kind of revenge for humiliations inflicted upon him by his wife in the past. But to the child he is dealing a double and terrible blow. In the first place, the child discovers that a wall of rancour and recrimination separates his parents; secondly, there is implanted in his mind at the same time the idea, 'I have an evil character.' Such a thought can easily breed self-doubt, and bids fair to make the child a weakling, both in the struggles of social life and in those which he must wage against himself to master his own character.

So the plan of my book is somewhat altered. But is not this little spectacle more alive than all that I had prepared? It raises the very problem which I wish to tackle, in a way in which it is constantly presented to us. In the space of a few seconds a whole complicated network of conflicting forces has been revealed. In spite of the formidable handicap of his physical weakness in the face of adult strength, the child has won the battle, thanks to the secret alliance of the public and the tacit complicity of the father. At any given moment, when two people are face to face, a sort of balance of power is established. We know intuitively that as it swings from one side to the other it will determine their behaviour towards one another. This does not apply only to open conflicts like that which I have just described, but also to those that are masked and muted. It also applies, moreover, to quite peaceful personal relationships, for example to the mutual influence exercised by husband and wife. The question arises constantly as to which is the dominant partner.

The problem with which we are concerned is thus far wider than that of the antagonism of two opposing wills. The word 'will' suggests certain more or less violent traits of character. But there are people who, without ever being anything but gentle, dominate everyone around them, through the irrefutable logic of their arguments, their moral prestige, the fascination of their beauty, the weight of their reputation, their exquisite manners, or even because they have a fragility and sensitiveness which no one dares to injure. Often a wife will say to me: 'My husband ought to be a lawyer; he always has the last word; I feel powerless to explain myself in front of him; he is always right.' Often a husband will say: 'I have quite given up offering advice to my wife; she asks my opinion, but won't listen to my answer; she sees things as she wants to see them, and nothing will make her take an objective view.' There are parents who grovel before their child; and if one examines the situation carefully one sees that the child has not arrogated power to himself, but has been made king in spite of himself. It is the weakness of doting parents that has conferred upon him his absolute power. And if he gradually becomes self-willed and tyrannical they are more to blame than he is. His character is the consequence, much more than the cause, of the sovereignty he exercises.

There is, too, a certain type of mother who without ever giving her child a categorical order or a blunt refusal brings him up so discreetly that he becomes entirely dependent upon her. He thinks her a saint; he adopts her tastes in everything; he chooses the career, or the wife, that she secretly wants for him; he faces life without defences, because he has relied utterly on his mother to make all his decisions for him. Such a mother would be quite surprised, were she ever to subject herself to a rigorous self-examination, to discover that this prudent solicitude was not so disinterested as she thought, and that behind her high-minded desire to bring him up well and keep him on the right path there lay an unconscious pleasure in maintaining his dependence upon her and playing in his life the providential role that belongs only to God.

In personal relationships what swings the balance to this side or that is, then, a complex of factors so numerous and subtle that it would be impossible ever to assess them all. In the little conflict I have described, I have limited myself to noting those that are most obvious. Doubtless a large number of other conscious and unconscious elements entered into the balance which established the child's victory. The patient work of a psychoanalyst would uncover many more—those connected with the unconscious relations between the father, the mother, and the child, and the relations of each of them with the world, represented by the diners. And that was no more than a still from the uninterrupted film of an historical development in which every episode increases or lessens each actor's chances of victory in the future.

It is the same the world over—in a family, in an administrative council, in a workshop, in a school, in the committee of a charitable organization, between nations. The whole of society is seen to be subject to the interplay of clashing forces, sometimes balancing, and sometimes dominating one another. It is like an infinite series of equations, each expressing the inter-relationships of its members. And each of these equations is composed of many terms, positive as well as negative. Among the positive may figure the prestige of an illustrious name or a fine new car (even if bought on hire-purchase), a university degree or a well-deserved reputation for integrity—or even a reputation as an unscrupulous go-getter. On the other hand, as Adler has clearly demonstrated,[1] among the negative terms may appear the dragging weight of a secret or obvious infirmity, poverty, ignorance, the shame inherited by a child from a despised father, or an exaggerated hunger for affection, which keeps him in a state of

[1] A. Adler, *The Neurotic Constitution*, translated by Bernard Glueck and J. E. Lind, Kegan Paul & Co., London, 1921.

dependence. We are not after all dealing with fixed, dead mathe-matical formulae, but with life, with subtle movements whose course the faintest smile of confidence or sarcasm suffices to modify. The fact that one belongs to this or that party or church may be a mark of authority for one person, but for another it may merit only scorn.

But nothing of this is decisive. One man, who seems to hold all the trumps in his hand, allows himself constantly to be im-posed upon. Another has none, and perhaps for that very reason plays a bold game and dominates everyone around him. What does seem to be the deciding factor is a certain psychological strength which stimulates one man, so that he hides his defects and makes the most of his resources, while another is paralysed by a psychological weakness which makes him miss his oppor-tunities and clumsily reveal his failings.

In the same way a good chess-player can recover his position in an apparently hopeless game by careful placing of his few remaining pieces, so that he mates his opponent before an attack can be pressed home at his weak points, while the opponent's play is encumbered by his own pieces standing uselessly blocking each other.

We are all in the habit of classifying people into two categories, the strong and the weak. There are those who seem doomed to be defeated and trampled upon. They have been so often beaten in this universal free-for-all that they are always expecting it to happen again, and this saps their strength. Those who know them also expect it, and gather strength and assurance for them-selves from the fact. Even a stranger has an immediate intuition of their weakness, and treats them either condescendingly or aggressively—to do either is to humiliate them. On the other hand, the same intuition warns him of the strength of the strong, so that he adopts towards them an attitude of timidity or defer-ence which confirms their strength. *Audaces fortuna juvat*, as the Ancients used to say.

In reality, the facts are more complex: we are all weak towards some and strong towards others. A man who at the office is constantly humiliated by an unjust superior may take his revenge at home by bullying his wife and children. And the superior is perhaps avenging himself in the office for the tyranny exercised over him by his wife at home. In the office the subordinate is paralysed in his defence by the fear of dismissal, and this feeling that he is a coward, sacrificing the justice of his cause to material interest, increases his humiliation, adding to it an element of self-contempt. This in turn increases his irascibility at home. But no one tyrannizes those around him without suffering remorse as a result, and this very feeling of remorse, repressed more often than not, aggravates still further his ill-temper.

One can see how reactions of strength and reactions of weakness are interwoven, so that there develops the twofold progression I mentioned just now: from defeat to defeat, the weak become yet weaker; from victory to victory, the strong become yet stronger. One ends up with the feeling that it is all inevitable—some people seem predestined to success, others to failure.

*   *   *

Can we truly say, then, that there are two kinds of men? What, in the last analysis, is the origin of the marked contrast between the strong and the weak? Are they really so different? Such are the questions that have been in my mind over the last few years, and which I wish to discuss here in the light of my daily observations. It is with a deep sense of its importance that I approach the subject, involving as it does two of the most fundamental problems of our times.

First there is the problem of the neurotics, whose number increases constantly in spite of the prodigious advances made in scientific psychology. It is a fact that these people, for the most part, present an appearance of being weak and overwhelmed by life. They feel they belong to a different race of beings from the strong, who succeed in life. Every doctor can testify to the difficulty of overcoming this sense of defeat and restoring self-confidence to such people. The trouble is that in order to be successful they need confidence, but in order to recover their confidence they need success. What is worse is that this idea of being destined to failure gives them a warped view of themselves and of the world. They exaggerate their failures and the successes of others, and discount their own victories. I spend weeks attempting to encourage a student who has failed his examinations several times. I analyse with him the underlying causes of his inferiority and his apprehensions. He regains a measure of self-assurance, and passes his examination. I am overjoyed, and expect to see him proud and happy at last. I believe the game has been won. Nothing of the kind: he is convinced that the examiner has awarded him a pass-mark out of pity, that all his comrades were better prepared than he, that in life he will be all the more likely to disappoint people who will expect him to have knowledge which he does not possess.

But this question of the strong and the weak touches the whole problem of our society, and, in the last analysis of war and peace as well. War between nations, between coalitions of nations, between parties and coalitions of parties, is merely the final consequence and supreme expression of the universal conflict which I have described. If weakness leads to a sense of failure, strength too has its vicious circle: one must go on being stronger and stronger for fear of suffering an even more crushing defeat, and this race in strength leads humanity inevitably to general collapse.

For this reason I am writing not only to bring some hope to the weak, but also for the strong, who all feel vaguely that the victories which they must constantly be trying to win for fear of being themselves defeated, sustain the atmosphere of violence, the nervous tension, the threat of catastrophe under which we live in the modern world.

I believe that there is a great illusion underlying both the despair of the weak and the unease of the strong—and the misfortune of both. This great illusion is the very notion that there are two kinds of human beings, the strong and the weak.

The truth is that human beings are much more alike than they think. What is different is the external mask, sparkling or disagreeable, their outward reaction, strong or weak. These appearances, however, hide an identical inner personality. The external mask, the outward reaction, deceive everybody, the strong as well as the weak. All men, in fact, are weak. All are weak because all are afraid. They are all afraid of being trampled underfoot. They are all afraid of their inner weakness being discovered. They all have secret faults; they all have a bad conscience on account of certain acts which they would like to keep covered up. They are all afraid of other men and of God, of themselves, of life and of death.

Even the most gifted, even those who claim to be surest of themselves, have a vague feeling that their reputation does not correspond to reality, and they are fearful of the fact being observed. The most learned professor is afraid of being questioned on something he does not know. The most brilliant psychologist is afraid of being found to be the slave of some commonplace complex. The most eloquent theologian is afraid that the doubts that still haunt him will be guessed at. All know that their close acquaintances have discovered in their private lives failings which have escaped their crowds of admirers. All feel the mystery of life to be much deeper than they make out, and that what tomorrow has in store may suddenly reveal their weakness. What distinguishes men from each other is not their inner nature, but the way in which they react to this common distress.

I am driving my car: if there are some pigeons on the road I have no need to brake; I know that fear is their safeguard, and that they will fly away just in time to avoid being run over. But if I see hens on the road I take care, for I know that fear makes them panic, so that they are liable to rush straight under the car wheels.

Similarly among human beings there are two opposing types of reactions to the same inner distress: strong reactions and weak reactions.

Let us take the case of two pupils who each know one half of what they ought to know and are ignorant of the other half. One, obsessed by the gaps in his knowledge, remains dumb even when questioned on what he knows. Inwardly, he bitterly reproaches himself for his panic, and this inner conflict paralyses him all the more. He sees himself already as a subject of shame to his parents, and this thought so completely occupies his mind that he remains deaf to the kindly attempts of the examiner to give him a chance to rescue himself from failure. His comrade, on the other hand, is no less conscious of his ignorance, but danger acts as a spur to him. Even when questioned on a matter he does not know he throws himself boldly into a brilliant exposition which cleverly turns on to the topics with which he is more conversant. The feeling that victory is within his grasp imparts a sort of elation which increases still further his assurance and his intellectual energy, so that he finds the slightest detail of his knowledge ready to hand.

It is obvious that these reaction-mechanisms count in practice for more than the true value of the knowledge of the respective candidates. One has turned his 50 per cent. into 100 per cent., while the other sees his 50 per cent. estimated at nil. The result might be the same even if the 'weak' pupil went into the examination much better prepared than the 'strong' one. It is important to note that both are afraid of failing, but only one of them shows it, since their reactions to this same fear are quite different. Thus it is that what differentiates men in any given circumstance is their differing response to an identical anxiety.

The strong reaction is to give ourselves an appearance of assurance and aggressiveness in order to hide our weakness, to cover up our own fear by inspiring fear in others, to parade our virtues in order to cloak our vices.

The weak reaction is to become flustered, and thus to reveal the very weakness we want to hide; it is to allow our consciousness of our weakness to prevent us from bringing into play the concealment-reactions which permit the strong to dissimulate their weakness.

I have to admit that in this respect the weak always seem to me to be more honest than the strong. The strong, in fact, end up by deluding themselves. Always hiding their weakness from others, they end up by failing to recognize it themselves. They repress it without eliminating it. They retain, so to speak, an unconscious consciousness of their weakness, which brings in its train further concealment-reactions.

The weak, on the contrary, are hyperconscious of their weakness. That is why they have the appearance of being ill, failures, overwhelmed by life. The strong are not ill, but they make society ill through the fearful operation of their reactions.

The weak allow themselves to be crushed because they believe in the strength of the strong, not seeing that it is a cloak for weakness. The strong crush the weak in order to gain assurance from their triumph.

In reality we all react strongly or weakly, according to circumstances, but in varying degree. Sometimes, in fact, a weak reaction, such as an attack of nerves, represents a supreme weapon which is brought into play for want of strong weapons. Such was the case with the child we were considering just now, whose tears—a weak reaction—ensured his victory. At the other end of the scale a strong reaction such as anger never quite succeeds in cloaking the weakness it betrays. The subject himself always realizes this to some extent, and this projects him into a further train of strong reactions, of increasing violence.

So then strong reactions—the thump of the fist on the table, for instance—are an admission of weakness; and weak reactions are an indication that some power of reaction still remains. A touchy and impulsive wife heaps abuse upon her husband at the slightest difference of opinion. It is as if a sluice-gate had suddenly been opened to let through a rushing torrent. A flood of old grievances is released. The husband, on the contrary, reacts weakly in such circumstances: he is benumbed and speechless, overcome by inexpressible fatigue. But this reaction is one more method of defence. His wife is well aware of this, finding his obstinate silence irritating in the extreme. For all her shouting the victory will not be hers so long as she fails to break down this wall of silence.

'Why don't you answer me, instead of sitting there like a moron!' she screams at him. She threatens to divorce him. He thinks of suicide, the supreme weak reaction—though it too is a weapon, for the thought really means: 'Perhaps on my grave she will be sorry for the wrong she has done me.'

In spite of appearances, strong and weak reactions are closely related. This fact is more easily recognized if we observe how one can pass rapidly from one to the other. That silent husband may rise to his feet in a flash and strike his wife. She may as rapidly pass from her state of ungoverned passion to one of utter depression. Husband and wife will have changed weapons. Now it is he who talks of divorce, and she of suicide. About-turns of this sort are frequent in politics, where they always occasion acute astonishment.

Once again I have given an example of sharp conflict, but in reality a subtle interplay of strong reactions (veiled criticisms, mild irony, imperceptible bluff) and weak reactions (restrained admiration, delicate flattery, apparent acquiescence) forms the texture of a thousand and one social, intellectual, and commercial relationships. Clearly, strong and weak reactions are less antithetical than one would think; both are signs of the same fundamental distress, common to all men. And both, though by means of different mechanisms, lead to the same result: the crushing of the weak and universal war, until the strong themselves are crushed beneath the ruins they have heaped up.

*   *   *

A mother envelops her two daughters in a possessive and tyrannical love. Convinced that she is acting for their good, she arrogates to herself the right to direct every detail of their conduct, to preserve them from all the dangers and harmful influences of the world.

One of the daughters, generally the elder, responds to this maternal domination with weak reactions. She submits, loses all initiative, becomes hesitant and over-scrupulous. She takes up no career, becoming her mother's domestic servant. She gives up having a life of her own, renouncing all independence. Her submissiveness encourages the tyranny of her mother, who nevertheless, in spite of all her efforts, finds occasion to reproach her. She has an increasing terror of these complaints, and becomes more and more docile and distressed. She is dominated by the power of mental suggestion; she is afraid of men, of sex, of love, of life. She takes refuge in a dream-world. Her growing sense of 'spoiling her life' accentuates this tendency, which makes her even more embarrassed in face of reality, and more dependent on her mother.

The second daughter, on the other hand, responds with strong reactions. While still quite young she stands up against her mother's pretensions, and rebels. The latter is affronted by her impertinence, and in order to break her tries to tighten the screw of constraint.

Mother and daughter face each other in a still unequal combat which drives each to accentuate her position. In order to defy her mother, the daughter makes a show of going out, and mixes with young men of doubtful reputation. One day her mother comes upon her unexpectedly, and heaps abuse upon her. It is the last straw. The daughter leaves the house, slamming the door behind her. In order to bring her to her senses the mother refuses to give her any money. The daughter learns to manage for herself, and finds some means of support. She suffers cruelly, too, but she acquires a maturity which is in marked contrast with the infantile attitude of her elder sister. She slaves at her work to make a career for herself and become independent. She has affairs with men, and learns to profit from their weaknesses. Soon she is saying to her sister: 'You are a ninny—it's your own fault that you are spoiling your life. Do as I do—break loose, have a will of your own!' These reproaches only increase the elder sister's lack of confidence in herself, while the younger sister finds satisfaction in repeating them in order to persuade herself that she is in the right, in spite of her uneasy conscience.

Naturally the mother seeks compensation and consolation in the daughter that remains devoted to her. She showers her with complaints about her unworthy sister. She awakens her pity, her eagerness to comfort her and her limitless devotion. But the mother is inconsolable, for nothing her elder daughter does can wipe out the offences of the younger. Then the confused, repressed anguish of the elder—the inevitable result of a thwarted affective impulse—crystallizes into obsessions. From then on she feels ill, and therefore unable to face the struggle of the world, in which the victory always goes to the strong and the wicked. And when she consults the psychiatrist—the supreme confirmation of her social failure—she accuses herself of weakness, cowardice, and lack of love towards her mother.

Meanwhile, impelled by an unconscious impulse to get further away from her mother, the younger daughter goes abroad. Unexpected opportunities come her way, and she makes a brilliant career for herself. She does indeed have an occasional qualm about having hurt her mother, but such feelings she promptly represses, submerging them under the flood of her own grievances. Dr Baruk has admirably described[1] the mechanism of aggressiveness resulting from repression of the moral conscience. The strong can be caught in the awful toils of their own reactions, just as can the weak. A strong reaction leads to unjust and violent acts which leave behind them a painful feeling of guilt. This guilt feeling is then repressed, giving place to redoubled annoyance directed against the victim of the violent action. This is the origin of the preventive type of attack which plays such an important part in every human relationship, recalling the fable of the wolf and the lamb. When we are in the wrong we make the first move, resorting to abuse or outright attack, or at the very least we nurse our private criticisms. But this attitude is not unmixed with some feeling of guilt, which in turn is masked by further and more far-reaching feelings of aggressiveness. Caught thus in the toils of her reactions, our emancipated younger sister overcomes every obstacle in her path. She has become a strong woman, repressing every feeling of pity and imposing her will on all and sundry.

[1] Henri Baruk, *Psychiatrie morale expérimentale, individuelle et sociale*, Presses Universitaires de France, Paris, 1945.

She despises her sister, who for her part secretly admires her. She dazzles a weak man, who is seeking refuge in her strength. She marries him and crushes him in her turn. Later on she will adopt a domineering attitude towards her own children, so great is her constant need to demonstrate that she is right.

You see how it works: one of the daughters is weak and ill. The other is not ill, but the chain of her strong reactions makes her a source of infection for others. One has repressed her 'aggressiveness' and turned it inward against herself; she is a prey to doubt, burdened with scruples and self-accusation; she represses into her subconscious her rancour against her mother, who has ruined her life, and compensates this unconscious rancour with anguished devotion.

But the other daughter has repressed her conscience, her warmth of heart, her femininity. She must constantly be winning new victories in order to maintain this unstable equilibrium. In reality neither of the daughters is free. They are captives, the one of her weak reactions, the other of her strong reactions and their ineluctible evolution. True strength, however, lies in being free. You will understand therefore why I affirmed earlier that the strong and the weak are less unlike than they seem. Both bear within them the same distress, the common source of their false reactions, strong and weak.

Neurosis, shyness, feelings of inferiority, lack of self-confidence, hypersensitivity, pathological feelings of guilt, emotional instability, obsessions, panic, functional disturbances, indecision, and depression are the expression of weak reactions. In their turn, all these unhealthy manifestations maintain in the subject a feeling of weakness which provokes him to further weak reactions.

But what of strong reactions? Are they not the domain of the moralist and the sociologist, rather than the doctor? By no means. Certainly their immediate fruits are social and political conflicts, social injustice, violence, intolerance, calumny, vengeance, cruelty and war. But there is something more. We may well find that the daughter who rebelled, and whose good health forms such a marked contrast with her sister's neurosis, falls a victim to one of the relentless diseases which attack the strong: high blood pressure, arteriosclerosis, rheumatoid arthritis, or cancer. This is indeed a delicate and complex problem, which I do not claim to be able to settle with a stroke of the pen, but which ought to be raised. It merits serious scientific investigation, as yet scarcely begun. Such a study would go far to revolutionize modern medical thinking.

In order to understand it we must conceive of the human person as a unity. These strong and weak reactions of which I have been speaking are not only psychological. They are reactions of the entire person, in which the body participates equally with the mind. The reader will be well aware of this, having doubtless had a mental picture, as he read my account, of the difference in the physical appearance of the two sisters: the one neurotic, asthenic, thin, morose, pale, her hands emaciated, her blood pressure low, her vegetative nervous system unstable; her sister powerfully built, her head held high, healthy-looking, her complexion florid, her blood pressure high.

In their studies of morphology Kretschmer,[1] Sigaud,[2] Allendy,[3] Carton,[4] Corman,[5] and others have stressed these psychophysical correlations. Whatever the precise terms they employ, they all classify men as strong or weak. The strong reaction is not only a reaction of the character; it is also a reaction of the body, an exaltation of its vitality, which expresses itself in the first place in physical well-being. I have no doubt that evidence of it could be found in the vigorous stimulation of the chemical metabolism of the tiniest cell in the organism.

However, although a supercharged engine has a high output, it wears out rapidly. In the same way it is not with impunity that one is led, through one strong reaction after another, constantly to mobilize all the physical and mental resources of one's organism.

[1] E. Kretschmer, *Physique and Character*, translated by W. J. H. Sprott, Kegan Paul & Co., London, 1936.
[2] Claude Sigaud, *La forme humaine*, Maloine, Paris, 1914.
[3] René Allendy, *Les tempéraments*, Vigot, Paris, 1922.
[4] Paul Carton, *Diagnostic et conduite des tempéraments*, Le François, Paris, 1926.
[5] L. Corman, *Quinze leçons de morphopsychologie*, Nantes, 1937.

The experienced doctor knows this well. One patient, sickly, suffering from one indisposition after another, always coming to see him about some new functional disorder, will live on for years and years, while his vigorous brother, who boasts of never having a day's illness and of not coddling himself, will be suddenly laid low by some serious disease.

It would seem that there are 'weak' maladies and 'strong' maladies. At first sight the former seem to be mainly functional, nervous, and psychological, whereas the latter seem to be organic and unyielding. But they are both maladies of the whole person, which has its own way of reacting to life. Strong reactions and weak reactions are both psychosomatic.

One point is worthy of note here, by way of illustration. It is observable that nervous, sensitive people also have a very fragile capillary system; they bruise at the slightest blow. I have just this moment received a note from a patient of this type. 'Why, is it,' she writes, 'that I often have black and blue marks without having bumped into anything?' During the recent study-conference at Bossey on the medicine of the person, Professor Vogelsang proposed that in order to throw light on the problem of man's psychsomatic unity vigorous research should be carried out into the delicate anatomical and physical connections between the nerve ends and those of the capillaries.

We see, then, how the moral and the physical problems are interwoven. The doctor observes two opposite forms of psychosomatic reaction. Some of his patients have little defence against either pathological agents or social aggression. Their physical and psychic ills tend to be chronic, the one bringing on the other. Their physical debility determines their psychological weakness, and their psychological and social failures provoke fresh physical disturbances as the expression of their weak reactions. No sooner are they cured of one malady than another makes its appearance. They are caught in an ever more complex web of successive problems.

Other subjects on the contrary have vigorous reactions. To them they owe prolonged and robust health, physical as well as psychic. Everything seems simple to them. They set themselves up as an example to their weaker brethren, mortifying them with the challenge they fling at them from the height of their superior health. If they fall ill, it is a question of some serious disease, of a paroxysmal crisis in which their vigorous defence clashes with the pathological agent. They either recover promptly or prematurely succumb. These two types, speaking generally at least, are opposites both in psychic and in physical health. Think for example of the acute mania which attacks the cyclothymic, so uncomplicated in character compared with the subtle complexity of neurosis.

Socially, the strong go from success to success. Everything seems easy to them. They do not even notice that the price of their victory is often the tears of others, and a host of injustices which may one day lead both them and society to some sudden catastrophe.

It is the weakness of the weak which encourages the strong in their headlong course, and it is the strong appearance of the strong which fosters the apprehensiveness of the weak.

In any workshop you care to enter you will find the 'smart' workers, who know how to get themselves the easiest tasks that are soonest done, and who, not being over-scrupulous, do not lose themselves in a mass of detail, and so get on quickly. They are much appreciated by their overseers, earn more money, are held in honour, and marked out for advancement. Their success stimulates and fosters their ambition. Beside them, on the other hand, the rest are left straining futilely in the constant efforts they must make to control themselves, an effort which is never appreciated at its true value. They themselves underrate it: their scrupulosity prompts them always to find fault with their own work. They waste time by starting it all over again, and consider themselves incompetent. They imagine that the smart ones are the better workers, which is not the case. They take a dislike to the factory in which they work, and their discouragement reduces their output still further, or else they go from factory to factory, their lives disjointed and unsatisfying.

*　　　*　　　*

But all these reactions are only a façade. The fundamental problem of all men is the moral distress which they hide under these strong or weak attitudes. Psychological salvation consists in causing the weak to go over to the camp of the strong. The doctrine of aggressiveness developed by Freudian psycho-analysts is well known: neurosis originates in the repression of natural aggressiveness, and morality and religion are merely social constraints which crush the individual, depriving him of his weapons and making him in advance the loser in the battle of life. Perhaps the psychiatrist consulted by our neurotic daughter will succeed in inculcating her with his doctrine. He will have no difficulty in making her discover in her dreams the evidence of a fierce rancour against her mother. In order to cure her he will help her to realize and admit it. I am far from decrying this treatment, which may be a necessary stage. The sick must be treated. And the daughter will be more honest towards herself when she in her turn stands up to her mother as her sister does, than when she weakly submitted to her domination.

I have seen many neurotics thus pass as a result of a course of psychoanalysis from the camp of the weak to that of the strong, and thereby they are cured in the clinical sense. This is indeed a worthwhile result, at least for the subject, if not for the old mother who is at a loss to understand the flood of grievances poured out upon her by her child. But it is clear that the change that has taken place is only in the reactions of the person, and not at the deeper level of the person itself. Such patients have gone from repression of aggressiveness to repression of the conscience. They have not resolved the fundamental inner conflict of the person. It is merely being translated into a different type of reaction. This fundamental conflict is one in which our aggressive instinct is ranged against our moral conscience, our need to express our personality against the restraining influence not only of society or the will of others, but also of our own judgement of good and evil. It is in that deep-seated conflict that the human drama consists. It is the cause of the intimate malaise which we saw to be lying at the root of strong as well as weak reactions.

This, in my view, is the link between the medical and social problem of man and his moral and spiritual problem. The fundamental conflict which I have just described is the great human fact, which cannot be burked. Two forces confront each other in man: the need to live as if he were alone, to brush aside everything which stands in the way of his growth and his ambition to dominate others and make them the docile instruments of his power or to crush them if they resist; and a moral conscience no less powerful, which penalizes every unjust act with ineffaceable remorse, the need to love and be loved, an intuitive sense of the divine order which sets harmonious limits to the living-space of each person in nature and society. If men are all weak, that is because they all feel themselves torn between these two forces, and powerless to resolve the resultant inner conflict.

The majority manage after a fashion by means of compromise —a mixture of strong and weak reactions. Turn and turn about according to circumstances, they press home an attack or beat a retreat. They elbow their way forward just so far as the moral conventions, the law, and public opinion allow. They have fits also of kind-heartedness, and conscientious scruples, so long as these do not compromise their essential interests.

The strong and weak reactions which we have studied mark two opposite positions: that of silencing one's own conscience and one's feelings in order to give free play to one's vital instinct, and that of blocking the instinct and allowing oneself to be crushed by others. As extreme positions, they are pathological; and both destroy the harmony of the person. They lead on the one hand to the maladies of the weak (to tuberculosis or neurosis, for example), and on the other to the maladies of the strong, such as those organic diseases of attrition which I have mentioned, or to the 'lucid madness' described in Dr Baruk's book,[1] where he uses the expression in reference to typical cases of repression of the moral conscience, animated by a formidable and unscrupulous dynamism which can lead to political and social disaster.

But neither extreme solutions—whether strong or weak—nor

[1] Op. cit.

compromises between them afford to man the profound healing he needs. Compromise will not bring deliverance from the obscure anguish caused by the conflict within him. Even if the law and the moral conventions of society do not, his own conscience accuses him of many a secret fault; and even when through cowardice he has chosen to show generosity, he feels ill at ease in the knowledge that he has acted only out of weakness.

I have described in the elder sister the extreme attitude of the weak. Far from putting an end to the inner conflict it exacerbates it. The instinct of life cannot be destroyed; one can turn it against oneself, but it will not be silenced. It gnaws on inside us, accentuating our malaise and provoking further weak reactions.

The extreme strong attitude—that of the younger sister—invigorates the individual, but it too does nothing to resolve his inner conflict, since the moral conscience is as indestructible as the vital instinct. We cannot entirely silence our conscience or our feelings, though we can repress them. They then become the unconscious source of a series of strong reactions aimed at hiding them, but which only make the repression worse.

Thus in both the strong and the weak the inner conflict remains unresolved. Proof of this is the need, common to both, to reassure themselves by adopting certain beliefs and passionately defending them. The weak are pacifist, idealist, utopian; they set up their weakness as a virtue and vainly denounce the injustices of the world without daring to combat them. The strong believe in the will to power, the superman, war, and progress through struggle; they are materialists and realists. The doctrine of aggression has no more fanatical proselytes than former neurotics who have gone over to the side of the strong as a result of a course of psychoanalysis. Their ardour betrays the torment of their suppressed moral conscience. So true is it that all men feel the need to justify their conduct by the beliefs they profess, and to convert others to them in order to persuade themselves of their value.

True inner healing is not to be found either in weak or in strong reactions, since it depends on a real solution of the fundamental conflict. It is not to be found on the level of psychology, but only in the realm of the spirit. For God has given us our instincts as well as our moral conscience. That is why both are indestructible. God alone harmonizes them, when man obeys him.

Though psychological salvation consists in crossing over from one camp to the other, religious salvation lies in the rediscovery of the divine purpose, in which the instinct of life and the moral conscience each have the proper function in the person for which they were designed by God. No doubt that purpose is never fully realized in this world. But case after case has shown that the road to health both for the person and for society lies in a genuine experience of the grace of God. Such an experience delivers the weak from the toils of their weak reactions, and the strong from the vicious circle of their strong reactions. It restores the courage of the weak and breaks the pride of the strong. The weak man is reconciled with life, with himself, with his sexuality, with his instincts; the strong man hears the voice of his conscience, and is given a new and different strength, the strength that comes of the recognition of the secret weakness he has been concealing under his appearance of strength. It helps the weak to discern the cowardice in what they thought to be generosity, and the strong to recognize the injustice in what they claimed to be their rights.

Let us look again at the two sisters. If it is given them to experience this decisive encounter with Jesus Christ, we shall see the elder become sincere with herself once more, admitting her rancour against her mother, and forgiving her. She will thus be liberated from her weak reactions without going to the opposite extreme represented by the strong reactions of aggressiveness. We shall see the younger asking forgiveness of God and her mother—and this will be in no sense a weak reaction, but, on the contrary, freed from remorse she will find inner peace and love for her mother.

As their experience of God's grace increases, in spite of frequent returns to the old natural reactions, we shall see the elder assert herself more and more, and the younger become gradually gentler.

All this is true not only of extreme cases and acute conflicts such as I have used as examples for the sake of clarity. In every social relationship, in fact, there arises the question as to which party is going to have more influence on the other. In every social relationship there is a confrontation of wills, each setting limits to the other. This is so whether they clash in conflict, or whether each, confident that he is in the right, seeks by more kindly means to win the other to his point of view. In every social relationship, therefore, all three attitudes are possible: the weak reaction which passively submits, renouncing all attempt to influence the other; the strong reaction which tries by pressure, either violent or gentle, to have its way; and thirdly the God-directed way, the harmonizing of the two wills through their submission to his divine will, which marks their just limits.

I know, for example, a married couple who are believers, intelligent, full of good will and the desire to understand each other. But they are radically different in temperament. The husband is of a passive, contemplative nature; his wife is strong and active. The powerful and tragic interplay of their respective reactions, strong and weak, has brought many difficulties to their married life. In spite of the good qualities that each possesses, this has been an obstacle to true union. Nevertheless the wife did not try to dominate her husband, or at least not consciously. She wanted to help him; she urged him to be more enterprising, to open out, to make more of himself. But the result was the opposite. Under this pressure, affectionate though it was, the husband felt himself inferior and misunderstood; he retired further into his shell, and seemed drained of energy. At heart, each hoped the other would change.

Today I have received a letter in which they tell me of the change which the experience of God's grace has wrought in their lives. While at her prayers the wife realized that God was asking her to renounce the pressure to which she was subjecting her husband 'in a spirit of impatience, self-pity, and reprisal', she remarks. As for the husband, he has seen that he must stop 'taking so readily to heart the things that upset him'.

Now at last the atmosphere between them has changed. The

voice of God has delivered both the husband from his weak reaction and the wife from her strong reaction, reactions each of which fostered the other. The power of prayer has rescued them both from the blind inflexible mechanism of their natural reactions, lifting them to a new plane of real unity in the harmonious diversity of their complementary temperaments. They joyfully add: 'It is no longer a question of changing each other—but of changing ourselves, with God's help.'

2

THE DEFEATED

WHAT WE HAVE said so far raises the question as to the cause of this diversity of reaction in different people. How is it that to the same inner anguish some react strongly and others weakly, the former taking pride in a deceptive health and strength, while the latter find their way to the doctor defeated by life?

Defeated. How often have I heard that word spoken by those who come to tell me of their sufferings! 'I have spoilt my life. Ten years ago you could have helped me; now it is too late.' Crushed by all the misfortunes which have broken them, by the succession of disasters which life has brought them, they feel that these things are somehow inevitable, that they are living under some sort of curse. They expect only fresh catastrophes. They spoil everything they touch, they darken the lives of those they love; they blame themselves, and this gives them a bad conscience which aggravates the awkwardness of their reactions. They are the 'black sheep' of the family. They feel that happiness is not for them. Everything goes wrong for them—sex, marriage, work, their efforts, their judgement. They are crushed by life, by society, by money, by morality, and, worse still, by the very people who wish to help them and try to put them right, who call them selfish, proud, over-sensitive, hypocritical, or perverse. They are crushed by the element of criticism in all this advice, and by social, moral, and religious formalism. They fight against it with the energy of despair, rushing headlong against the barricades, only to fail once more and so draw fresh criticism upon themselves.

What is even more tragic is that they are crushed even when someone seeks to help them with kindness and love. The pity they inspire in such a person humiliates them. His solicitude only makes them feel their abject state more keenly. I myself have often noticed how the weak reactions of my patients become more pronounced and more numerous just when they are beginning to feel that their condition is being understood.

I am talking to a woman who has always felt unwanted in her family, who has doubted her parents' affection, felt herself weaker than her brothers and sisters. Going from one weak reaction to another, she has finally fallen victim to an obsessional neurosis. Between her and me there is an obvious disproportion which contributes to her sense of defeat. In our inmost selves each of us is as wretched as the other; but this she cannot believe. She considers that she is the one who has failed, and that her doctor has been successful. She is the patient, needing help; I am the doctor, giving it. Our exchange of views seems to her to be all in one direction, even though I am learning a lot from it. To her it is like a lesson. My reputation, my professional knowledge, even my faith, prevent her from feeling herself my equal, and so she cannot believe that God loves her as much as he does me—he loves her more, since he has a particular care for the sick and the outcast. It is only because of my need that God is gracious towards me, but she thinks that it is because I deserve it, whereas she dare not even pray to him. Thus her feeling of inferiority towards me is projected even into the spiritual sphere, and deprives her of the religious experience which would deliver her from it. She thinks herself unworthy to take up so much of a busy man's time, as if my job in life were not precisely that. The more time I devote to her, the greater her fear of disappointing me after I have taken so much trouble, and the more this possibility promotes her lack of self-confidence. 'Why don't you attend to your other patients, who will give you more satisfaction than I can?' she says, at the very moment when she most needs attention.

Thus the weak can be crushed both by criticism and censure, and by understanding and kindness, while others stand firm both under criticism and when treated with affection.

The weak are sensitive and emotional; but is their liability to emotionalism the cause or the result of their failures? In any case, they are usually subjected successively to pity and to censure. Is their trouble one of nerves, or one of character? The question is a futile one, constantly asked and never resolved, because there is some truth in each of its terms. In order to remain neutral and open to all the aspects of the problem, let us call their trouble one of affectivity.

Affectivity—joy and sadness, enthusiasm and dejection, confidence and despair, imagination and mental inhibition—is a complex, delicate, and powerful force, easier to name than to define. It seems to me to have been given originally to man for his good; that is, as a guide to the fulfilment of his destiny. Each step towards that end normally calls forth its positive aspects; each step in the contrary direction, its negative aspects. This is why it is such a powerful force, governing, in fact, the whole of man's behaviour.

When it is disturbed, it provides no sure guidance, creating only disorder and paradoxical reactions. It is just when he is entering upon the right course that the nervous person is most beset by anxiety. He is led to act—and is often conscience-stricken as a result—in precisely the way that will draw down upon himself the ills from which he suffers. He loses his way like a man in a hall of mirrors, who cannot find the way out, seeing only his own reflection, multiplied to infinity. His panic increases his confusion. He feels powerless, defeated.

But once again we ask what is the origin of this disturbance. Have such people been destined to defeat even from the cradle— as they themselves often think—owing to an inborn tendency to weak reactions? Or is the disorder of their affectivity due rather to the adverse circumstances of their life? Or again, have both factors—the innate and the accidental—diabolically conspired together? I think that this last is the case.

At the beginning of this century all nervous troubles were thought to be due to organic lesions, sometimes accessible to scientific investigation, sometimes not. Since then the analytical school has shown the extreme importance of accidental psychological factors, of emotional shocks suffered during infancy, of complexes and conflicts. I cannot study here the genesis of weak reactions without going more thoroughly into the affective mechanisms which have been revealed to us by the psychoanalysts. But it also seems to me that, carried away by the enthusiasm engendered by their discoveries, the latter have in their turn failed to pay due regard to one aspect of the problem of nervous troubles. Large numbers of children suffer brutal and premature revelations of a sexual nature, are maltreated by fathers jealous of the affection lavished on them by their mothers, are persecuted by unjust teachers at school, without for that reason turning into neurotics. Many, indeed are on the contrary stimulated and hardened by such experiences. My story of the two sisters is an example of this.

We constantly come across neurotics whose condition is due to harmful suggestions received during infancy, but their brothers and sisters are not neurotic. On the contrary, they have reacted vigorously to the same suggestions, and have developed strong and self-reliant personalities. I have just seen a girl whose history is as tragic as that of the two sisters. Born before the marriage of her parents, she was entrusted to the care of strangers who maltreated her. Her parents suddenly took her back when they married. They were almost unknown to her, and she felt lost with them. Soon her parents began to quarrel and to be unfaithful to each other. The child lived among scenes of violence, and was used as the scapegoat in these family quarrels, until her parents were divorced. Then she lived once more with strangers who exploited her. She at last found a little affection in a new family, but very soon these adoptive parents were divorced as well! The only light that had ever begun to shine in the darkness of her life was transformed into a devastating conflagration. In adolescence she was taken back by her mother, now living with a lover, who soon began to persecute her out of jealousy, because the lover showed her too much affection. Her father took to drink and could do nothing to help her.

Now this girl, far from being crushed by all her misfortunes, was stimulated by them. She reacted strongly. While still quite young she went right away; and she made good: she found herself a good job, and now at the age of only twenty she is successfully earning her own living; she knows how to defend herself against importunate men, and has great plans for the future. Now she wants to travel, and has come to ask my advice.

It is the sick who go to see the psychiatrist; and he, as soon as he discovers emotional shocks in their childhood, sees in them the cause of their neurosis. He less often has the opportunity of examining the other type of person, who has also had such experiences without falling ill as a result.

The psychological traumas of childhood, in which psychoanalysts see the cause of neurosis, have therefore a real importance but not a decisive one. There is another factor involved, which we may describe as that of the terrain. This terrain is in fact the person's psychosomatic make-up, his inborn predisposition to weak reactions. Thus, after the period of organicist theories of neurosis, and after that of psychoanalytic theories, we must now, I believe, seek a satisfactory explanation on the basis of a psychosomatic conception. The neurotic does not feel himself understood by a materialist doctor who fails to recognize the importance of moral factors in the genesis of his condition: the sufferings he has undergone, the affronts he has borne, the tyrannies that have crushed him, the remorse that has sapped his strength, the disappointments he has experienced. Neither does he feel himself understood when his doctor, on the other hand, fails to recognize the part played by the innate factor. For the patient himself feels intuitively that a certain inborn disposition in his physical and psychic constitution has led him to react differently from other people to the shocks and difficulties of life, to allow himself to be defeated where others have been strengthened.

I once treated a melancholic who had been under a number of psychiatrists one after the other. He told me of the immense relief he had experienced when the last of these had finally frankly explained to him that there was in him a natural inborn disposition towards depression, for which he was not responsible, and which he must always take courageously into account.

It is only those, then, whose temperament predisposes them to defeat who allow themselves to be crushed. This is no longer a purely psychological problem; it is a medical, a psychosomatic problem—a problem of the person. Dr Widal has made a similar observation in regard to allergical affections: 'Sensitivity is a matter of the will.'[1]

A woman feels herself defeated by life. Psychological analysis reveals the part played in this by her mother, a strong and noble personality, who has dominated her, thwarted her desires and her vocation. As a result the daughter has a feeling of being paralysed by her mother, of being prevented by her from living freely. But when the mother dies she does not act any more freely, and is as crushed as before. She exhibits a sickly constitution. In spite of every effort she fails to put on weight, to improve her blood pressure, the condition of her heart or her digestion, and her neuritic pains continue.

If then in order to understand neurosis we must with Freud take into account the importance of accidents in the patient's psycho-sexual development, with Adler his psycho-social development, and with Jung his psycho-spiritual development, we cannot, like them, see in such accidents the sole cause of the disease. Borrowing a formula from the mathematicians we shall say that psychological traumas and pathogenic complexes constitute a necessary but not a sufficient factor. For the disease to break out there must be in addition a certain disposition to weak reactions, which has its basis in the psychosomatic temperament.

The question then is, what is the reciprocal part played by the two overlapping factors? How much is inevitable and how much is curable? And, finally, what is the nature of the innate factor?

The latter, is, I believe, psychosomatic, and doubtless depends on what are nowadays called the genes: on the physical side a certain constitutional debility; on the psychological side a high coefficient of sensitivity and liability to emotional excitement.

[1] See Pierre Salet, *Les livres de Confucius*, Payot, Paris, 1923.

Let this terrain be the scene of psycho-sexual, psycho-social, or psycho-spiritual traumas, and they will give rise to weak reactions. The more serious and numerous these traumas are, the more marked the reactions will be. Physically weaker and psychologically more sensitive than other people, these subjects will regularly respond with weak reactions. The weak reactions will in turn undermine their physical powers of resistance and increase their sensitiveness, thus setting up the vicious circle I have described.

These two classes of indication—physical debility and psychic sensitivity—are found in all neurotics, and also in the 'diseases of the weak', whose symptomatology is physical rather than otherwise, such as tuberculosis. A further proof of the part played by the body is the fact that a neurosis often shows itself following childbirth, an operation, an infectious disease, a period of overwork, or a psychological crisis such as puberty or the menopause.

The essential cause of this physical debility remains a mystery. I do not think that somatic medicine, perhaps just because it has been too analytical and materialist in outlook, has yet given us the key to the problem. It has succeeded in measuring anaemia, the blood-pressure, and the secretion of hormones, but has not penetrated the cause of all these disturbances. It is very possible, however, that there is a single psychosomatic cause of both physical debility and psychic sensitivity.

There is probably, therefore, a certain basic and inborn coefficient of physical debility and psychic sensitivity, which predisposes the subject to weak reactions, and which is in turn aggravated by them. It is this vicious circle which we can attempt to break with our physical and psychological therapies, this supplementary coefficient which we can annul. But the subject retains his temperament. This he must indeed accept, and take into account in the organization of his life. For if he rebels against his nature, if he flouts it by exposing himself to excessive physical efforts or acute injury to his feelings, he will see the reappearance of the train of weak reactions, to which he remains predisposed. But though such people cannot alter their temperaments, this does not mean that they are fated to defeat, as they often feel themselves to be. It is the vicious circle of weak reactions which gives them that impression, and if they learn how to break it they will become reconciled to their sensitiveness.

Thus the essence of physical debility still escapes us. It is even more difficult to evaluate the coefficient of sensitivity. It probably varies from person to person much more than we suppose. But there is no test by which it can with certainty be measured. How can I determine whether the noise I hear is heard more loudly or less loudly by my neighbour, or whether it is that he hears it equally loudly, but *feels* it to be louder? Again, what precisely is the difference between hearing a sound more loudly and feeling it to be louder? It is the same with pain: if one patient, an excitable southerner, gets so worked up about the prick of my hypodermic needle, while another, a German Swiss, remains unperturbed, is it because it really hurts him more, or because he reacts more intensely to the same pain?

Dr Dubois of Berne has shown[1] the part played by suggestion in sensitiveness. He tells amusingly of how a sufferer from insomnia came to his clinic, in which the window of the only vacant bedroom overlooked a noisy factory where work started at an early hour in the morning. He firmly assured the patient that one hears only the sounds one listens to, and that one listens because one is afraid of being interrupted. And the patient, who ordinarily awoke at the slightest sound, slept through the clatter and regained confidence in sleep.

Truth to tell, such a story does not solve the problem of the coefficient of sensitivity. One may admit that Dr Dubois' positive suggestion inhibited a very great inborn sensitivity, as one may also admit that the patient's sensitivity was exacerbated by his fear of noise and insomnia. What argues the existence of the inborn factor is neither the first state of sensitiveness nor the succeeding state of insensitiveness, but rather the astonishing contrast between the two and the capacity to go from one extreme

[1] Paul Dubois, *The Psychic Treatment of Nervous Disorders*, translated and edited by S. E. Jelliffe and W. A. White, Funk and Wagnalls, New York and London, 1908.

to the other. For suggestibility is indeed one of the signs of a predisposition towards weak reactions, since the latter show a tendency to submission to the ascendancy of others.

What inclines me even more to recognize the importance of the innate constitutional factor in sensitivity is its polymorphism: in general, those who are sensitive have greater acuity of perception in a variety of directions. They are sensitive to noise, to cold, to pain, to sympathy, to beauty, to nature, to joys as well as sorrows, to intellectual problems as well as to moral and spiritual questions. It is true that suggestion and psychological complexes play a considerable part, but they are selective. They increase sensitivity to a particular sensation or feeling, whereas the inborn coefficient of sensitivity represents a general predisposition.

Even in early childhood such people suffer unduly when they see a comrade punished or an animal treated cruelly. A typical case is that of a young woman who had been her mother's favourite, always treated leniently. She tells me how she spent her childhood in constant terror of the scoldings which her mother used to give to her sisters. Today it is she, rather than they, who bears the mark of those outbursts, which were not directed at her, and which, besides, were possibly not excessive. It would seem, then, that these candidates for defeat are endowed from the cradle with an excess of sensitivity.

*   *   *

When this terrain of innate sensitivity is invaded by the accidental factors of hypersensitivization, these then trigger off the process leading to the crushing of the individual which I have described.

Of all accidental factors, the most important in my view is parental discord. It makes no difference whether it is expressed in daily scenes and violence, or in those stony silences and bitter sarcasms which betray an undercurrent of conflict.

I have by me at this moment my notes on a dozen such unhappy cases, lives loaded with disasters after a childhood spent amid an atmosphere of parental strife. The conclusion is inescapable that there is a causal connection. 'My first disillusionment,' one patient tells me, 'goes back to when I realized that my parents did not get on together. It was terrible. I felt utterly alone and rebellious against life.'

By instinct the child demands the unity of his parents; he therefore strives in vain to bring them together. He suffers doubly, for the hurt done by each of his parents to the other falls on him; he is crushed between the hammer and the anvil. 'It is very rare,' writes a young girl whose parents are always lecturing her about morality, 'for a whole day to pass in peace, without a scene. Of course one wants to change things, but how is one to set about it?'

It is that feeling of being powerless to reconcile his parents which crushes the child.

He lives in terror of a fresh outburst. Furtively he keeps watch on his parents, gauging their mood. He knows the lies they tell each other, and is afraid lest the discovery of them should provoke yet another scene. His fear of contributing to this outcome himself makes him a party to the lies, racked by remorse. He dare not speak his mind to his parents, nor to his brothers and sisters, nor to his grandparents, for fear of making matters worse. He keeps it all to himself, wondering in anguish how it will end. He is reduced to spending long hours at night weeping in secret into his pillow.

Carried away by the passion of their conflict, each of the parents accuses the other in front of him. They each impart their scandalous secrets to him and try to make him share their resentment, and sometimes bitterly reproach him for not taking their part.

For the rest of his life the child will suffer from a mental conflict between the two sets of attitudes represented respectively by his parents. One symbolizes conformity, reason, common-sense, morality, and economy; the other, life, sensibility, caprice, enthusiasm, and impulsiveness. One symbolizes law, the other grace. The child takes after both his parents, and so it is as if their conflict were continued irreducibly in him, between the two sides of his nature which derive from these two sets of attitudes. A

46

young woman writes to me: 'I had my father's outlook and my mother's reactions'—reactions of contempt, on the latter's part, for the outlook of the former. Another young man cannot be convinced that reason and love can be conjoined in a marriage. Or else he wishes to get married, but believes himself incapable of love. Or perhaps he plunges into the folly of impossible love-affairs. The inner paralysis that is characteristic of weak reactions is the expression of this mutual neutralization between two opposing forces. 'All my life,' a young man tells me, 'I have felt torn between the life of the country represented by my father and that of the town represented by my mother. Even now I can-not choose between the farm and my studies. An atavistic instinct draws me towards all that is healthy in the life of the country, but I cannot get away from the disdain which my mother had for my father's ignorance, and which she has passed on to me.'

The root of the conflict between parents is often a feeling of guilt on the part of both because of the child having been con-ceived before marriage. Each harbours resentment against the other, but they also bear a grudge against the child, whom they persecute as the 'witness of past wrong' (Allendy).[1]

Dissension between parents leads to a situation which I find repeated in the antecedents of so many of these people crushed by their experience of life that I might call it the classic pattern: moral abdication on the part of the father, and emotional domin-ation by the mother. In practice the mother suffers more than her husband does on account of the conflict. She has neither the office nor the public house in which to take refuge; so she seeks to fill her emotional void by means of possessive love towards her child. The father holds aloof from the child, taking no further interest in him because he has become the private property of the mother. He leaves him defenceless in face of what amounts to emotional blackmail by the mother, who dominates the child with her arbitrary demands and her tears. Sometimes it is far more subtle than that. For, as Benjamin Constant wrote, 'what is left unsaid is not for that reason less real, and all that is there is guessed.'

[1] René Allendy, *L'enfance méconnue*, Editions du Mont-Blanc, Geneva, 1946.

Without saying a word, by means of imponderables, the mother makes the child feel that he is hurting her when he does not share all her feelings; she abuses his affection in order to savour his attachment to her, as a balm for her conjugal unhappiness. She tells him that he is free to do as he likes, but he is well aware that this is not true. It is a liberal tyranny. One of my patients once gave me a poignant account of how her mother would wield an all-powerful weapon—that of depriving her of her good-night kiss. The storm rumbled on until the sleepless child, defeated at last, got up and came and made her act of abdication in order to obtain the kiss.

A child who is watched over with tender solicitude often feels himself cut off from real affection because his mother loves him not for himself but selfishly, for her own satisfaction. The doctor, of course, can see that the mother suffers as much as her child. There lies the tragedy. The marks of his affection which she demands can never satisfy her, since the real cause of the trouble is her marital conflict. Looked at objectively, she is no more 'responsible' for making her child suffer than he is 'guilty', as she claims, of making her suffer by his reactions towards her.

The less the mother talks about her conjugal distress, the more she sublimates it in complaints regarding everything else. She sighs at the smallest task. I have seen several talented young grown-up girls sacrifice their chance of a career in the hope of assuaging those endless sighs by easing the pressure of household work on the mother. But in vain, for the cause of the sighs is elsewhere. The mother needs to complain, and goes on complaining just as much, however devoted the daughter.

In this classic pattern, however, the father is no less to blame. The child is weak. God has provided him with a protector in the person of his father, to defend him until he has become strong himself. When the father has abandoned his role of protector, it is understandable that the child is marked for life with a tendency to weak reactions. This can always be seen in the case of fatherless children, whether the father is dead, divorced, or has abdicated morally.

48

The mother, on the other hand, deprived of her husband's support in the bringing-up of the children, usually becomes too fearful of their physical and moral health. By being over-cautious she makes them weak. I can call to mind one such, aged nearly thirty, who was terrified at the prospect of a cycle tour of some hundred and twenty miles which I suggested he should undertake in order to go and visit his best friend. A pusillanimous mother constantly keeps her child away from school, and the result is that he develops a feeling of inferiority.

This classic pattern leads a sensitive child to an exaggerated dependence upon his parents—on the father, from a kind of perpetual yearning for some sign of affection which is never forthcoming, and on the mother who has encouraged it with her emotional blackmail.

One particular case was a man who seemed to have won his freedom. He had made a career for himself right away from his parents, in a different town. Nevertheless he collapsed into complete moral confusion when they died; his childhood memories revealed all the details of the classic pattern.

One often also meets emotional blackmail between husband and wife or between lovers. One of them dominates the other with the continual threat of a 'row' or of withdrawing his love. What he is relishing in this way is not the affection of the other, but rather the dependence in which the other is held. Another type of blackmail is the constant enumeration by parents of the sacrifices they have made for their children. This they use as a lever to force a flattering submission on the part of the children, playing on their sense of gratitude. I once caught myself doing it. The day after my son and I returned from a holiday he committed some peccadillo. 'Is that the way you thank me for the pleasure I have given you by taking you away on holiday?' I asked him. Later, during my quiet time, I realized that it was for my own pleasure and for my own peace of mind, since I was worried about his health, that I had taken him, and I went and asked him to forgive me for having distorted the facts in order to bring pressure to bear upon him.

49

This demand for gratitude may remain unspoken. One often feels it in the case of a child brought up by a widowed or divorced mother who has given up for his sake the idea of marrying again. Even if she does not realize it, she expects compensation from him for her self-sacrifice, and this demand is crushing to the child.

I once treated a hard-working and conscientious student who as the examinations approached suddenly showed signs of depression due to panic, which inhibited him completely in his work. I was at once struck by his false sense of guilt. He repeatedly insisted that after all the sacrifices made by his family to enable him to study he was being an unworthy son in shirking like that. Tranquillity, courage, confidence, and success returned only when he understood that the truth was quite otherwise: he was not in debt to his family for the sacrifices they had made; instead, the family was in his debt for the honour it was seeking in sending him to the university, an honour by means of which it hoped to wipe out a social disgrace it had suffered in the past. How many people there are who are crushed by the feeling of being the horse on which everything is staked, and which must at all costs win the race.

There was another boy who found his school-work hard, and had become really obsessed by the fact. I saw that the fear came from his father who had himself failed at school. He had pushed his son into academic studies in order to realize in him an ambition he had himself failed to achieve, and he used to await the results of each examination with contagious anxiety and nervousness. Allendy has pointed out[1] that parents are the more demanding in regard to the moral conduct of their children, the more they expect, albeit unconsciously, to compensate thereby for their own failings in the past.

We have come here to the idea of *'noblesse oblige'*, which crushes so many lives. It is the supreme expression of social formalism and of regard for 'what the neighbours will say'. It is prevalent among the aristocracy, especially in families which have come down in the world financially or morally, and even more among

[1] *L'enfance méconnue.*

circles which consider themselves smart without genuinely being so. There, the only—and false—moral code is that of living up to a name or a reputation, symbolized by some famous ancestor. The child feels that he has no freedom: he may not marry whom he wishes, nor enter upon the career he would like, nor sometimes even smile or weep. Even if he conforms successfully in all these things, he does not feel he is doing so from personal conviction, but because he has weakly given in. And if he flouts the family tradition, he never succeeds in stifling in his heart the malaise left there by his early upbringing. None of his actions, whether he conforms or not, seems to him to be free, but rather determined by abdication or revolt.

A similar sense of obligation weighs upon children of men who are highly respected either morally or socially. Such children have no feeling that their behaviour is governed by their own conscience, but rather that the guiding principle of their lives is the constantly-repeated admonition not to compromise their father's reputation.

Conversely, every shortcoming or abnormal situation weighs on a sensitive child much more than parents generally realize. The child often has an acute intuition of the uneasiness which is being hidden from him: the fact, for example, that he is illegitimate. But he may have a keen perception of much more subtle anomalies—that the father is under the thumb of a wealthy or domineering and jealous sister who directs the education of her nephew and reduces the parents to the status of marionettes; or that a friend of the family, constantly invited to the house, has in fact taken over control.

Every child who is ashamed of his parents is caught in the toils of weak reactions. It is well known how perspicacious and pitiless schoolchildren can be in their mockery of a fellow-pupil whose parents are poor or eccentric. I am reminded of a woman sufferer from depression, who when quite young had been entrusted to the care of an uncle and aunt who had become fond of her. At school her class-mates despised her as an 'illegitimate child'!

Even where there is no question of insults of this kind, a

51

predisposition towards weak reactions is observable in the case of practically all children brought up outside their natural home. Analysts have stressed the importance of repressed feelings of jealousy towards brothers and sisters who are still at home, or towards other children who are still living with their own parents. But I think that there comes in here a more mysterious and very important phenomenon—that of depersonalization. We have an instinctive urge to be ourselves, which is always injured if we are uprooted. This is especially true when a child is made to play a part other than that which is really his own; when, for example, an aunt has herself called 'Mummy'. It may be that the aunt has lost her own child and has been entrusted with a nephew in order to console her. In such a case she depersonalizes the nephew by identifying him with the child she has lost.

Similarly, I have had several patients who had lost their mothers at an early age, and whose fathers had remarried, and then they had been made to call their stepmothers 'mother'. This is done, of course, with the best of intentions, but it touches on a deep instinctive element in human nature. A child has but one 'mummy'; to make him give this name to an adoptive mother is to depersonalize him. A child's true parents can also deprive him of his personality by moulding him in the pattern of a dead elder brother or sister, whose tastes and career he is compelled to follow. Depersonalization can also take place when a widower unconsciously requires his second wife to reincarnate the first. I am reminded, too, of twin sisters who had become identified to such an extent that they formed, so to speak, but a single person. More than twenty years of age, they were still exactly alike in dress, hair-style, and gestures. But one of them was 'strong', and had imparted her personality to the other; and the other, incapable of living her life in accordance with her own real nature, had fallen a victim to nervous depression.

*   *   *

Shortly after their marriage a young woman said to her husband: 'You mustn't ask me to knit clothes for our children. I don't know how to knit, and I can't make head or tail of the complicated "instructions" you get in wool-shops or in magazines.' Her husband questioned her, and she told him how as a child when she first started trying to knit it was amid an august assembly of ladies who vied with one another in giving her good advice. These zealous ladies, instead of noticing ninety-nine stitches that were quite well-made for a first attempt, pointed out the hundredth, which was too slack. They added: 'You'll never learn to knit well if you go on like that.' This negative suggestion had sown the seed of lack of self-confidence in that little girl's mind. Now, as she told her husband, she understood the reason, and her self-confidence returned. Soon she became so expert that her friends came to seek her advice, and explanations of the obscure 'instructions' in the papers.

As a general rule a schoolmaster marking an exercise, instead of assessing its correctness, originality and thoughtfulness, confines himself to deducting marks for errors in accordance with a marking-scheme. This may seem less arbitrary than a real appreciation of the work, but it suggests to the child that the main thing in life is to avoid making mistakes. This gives him the wrong outlook; it is contrary to the Gospel, which speaks rather of bearing fruits, of cultivating our talents. How many employees, too, become discouraged because their employers never have a word of appreciation for their success in a difficult task, but are quick to point out some unfortunate slip in spelling.

Even gifts can be spoilt with this negative coloration. A child's pleasure in the gift of a watch is ruined if he is told at the same time: 'This is to teach you to be punctual at meal-times.' One can imagine the situation in an instance such as Allendy recalls,[1] where the parents offered their child a cane in the guise of a Christmas present. The choice of presents always constitutes an interesting problem. Thus, a certain intellectual husband always gave his wife a book as a birthday present. He was attributing his own tastes to her. Perhaps, too, he reckoned on having the pleasure of reading the book himself! One day he brought her a bottle of

[1] *L'enfance méconnue.*

scent, having taken the trouble of choosing it carefully for her himself. His wife was overcome—how her husband had changed! Now she was sure of his love.

Unhappily the fatal and lasting effects of negative education are to be found in those brought up by the most virtuous, pious, and well-intentioned parents, thoroughly conscious of their responsibility, and deeply concerned for the future of their children, in the most cultured families—particularly in the case of children of teachers.

Such parents load their children with recommendations, and especially with prohibitions. With their adult perspective they see evil where the child sees none, so that the latter often fails to understand why his parents attach so much importance to a childish action or gesture. For fear of evil, the parents suggest evil to their child and impel him towards it, by awaking in him, through their allusions, a false emotion. So far from giving him a clear and realistic vision of evil and a healthy vigilance in regard to it, they arouse instead a mysterious and vague anxiety which saps his moral resistance.

After parental quarrels, this negative kind of education is in my view the factor which most frequently provokes weak reactions.

Leslie Weatherhead tells[1] of a psychiatrist who was staying in a friend's house where the number of orders given to the child was so great that he decided to count them. In two hours a hundred and twenty orders were given—forty-six for things he ought to do, and seventy-three for those he must not do. Such an avalanche must destine the child to a life of defeat. Things are worse when all these admonitions are couched in a tone of irritation which reveals the wounded pride of the parents. As a result the child's discouragement at his failures in school work, in the realm of art and of social behaviour, is increased by his sense of being a subject of shame to his parents. They thus arouse in him a sort of panic which is the cause of further failures. They suggest the

[1] L. D. Weatherhead, *Psychology, Religion and Healing*, Hodder and Stoughton, London, 1951.

failure they are afraid of. They suggest the fear of failure which for the rest of his life will become the cause of a succession of failures. If the child pulls himself together, makes a fresh effort, and achieves some success, the parents break his spirit with 'provided it lasts'; and the child perceives all their doubt. If he fails, he gets an 'I told you so', which is still more crushing. Let those parents read Confucius, when he praises the virtue of perseverance: 'What does it matter if you arrive only after the hundredth attempt where another arrives at once? You will surely arrive if you do not allow yourself to be discouraged.'[1]

I shall be told that education used to be much harder in the past; that a child was forbidden to do many more things—like speaking at the meal-table, for instance; that a young girl's life was bounded by piano-lessons and embroidery in the afternoons under a mother's watchful eye; that many more boys were forced to go unwillingly into their fathers' businesses in order to keep the family tradition going.

All that is indeed true. But the problem goes deeper. It seems to me to be bound up with the spiritual recession of our time. Children used to be brought up more strictly, but they felt that the severity with which they were treated arose out of a real conviction in their parents, behind whose moral precepts they were able to see the spiritual zeal which prompted them. The parents imposed upon themselves the same austerity of life, the same self-control, the same moderation in liberty and in pleasures, because their religion required it. They imposed this moderation on their children, not in order to bully them, nor merely out of concern for social convention, but because they believed it was God's command, and the way to train the character. By detaching morality from its spiritual sources we have turned it into an irksome harness. When the parents no longer believe in anything, all their commands and prohibitions must seem purely arbitrary.

In the past, writes Dr Jean de Rougemont,[2] children were taught 'a living morality, made up more of exhortations than of

[1] Pierre Salet, op. cit.
[2] Jean de Rougemont, *Vie du corps et vie de l'esprit*, Paul Derain, Lyons, 1945.

prohibitions', and he tells the following amusing anecdote:

'Why mustn't I do that?' asks the five-year-old.

'Because you mustn't,' his mother replies. 'You never see me doing it.'

'But who told *you* you mustn't do it?'

'*My* mother, when I was your age.'

'Oh! And *her* mother told her she mustn't, too?'

'I expect so.'

'Well,' the child concludes, 'I wonder who can have made up such a silly game!'

It seems then, that as a result of the secularization of the modern world, education has lost its real value, and what is left is only a meaningless tradition, more hurtful than effective.

In the same way, when in the past a father spoke to his son of following him in his career, he spoke of it with conviction and pride, communicating to him the fervour of his own professional dedication. But today most young people hear from the lips of their fathers and their elders nothing but bitter cynicism about their work, which they look upon as a curse, a life of slavery from which they would gladly escape were it not for the need to earn their daily bread.

There is a certain negativeness and disillusionment about modern man, which impels him to crush the joyous upsurge of life in the child. But, as Dr de Rougemont says again, 'the child is right, and the adult is wrong. The child believes in life, and the adult has stopped believing in it.' The fact that there are in our day so many neurotics, that so many of our patients are the prisoners of their own weak reactions, is doubtless often due to the cynical influence of too many adults who take an unhealthy pleasure in the destructive work of what they claim is rescuing their children from their naïve illusions.

To make a child feel small is, for the adult, an easy way of making himself feel big, and he gives way to the temptation all the more readily because he is conscious of his own shortcomings. Often jealousy is at work. A father forbids his son to take up the career he wishes to go in for because he unconsciously fears that the son will outstrip him in social esteem or be happier than he is, when he himself was similarly obstructed by his own father. Parents, too, often encourage jealousy between their children, in order to keep a tighter rein on them, or to humiliate one of them whose brilliance puts them in the shade.

*   *   *

One occasionally comes across cases of sensitive, artistically-minded children, rich in possibilities for a brilliant future, to which their mentally more circumscribed parents are blind. Such children frequently do not fit into the rigid pattern of school or of their family tradition. Misunderstood, the victims of angry outbursts, blows, and invective, their reactions are those of rebellion or despair, reactions which are met by threatening allusions to the reformatory or the lunatic asylum. Treated as hysterical, they are turned into neurotics. Such a child is unable to believe in the affection of his parents, and this feeling of abandonment may well set up in him dangerous compensatory mechanisms. An impulse to steal, for instance, may have this origin. Since he is not given that to which he has a right, he takes something to which he has no right. This terrible chain of cause and effect can easily bring disaster to the life of the very child who, more perhaps than others, stands in need of tenderness and confidence. And when repeated threats have exacerbated the child's reactions, it becomes necessary to put them into effect. The head of the approved school or the doctor in the mental hospital finds himself up against a stone wall of resistance, since he has always been presented to the child's mind as a monster.

One of my patients, suffering from nerves and obsessions, says to me: 'Throughout my childhood my father used to repeat everlastingly, "You are an imbecile".' Another, a girl, says: 'My mother kept telling me I was stupid, wicked, and ugly.' Yet another: 'I was constantly told that I was good for nothing.' And many more: 'You have a bad character.'

To put a label on someone is inevitably to contribute to making him conform to the label, especially if the person is at the impressionable age of childhood. To treat him as a liar is to make him one, and it is the same with selfishness or pride. I no longer believe that there are bad characters—I do believe that there is sin, which is quite another matter. The first of these two concepts belongs to the realm of social formalism, the second to that of moral realism. We are all sinners—equally sinners: the decent, honourable, respectable folk equally with those they despise; and cruel, unjust, proud parents equally with the children they crush with this talk of bad characters. In the true perspective of sin they would show the child that the weaknesses from which he suffers are common to all men, even if they hide them under strong reactions. This would help him to take heart and mend his ways. If, on the contrary, they treat him as a black sheep, they give him a terrible feeling of spiritual loneliness, of being bad whereas the rest are good. In this guilty solitude he has reactions which bring down upon him ever more humiliating reproaches. Such are the circumstances, the physical conditions, and the psychological chain of cause and effect in a person's life which result in the same universal sin taking the form of smug self-satisfaction in one, and weakness of character in another. Seen in the light of the Gospel, the former is worse than the latter!

There is such a thing as a Cinderella-complex. One can have no idea of the injustices which can fall one after another on the head of a child once he has begun to be the lightning-conductor of every family storm, the scapegoat on whom every score is paid off. If a toy is broken, if a glass is smashed, if his brothers and sisters quarrel, it is always his fault.

As a child one of my patients used to go out to play with her cousin. They would be told to be back at a certain time. When the time approached she would try to persuade her cousin that they should go home, pleading with an anxious insistence prompted by the fact that she was frequently scolded. But her cousin, who was never scolded, used to pay no attention. A terrible struggle then took place in her mind: should she go back alone? She dared not do so for fear that her companion should be scolded. Her increasing anxiety amused her cousin and incited her to further delay. When the two girls at last returned, my patient's mother would accuse her of being responsible for their being late, and of having a bad influence on her cousin.

Another of my patients was very anxious to help her parents, and toiled without respite while her parents indulged in foolish extravagances, and spoilt her brothers and sisters, who laughed at her.

An intelligent young girl is paralysed with misery over a French composition. I learn that the teacher always makes a practice of reading aloud in class, giving the names of their authors, the best and the worst compositions—in her opinion, of course. One can imagine the psychological shock sustained by our little girl when her composition is read out in front of her classmates as being the worst. One of my patients, who did extremely well later on in his career, though only after surmounting tremendous psychological difficulties, told me of the effect on him of seeing on his school report the following remark: 'A bad pupil; I have no idea what he will be able to do when he leaves.' This remark had burnt itself into his brain, and one could see that it still hurt when he repeated it. Allendy also quotes[1] the case of a child whose teacher had said to him: 'You'll turn into a gangster.' He rightly points out that the effect of negative suggestions of this sort is the more harmful and lasting the greater the prestige, in the child's eyes, of the person who makes them. This is not always the father or teacher; it may be the elder brother whom a little girl admires so much that she makes him her arbiter in everything. If she is fat, whereas her brother likes slim girls and is always comparing her disparagingly with them, she will grow up into adulthood with doubts about her own good looks, and feeling that no man can ever love a stout girl like her. She sees herself as stouter than she really is, and her efforts to conceal it spoil the naturalness which is so necessary if a woman is to be attractive. She dresses badly, and has no idea of how to make the most of her style of beauty. This can go very deep; the girl begins to be afraid she will never marry. The subject thus becomes so charged with emotion that it sets up in her a feeling of general inferiority which makes its presence felt in every domain of her life, including

[1] *L'enfance méconnue.*

even her religious life. Such was the case of a woman who came to me with her distress at having lost her faith. Of course, behind her religious crisis there were other causes which I cannot analyse here. Here I am concerned to show the pernicious pervasive influence of a negative suggestion received in childhood. It had made this young woman susceptible to every other ground for doubt. Love and religion are the two spheres that are potentially the most highly charged with emotion. That is why so many people associate them in their minds. If they are afraid of losing love they are afraid of losing faith; if they have faith in love, they have faith in faith.

Unhappily there are countless women who from childhood doubt their own good looks. This idea warps their whole lives, for beauty is one of the most precious of God's gifts to woman, and one which she cannot disregard with impunity. If this doubt does not prevent her from marrying, it will persist in marriage, and will make it difficult for her to believe in her husband's love and to give herself to it whole-heartedly. It can, furthermore, have physical repercussions, in virtue of the psychosomatic corres- pondences whose existence is now generally recognized. In such women we often find signs of ovarian insufficiency, dysmenorr- hoea, excessive pilosity, etc. The state of doubt has acted as a brake on the functioning of the endocrine glands which control woman's femininity and beauty.

A girl may have such an admiration for her mother's beauty that she despairs of ever equalling her, and this lack of confidence also can block her development. Similarly I have met the case of a man who, in spite of a brilliant career, still preserved this sense of defeat whose mechanisms, at once so diverse and so similar, we have been studying. I observed that this feeling arose from the excessive admiration he had always had for his father. It was true that the latter was an eminent man, worthy of the greatest esteem for his numerous and well-integrated qualities. But just as the girl I mentioned saw her mother as a veritable goddess, so this patient still regarded his father as a god. He was always mentally comparing himself with his unreal model, and could not but be inferior to it at every point. What I want to bring out here is that these distortions of the truth, to which parents sometimes contribute by hiding from their children their own difficulties and weaknesses, far from stimulating a child, paralyse him in his physical, intellectual, and psychological development. Many young women have said to me: 'I can't do anything; my mother did everything to perfection, and I never dared to touch a pan or a broom in her presence.' Another compares herself with her mother in quite a different sphere: her mother has never expressed her love for her by means of caresses, but only by devotion to her welfare. The daughter's nature is quite different: love does not lead her to feverish activity, but to passive and sentimental tenderness. And so she says to me: 'I always wonder if I am really capable of love.'

Even more frequently parents make systematically invidious comparisons of one child with a brother or sister. The temperament of the other child is quite different—docile and submissive, successful at school because of the absence of particular likes or dislikes or any overriding enthusiasm which might prove a distraction from work. He may not have more to give in life, but is for the moment a great credit to his parents. And the esteem in which they hold him actively encourages him in his docility. The younger child, of a more lively and original turn of mind, sees himself constantly compared with his elder brother or sister, in regard to whom he will retain a serious feeling of inferiority which will inhibit him in all his social relationships.

Another case is that of a man who almost exactly represents the grasshopper of the fable, while his brothers resemble the ant. Like the ant, the latter offer him wise advice which, even though it is very affectionately given, comes from the height of their social success and from the pedestal on which their parents have set them. Nevertheless their brother feels that he has in his heart a treasure of which they know nothing, but the force of the old suggestion is so great that he is ashamed rather than proud of it.

Then there is the girl who is artistic and contemplative, while her sister is a woman of action. Though she criticizes this sister, she also admires her, and is always measuring herself against her rather than developing her own gifts.

Some parents, who never speak to their children of anything but their shortcomings, with never a word in praise of their good qualities or to thank them for their little acts of affection, take great pride in boasting about them—in their absence—to friends and acquaintances. Meanwhile the children imagine that they are a complete disappointment to their parents. The misunderstanding is unnecessary and tragic. For the parents think they are acting for the best. They adopt this attitude intentionally. They are afraid of making their children conceited if they let them see that they recognize and appreciate their good qualities. Of course they do not after all succeed in preserving them from pride, for everyone is proud, totally proud. But the feelings of inferiority which they thus implant in them are the most damaging form of pride. It is very much easier to appear humble in success than in failure. This has often been borne in upon me by the sight of poor souls full of feelings of inferiority, prostrated by their failures, yet who still have reproaches heaped upon them, accusing them of being vain and proud because they try, awkwardly enough, to find some compensation in making what poor show they can of the few talents they possess. While alongside them their brothers and sisters, constantly flattered by adulation and success, can easily conceal the secret satisfaction they get, and appear modest. The Gospel teaches us, however, to be unaffected and sincere; to see our children as they are, with their qualities both good and bad; to speak frankly to them about both, as well as about our own which they too can observe; to confess that we are all full of a pride which none of us can cast off by our own unaided efforts, or by pretending that it is not there; and to rely on God's forgiveness for it, and his grace to protect us from it.

One mother stressed recently that it is quite as dangerous to idolize children as to denigrate them. There is nothing like the truth.

Nor is there anything like being honest with oneself. I have seen many people who adopt a negative attitude towards themselves. In their own minds they constantly call themselves fools; they discredit and despise themselves. While protesting against the widespread tendency to judge other people, they will not forgive themselves their own shortcomings. They do not treat themselves with love.

The Gospel does not condemn love of oneself; it only requires us to love others as ourselves; it asserts the value of the human person as being the creation of God. To esteem oneself as such, while at the same time frankly recognizing one's sinfulness, is the essential precondition of the experience of God's grace.

'*Maxima debetur puero reverentia.*' Education, to be fruitful, must be animated by respect for the child. It must indeed open his eyes to the seamy side of his nature, but it should also encourage him by helping him to recognize his talents. It must seek to understand him instead of criticizing him. Behind what has been denounced as wilfulness it should see 'the explosion of a vital conflict' (Montessori). It must try to let him discover the truth for himself instead of imposing it dogmatically upon him. It must encourage him in his first attempts instead of crushing him by showing him that after thirty years' practice one knows how to do things better than he does. It must respect the child's own person. As Pestalozzi says, 'Make the child seek what he is capable of discovering by his own efforts.' Lastly, it must respect his own rhythm. How many parents and teachers are there who remember that in the scale of 'physiological time' one hour's concentration by a child corresponds to three or four hours in an adult? So it is that I have seen many a one crushed and defeated simply because he has always been hustled. Endowed with a slow temperament but brought up by keen and active parents, amid equally lively brothers and sisters, he has always been late, always been beaten to the post, if I may put it so, by someone else, so that it has been said of him that he is incapable of doing anything.

It is striking to discover how rare are those parents who are really interested in understanding a child who is different from them. Every time he shows any originality he is promptly denounced as perverse. Parents like to see themselves in their children, and are quick to victimize a child who does not take after them. It often happens too that parents who are at odds each victimize those of their children who take after the other. It even happens quite often that a child is victimized by both parents— by his mother because of his physical resemblance to the father, and by his father because his personality resembles that of his mother.

Many intelligent and well-intentioned parents have a vague feeling that there are psychological factors blocking the expression of their affection towards their children or towards one of them. They do not always succeed in recognizing the unconscious mechanism which is at work. And even where they do perceive it they do not succeed in freeing themselves from it. It may perhaps be an impulse of revenge for lack of affection in their own childhood. They strive hard to overcome the obstacle, but the very fact that they have to make an effort mars their success. The intuition of a child is incredibly quick to sense the mysterious barriers which separate him from his parents.

I have seen many patients who have become crystallized in an infantile attitude to life through lack of maternal love. They prolong their childhood indefinitely, because in it they did not receive what their instincts claimed. One of these told me that she had never once in her childhood received a present. Except once, when she was given a bar of chocolate which, however, was at once taken away from her to be given to another child. She was told she would be given another one instead, but she never got it.

Unconscious factors can also be at work in parents who worry too much about their child. If he is late home in the evening their disquiet can speedily take on fantastic proportions. This anxiety is quite illogical and quite outside the control of the will. In vain does the mother tell herself again and again that there are perfectly good reasons for her child's lateness, and reproach herself for her lack of trust in being so anxious, telling herself that this atmosphere of apprehensiveness may be harmful to the child. Her self-reproaches seem only to increase her fear. Her husband, moreover, cannot positively assure her that an accident has not happened. So it is not in discussion that they will find peace, but only in prayer. And it is also through prayer that the mother will be able to understand the true cause of her anxiety. It may be that as a child she suffered because her own mother worried too little about her. Her present distress is the projection of her own unsatisfied demand. And this discovery will help to restore her tranquillity.

Finally I must give some consideration to the important problem of the only child. The fact that they have only one child is very often already due to false timidity on the part of the parents —fear of pregnancy, of childbirth, of the financial burden of a large family. More often than not it is actual disobedience to God's will, and parents and child both pay heavily for it. The parents stake all their hopes on the child; they want him to be perfect, they inundate him with advice—excellent advice, of course. They dream of a distinguished career for him; they suggest, perhaps mistakenly, that he has a vocation for the Church, or make him follow a course of studies for which he is not fitted. They allow him no initiative, for fear of his making a blunder, no independence for fear of 'something happening to him'.

One young woman was incapable of reading a railway time-table, because her father, for fear of her making a mistake, had always laid down the itinerary even of her shortest journeys. Another of my patients had been brought up by an aunt. He was already a grown man, and his aunt, at the age of eighty, still accompanied him on all his journeys, for fear of his falling into evil company. Much more serious is the case of the illegitimate child, brought up by a mother who watches over his education with a solicitude and fear that are the greater because of her wish to recompense him for the wrong she has done him. Even if, as often happens, she makes a child prodigy of him, his attitude to life remains self-conscious and awkward.

And then parents always tend to spoil an only child. The result is to make him afraid of life, afraid of failure, afraid of being alone; and he will never rid himself of these fears unless he experiences the liberating power of God's grace.

A husband also often spoils his wife and weakens her self-confidence by doing for her everything she could do for herself. If he dies he leaves her to face life defenceless.

3

FEAR

I T IS CLEAR that whether a child has been frightened by his parents' quarrels, whether he is misunderstood and persecuted by them or by a teacher, whether he lacks self-confidence as a result either of a restrictive upbringing or of fear inspired by worrying parents, we find that the basic cause of his weak reactions is always fear.

Adults are unaware of the extent to which their very size frightens a child. In order to understand this, let them imagine what would be their own reactions if they lived among giants more than twelve feet high, whose strength seemed greater than that of Hercules, their intelligence keener than that of Minerva, and with voices more powerful than the voice of Jupiter; people whose actions seemed to verge on the miraculous, whose mutual encounters were brutal clashes, who kept innumerable secrets from them, replying to their questions with a curt 'That's none of your business', 'You ought to be ashamed of asking such a question', or 'You are too little to understand'.

This is especially the case with the father, and I know many people whose inability to face up to their lives derives ultimately from this ineffaceable fear of their fathers, a terror which has been carried over into a fear of all men, and especially of all in positions of power and authority.

Dr Allendy describes[1] as criminals parents and teachers who use this fear as an all-powerful weapon with which to dominate the child, to stifle his personality and obtain his submission to their unjust demands. Leslie Weatherhead writes: 'Deceitful methods which appeal to fear are particularly harmful and

[1] *L'enfance méconnue.*

odious: "If you do that the bogey-man will eat you up." "If you do this you will die." "If you are naughty God won't love you any more." '

One young woman used to quote, still trembling with emotion as she did so, her mother's oft-repeated phrase: 'You will be cursed.' Another used often to say to me: 'I feel I have no right to live.' Finally she told me that when she was a child she had heard her father say of her: 'That one ought not to have been born.' And there was the case of a man who had been to a quack-doctor, who in order to cover up his own failure had told him: 'The reason why I have been unable to cure you must be because you are possessed by a devil.'

Fear is the catalyst of suggestion, and suggestion implants all kinds of stubborn and absurd fears in the hearts of even the most intelligent and courageous men. Fear sends them hurrying to the palmist; and some foolish remark by the palmist inoculates them with a fear which falsifies all their reactions: 'You will come to a tragic and horrible end.' Sometimes suggestions of this sort are thrown out with the best of intentions. In order to reassure a patient who is 'afraid of being afraid of committing suicide' a doctor may tell her she has a 'temperament' which inclines her to the thought of suicide. It is scarcely necessary to say that instead of calming her this remark is one which she will be unable to put out of her mind.

The tragedy is that it is just those children who are sensitive, impressionable, and timorous, with whom one is tempted to have recourse to intimidation. Their comrades tell them fantastic stories because it is amusing and gives a sense of superiority to see how easily frightened they are. But even adults, nurses and parents, have been known to appear suddenly in the children's room dressed up as ghosts!

There are mothers who, in order to maintain their hold over a child, dangle the spectre of future remorse before him: 'You'll see,' they say, 'when I am dead you'll never be able to forgive yourself for the trouble you have caused me.' Others do not know how to control themselves in front of their children. I know of one young woman who still shudders at the memory of the unspeakable terror she experienced one night when her mother went out saying she was going to throw herself into the river. The child ran after her in the darkness, howling in despair. She stumbled into a ditch, gnawing the earth, and a passer-by, taking her for a disobedient child in a tantrum, hurled invective at her.

Add to this such accidental terrors as fires, bombs, and lightning; or punishment by being locked in the cellar or in a dark room; or meeting a lunatic, or seeing a schoolmate having an epileptic fit. Such experiences play an enormous part in the history of our patients, for they find fertile ground in every human heart, where nothing grows more readily than fear.

I cannot of course enumerate all the fears which beset men and women and dominate them to such an extent that they are afraid to acknowledge them. They range from a vague anxiety which is all the more persistent because it has no precise object, and involves a hopeless struggle against an invisible enemy, to those more specific fears which derive from an association of ideas which may or may not be conscious: fear, not only of disease in general, but of particular diseases which happen at the moment to be the subject of frequent public comment, such as tuberculosis, mental disease, or cancer; the fear of dying at the same age or of the same disease as one's father; fear of the menopause; fear of germs; the fear of going to the doctor because one is afraid he will confirm the diagnosis one dreads, when in fact it might mean being freed from groundless fear; the fear of having an abnormal child, which makes so many women fight shy of motherhood; the fear of dying in one's sleep; or of being buried alive while in a coma, which causes insomnia; fear of nightmares, a further cause of insomnia; the fear of an operation, the fear that under the anaesthetic one may involuntarily reveal some secret; the fear of death, which spreads to those around the sick person and prevents them from helping him to face death; the fear of losing a father, husband, or child, which brings in its train a false sense of dependence in regard to him; the fear of loneliness; the fear of having

68

no home, or of leaving one's habitual surroundings; fear of responsibility, of the unknown; the fear of being without money; the fear of hurting someone, which militates against sincerity, or the fear of being misunderstood, which prevents husband and wife being frank with each other and digs a ditch of misunderstanding between them; fear of being left alone, which prevents the breaking of an engagement that is empty of real love; fear of being disappointed in a friendship, which kills friendship through the constraint it entails; fear of the inevitable end of pleasure, which prevents the enjoyment of that pleasure; fear of being disappointed by reality, which makes us take refuge in illusion; fear of advice, fear of being influenced, fear of having neither the credit for the good which will come of following the advice, nor freedom from the evil that will come of not following it; fear of disappointing others, or of being reprimanded by them.

Every fear nourishes all the others, down to the 'fear of fear' of which St Francis de Sales spoke.[1] They grow snow-ball fashion until the mind is made dizzy with them, losing all its resistance to fear and all its capacity for common-sense. We are tormented by mutually exclusive fears—the fear of success at the same time as the fear of failure. One of my patients used to say to me: 'I am afraid of death, and I am afraid of life.' Others are afraid of continuing illness, but they are also afraid of getting well and having to face life again.

Fear creates what it fears. I have pointed this out elsewhere, in regard to war. It is confirmed daily as I observe the behaviour of individuals: stage-fright inhibits speech; the fear of being like one's father or mother leads to an ever-increasing resemblance, and plays a part at least as important as true heredity; the fear of not keeping one's resolutions prevents them being made wholeheartedly, so that failure is inevitable; the fear of succumbing to masturbation makes it certain that one will succumb; the fear of going mad makes us so nervous that those around us assure us

[1] See V. Raymond, *The Spiritual Treatment of Sufferers from Nerves and Scruples*, translated by Dom Aloysius Smith, R. & T. Washbourne, London, 1914, p. 26.

that we are heading for madness; the fear of 'cracking', of not having strength enough for a task, saps our strength so that we do 'crack'; the fear of disappointing her fiancé prevents a girl acting naturally, so that she does disappoint him; the fear of not being loved warps a woman's outlook, so that her husband wearies of her and becomes estranged; the fear of not being pretty enough makes her lose her good looks and impels her to disfigure herself with ridiculous make-up; the fear of growing thin stops her putting on weight; the fear of losing his wife's confidence turns a man into a dissembler, so that he arouses her mistrust; the fear of growing old makes us grow prematurely old; the fear of suffering leads us into a thousand errors which bring endless suffering in their train; the fear of penury leads us to speculations in which we lose the little we have; the fear of unemployment makes a young man change his job, so that he finishes up without one; or his fear of not being able to marry, through not having a good enough job, deprives him of the energy he needs to succeed in his career. 'I have come to realize,' a woman told me once, 'that my fear of death was really a fear of dying before I had done what I most wanted to do.' And it was just that fear that was preventing her doing it.

*   *   *

It is in the realm of sex that we find the most harmful childish fears. Both the scandalized howl that went up when the psychoanalysts demonstrated the frequency of sexual shocks in childhood, and the accusation levelled at them of projecting their own impudicity into baseless theories, were hypocritical. The truth is that objective examination of our society confirms their observations. It is precisely because society affects ignorance of the facts, wrapping in a cloak of silence the sexual laxity that is so widespread today, that those who have fallen victims to it believe themselves to be exceptional. Only with the greatest difficulty can they bring themselves to talk about it, as if it were an unspeakable disgrace. Sometimes it takes months of interviews for the experience that has been warping a person's whole life to come to light in all its crudity. I have here twenty-four cases of serious sexual shock, such as violation of a girl by a father or brother, or the sexual initiation of a boy by his sister. One can imagine, then, how frequent such shocks must be, when one takes into account all those due to encounters with sexual perversion, exhibitionism, inversion, and so on. The emotional shock is especially serious when the perpetrator is a person hitherto haloed with respectability, for it is often people of the highest reputation who indulge in the most vulgar sexual assaults on the young. Too often, when we speak of sin and its power, we are suspected of pessimistic exaggeration. If the Church wants to recover its influence, it must become realistic again. The atmosphere of mystery and shame in which it helps to envelop the whole problem of sex is as harmful as the smutty jokes of immoral people,. the double meanings of the cynics, or the advice of those psychologists who advocate unrestrained surrender to the impulses of instinct.

This is why we find that the past histories of so many of our patients contain psychological shocks due to some experience connected with sex, apparently less serious than those I have just mentioned, but nevertheless heavily charged with emotion. Such was the case of a man whose indefinable anxiety dated from a certain Sunday morning when he half guessed the meaning of the sounds he could hear from the next room. One is astounded at how many parents there are who keep a child sleeping in the same room with them, until he is quite big, naïvely imagining that he notices nothing, even if they do not make matters worse by scolding him sharply if he opens his eyes. Another case was that of a mother who had never herself come to terms with sex, and who in a thoroughly negative manner shared premature confidences with her daughter concerning the sufferings of a woman pursued by a husband's sensuality.

Such is the atmosphere of shame which surrounds the whole subject that I receive countless letters from unknown sufferers recounting experiences and memories of which they have never dared to speak to anyone before, and which have been poisoning their lives. But simply to tell someone about these things does not always bring relief. I am thinking of a man who followed up his letter with a visit to me in person, for it was only in living spiritual communion that he could lay his trouble at God's feet, and recover a free and positive attitude to life and sex. Sometimes what is needed is the assurance of forgiveness, since many people suffer less from the emotional shock than from the resentment it has aroused in them towards the person responsible for harming them in this way.

All these difficulties provoke such a close mental association between sex and fear that they combine to crush the spirit. Many a child suffers secret torment because he is afraid to ask certain questions; this may give rise to stubborn sex complexes. A perspicacious primary school teacher has written to tell me the startling results of her tactful investigations of the preoccupations of her charges, both boys and girls.

Fear plays a decisive role in all psycho-sexual troubles. It sets in motion the mechanism of auto-suggestion, which in its turn engenders fear: fear of not enjoying the sex life (frequently the sole and simple cause, apart from serious physical disorders, of impotence and frigidity); fear of being fatigued by the physical side of sex, whereas when it is in accordance with God's will it acts as a tonic; fear of marriage, or of not being able to remain chaste outside marriage; the fear of being unfaithful, which saps resistance to temptation; the fear of not being able really to love, which impels people to engage in 'trial' affairs in the artificiality of which true love cannot flourish; fear of giving way to the temptation of impurity, a fear which leads to excessive exertions in sport or in work, and in some cases even pushes a man into an ecclesiastical career for which he has no vocation, in the hope that thus his fears will be exorcised; the fear of recovering their health which one meets in some patients who are afraid that their return to normal life and health will also mean the reawakening of the powerful appeal of the senses; and, lastly, fantastic fears prompted by baseless ideas and misconceptions, such as the fear of disease, of frigidity or of sterility as a punishment for masturbation.

These things are so heavily charged with emotion that the most commonplace remark and even quite well-intentioned explanations can give rise to endless misunderstandings. A girl is afraid of becoming pregnant simply as a result of having danced with a young man, because her religious teacher has warned her against the disgrace of a pregnancy before marriage. The suggestive force of this idea is enough to bring on in her the few signs of pregnancy that she knows—amenorrhoea and vomiting—so that she feels her worst fears are confirmed.

It is appropriate to underline the important part played by auto-suggestion in the genesis of all kinds of sexual trouble, masturbation, impotence, and perversions. Auto-suggestion finds in fear fertile ground for its development, and it flourishes in the moral solitude brought about by the fear of speaking of these matters. I have seen men and women who without any objective reason have been seized suddenly with the fear of being homosexual. This is enough to turn their thoughts towards the corresponding mental images, or to arouse in them, in the presence of a man or woman friend, an uneasiness which they take as a confirmation of their fear.

More than once a man has come to see me declaring that he has been homosexual from birth, and we have discovered, going back calmly into his childhood memories, that he had once made advances to a little girl, who had slapped his face hard. From that moment the course of his imagination had been turned aside towards his own sex, in an unconscious effort to hide the injury to his self-esteem. It is a case of sour grapes.

Another such man had simply been revolted by a girl who was too provocative—another case of wounded self-esteem, because the man wishes to have the initiative in love. In a somewhat similar way one comes across impotence in a husband whose wife is too sensual; the more she claims sexual satisfaction the more the husband is paralysed. He is paralysed both by his bad conscience with regard to his wife and by his own humiliation. He may even go as far as adultery in an attempt to reassure himself. In such cases what is needed is a real relaxation of tension, to break the vicious circle, and to go back as it were to that stage in the evolution of their love when they exchanged their first lovers' kisses.

Another man has been afraid of being a homosexual since the time when he was the passive victim of a sexual pervert. Others suffer from the same fear simply because they are too shy to approach a woman. In the case of one young girl, her fears were the result of auto-suggestion set in motion by the unfounded suspicions of a boarding-school mistress in face of her attachment to a fellow-pupil.

Seeing all this, one realizes how unjust society is when it crushes all these anguished souls with its contemptuous accusation of 'perversion', a term heavily charged with ideas of shame and obloquy, whereas these people are no more sensual than any normal respectable person.

Some evangelists have taken me to task for speaking out against the verdict pronounced in the name of social convention in this matter, pointing to the story of Onan in the book of Genesis. I do not of course deny that to give way to every impure impulse is a sin: to *every* impulse, mark you, whether normal or perverted. Sin is common to all men, both normal and perverted. All men therefore may, through the same prompting of conscience and true repentance, experience the genuine liberating power of God's grace. But the false sense of guilt which comes not from the patient's impurity, but from his perversion, for which he is not responsible, is the source of nothing but despair, fear, and moral degradation. Even to tell a man suffering from some form of perversion that his trouble is much less rare than he thinks, is an immense relief to him.

Perverts are in the habit of trying to justify themselves by referring to theories frequently put forward as to the legitimacy of abnormal sexuality. It is not difficult to see that in spite of all their arguments they are still thoroughly imbued with this false shame which derives from conventionalism. Here is one, haunted by the idea of committing suicide at a propitious moment—a moment of victory—because he is afraid of reaching heaven in a state of sin! Such a case shows the terror to which this false and formalistic sense of guilt can give rise. The healthy emotion provoked by a genuine conviction of sin is salutary. But that suggested by society, which relates not to sin but to perversion, is fatal. The first leads to freedom from the fear of men; the second brings a host of fears in its train. In the realm of the moral conscience, the sufferer from abnormal sexuality discovers that what is sinful is this fear, so far removed from the teaching of the Gospel, of what others will say, and that liberation from it will bring him victories. Confession remains, for the abnormal and the normal alike, the only road to deliverance; but confession is rendered more difficult for the abnormal by this false social shame, which sets up barriers of psychological censorship.

The Church is accused of propagating the fear of sex. We must admit the truth of the accusation. A pious woman who had been initiated into the sex life by a vulgar person whom at bottom she despised as being less 'spiritually-minded' than herself, was profoundly humiliated to realize the hold he had over her by means of the senses. Her feeling of humiliation was becoming an obsession, in what was really a gigantic effort to preserve the false and ethereal picture which she had formerly had of herself. Cases of this sort, which are very frequent among us, arise from the habit, common to many, of considering sexual sin as being different from all other kinds of sin. There are many parents who make an excessive fuss about their child's masturbating, instead of treating it as a very ordinary manifestation of infantile sexuality—a sort of groping exploration of a nature not yet fully developed. It is just the excessive shame with which we surround masturbation that arrests sexual development and perpetuates this infantile manifestation. Take the case of a mother who drags her daughter in front of me as if I were a judge, saying to her in my presence: 'The doctor will tell you; you'll die if you go on.' Another comes in tears to tell me of the 'mortal blow' she received when her son confessed that he masturbated. She believes that his 'salvation' is irretrievably compromised, and adds that she herself has been unable to pray since then. In other spheres people willingly admit

75

their failings without feeling greatly ashamed of them; but to feel in themselves the power of carnal lust wounds them with a quite special shame which has much less to do with the true moral conscience than with social convention. It is not of sinning that they are ashamed, but of having a sex instinct. In this negative attitude, permeated as it is with fear and pride, temptations are only made worse. Christian people must renounce all this formalism and learn again to understand the divine meaning of sex. Happily there are now some excellent writers who ar turning their attention to the task, addressing themselves both to the educated classes, as does pastor Leslie Weatherhead,[1] and to a more popular readership, as in the case of Dr Jouvenroux,[2] for example. Such writings form a welcome contrast with a whole tradition of moralistic literature which has been responsible for countless psychological catastrophes because it intensively cultivates the fear of sex.

To sow fear of something divine is to turn people away in fear from God. It is for this reason that so many of our young people, even when they pray about it, struggle against sexual temptation in an atmosphere of fear instead of one of faith.

There comes to me a woman who was brought up in an atmosphere of repression as regards sex. So successfully did she repress her sex instinct that she came to believe herself exempt from it. Several men courted her, but their too direct advances left her absolutely cold. She entered upon a brilliant social career, not, however, without experiencing from time to time a strange malaise at finding herself caught up in conflicts which remained inexplicable to her, since they had to do with her repression. But suddenly, terrifyingly, everything is turned upside down for her when in the course of a discreet friendship she feels the first promptings of an instinct of which she knows nothing. In her former artificial attitude she had always criticized, even despised, women who jeopardized their careers for the sake of a love affair, who allowed themselves to be ruined by their feelings, who 'lost

[1] L. D. Weatherhead, *The Mastery of Sex*, Student Christian Movement Press, London, 1945.
[2] Dr Jouvenroux, *A la découverte de l'amour*, Editions Ouvrières, Geneva, 1943.

their heads'. Up to then she had considered the head to be stronger than the heart. That had been one factor in the success of her career, though it had also caused difficulties, since it had been done only at the cost of a certain blindness about herself. Now she is quite overcome, because she has discovered that she herself has a heart which could well be stronger than her head. She realizes that, like those others whom she used to despise, she too is quite capable of losing her head. She is afraid; afraid of herself; afraid of these impulses she has found within herself.

But our talks together develop. She finds a new courage, the courage to look at herself as she really is, to look her fears in the face. Old memories return. She sees now that those impulses were always there within her, and that she has been hiding them from herself. She realizes, too, that they were the unconscious cause of the inexplicable conflicts she had experienced. The picture of herself that she had invented—that of a person exempt from instinct and from the danger of giving way to it—was an illusion. Rather than a sign of strength, it was a sign of weakness, since it was a kind of escape. True courage consists in accepting ourselves as we are, with these permanent dangers that are in us and which could quite easily entice any of us into some betrayal of our ideals; it consists in accepting the permanent struggle against those dangers—accepting it consciously instead of avoiding it by repressing our instincts. That woman has found peace again; and she finds herself stronger than before, now that she accepts the reality and the struggle.

The Christian position is simple and clear in this respect. It is not, for the Christian, a matter of being on his guard against the explosions of an instinct which he despises, ingenuously deluding himself that he is safe from its dangers—nor is he to give way to it outside the limits which God has assigned to him in marriage. The Christian values so highly the instinct implanted in him by God that he is careful not to profane it by abusing it. It is precisely because we have a positive attitude towards sex, because we look upon it as one of God's masterpieces, that we wish to submit it to him.

77

'Is it possible to remain chaste until marriage?' a French student once asked me, adding: 'I maintain among my friends that it is, but I doubt it myself.' Of course chastity is possible. Its effect is infinitely tonic for both physical and moral health. It is in order to justify its conduct that the world maintains the contrary. Chastity is harmful only when it is motivated by fear and false shame of sex, in which case the slightest slip becomes the subject of obsessive despair: 'The danger,' said St John Chrysostom, 'is not that we should fall while fighting, but rather that, once fallen, we should remain on the ground.' When the source of chastity is faith, it becomes stronger and stronger, and in turn fortifies the mind. Then a man can thank God for the strength he has been given, and rely on God's grace to protect him from misusing it, and to raise him up again should he fall.

We must therefore free men from all false fear of sex. Though I recognize that the Church is often responsible for these false fears, I ought to add that we often find them also in patients who have been brought up outside the Church's influence. These groundless fears prevent that blending of romantic and carnal love which is in accordance with the will of God.

But, paradoxically, in order to deliver man from a false fear of sex, we must help him to accept the true fear—that of giving way to the abuse of sex. This point is so important that I must beg the reader's whole attention. Here, for example, is a patient who tells me that as far back as she can remember, even at the age of two or three, she was troubled by a vague emotion made up of curiosity, desire, and fear, with regard to the truth about sex. She believed that she was alone in bearing this affliction, which up to now she has kept secret. You know well that she was not alone, that every child in the world knows the same fear. What has made her ill is not the fear, but its secrecy—her fear of the fear, which prevented her admitting it.

In company with all those psychologists who in the last half-century have drawn attention to it, I have pointed out that social conventionalism aggravates this fear. But I cannot agree that it is the sole cause. I do not believe that any child, even one brought up in ideal conditions, could approach an awareness of sex without experiencing this fear. He would know it even in a desert island.

The child's keen intuition tells him that there is awakening in him a formidable power which is capable of dominating and overwhelming him. It inspires him with a fear that is inevitable and universal. The conventionalist attitude says to the child as soon as he confesses or shows signs of these impulses: 'Aren't you ashamed of yourself?' This makes the fear worse, because it encloses it in secrecy and arouses a supplementary fear—the fear of his fear; and also because it is a lie. The truth is that the person who says to him: 'Aren't you ashamed of yourself?' has himself known, and still experiences, the same impulses and the same fear.

Conventionalism makes matters worse; it adds a further fear; but it is not a complete explanation. There is a basic, primitive kernel of fear which owes nothing to conventionalism, since it is part of our very nature. Psychologists who, like Freud, maintain that the fear of sex comes solely from social constraint seem to me to be living in the clouds.

There is no life without desire; there is no desire without fear; one cannot desire a thing without being afraid of not obtaining it.

We cannot obtain in this world all that we desire. Therefore we cannot live without fear; without the fear of being obstructed from without or from within in the accomplishment of our desires—from without by the forces of nature and the will of others, from within by our moral conscience.

Freud defined dreams as being the realization of repressed desires. I think one can define fear similarly: the screen of a repressed desire. Consider one of my patients, who when quite a little girl, was overcome by a feeling of anxiety when she went out of the house. The fact was that she had certain grievances against her mother, and was repressing them. She wanted to go away, to get right away from the house, but her conscience condemned this desire. And so, even when her departure was legitimate it evoked in her the guilty desire, and with it fear.

Nor can we desire a thing without being afraid that one desire will lead to another until the permitted bounds are overstepped.

The primitive kernel of fear which is present in all of us is linked with our moral conscience—a concept ignored by the Freudians. It is the fear of committing sin, of being carried away by the power of our instincts and doing acts which our moral conscience condemns.

In order to liberate their patients from fear the Freudians try to persuade them that it is a creation of social constraint, that all guilt is the result of suggestion. If a person is suffering remorse at having given way to masturbation, they tell him to forsake these false scruples because they are only the result of social prejudice. In a penetrating study of the feeling of guilt in connection with masturbation, Dr Maeder has clearly demonstrated the worthlessness of such theories.[1] There is no man living who can escape the inner voice which accuses him of violating the order of nature in using his instinct contrary to its purpose—for solitary pleasure instead of for a shared pleasure which generates community. A man can be moved to repress the voice of his conscience, but he cannot be freed from it.

Moreover, this does not apply only to sex. I have taken sex as my example, because it is the most typical. The inner force which inspires fear in us is life itself. It is not only sexual desire, it is the desire to live, to possess, to expand. Which of us does not desire, from our childhood up, to be the strongest, the richest, the biggest? And from childhood we feel also that that is impossible without riding roughshod over others, without violating the order of nature, without transgressing against that sense of order which is our moral conscience. And so we are afraid of our desire, afraid of giving way to it, afraid of ourselves.

This is a fear from which no theory in the world will deliver us. It is normal, universal, and healthy, as we shall shortly see. It is part of our human nature.

*   *   *

I received a visit one day from an English friend, a cool phlegmatic Englishman, just the type of man who seems not to be

[1] Alphonse Maeder, *Ways to Psychic Health*, Hodder and Stoughton, London, 1954.

afraid of anything. Furthermore, he enjoyed in the intellectual and political circles of his country the sort of eminence which might well give him every confidence in himself. Before I had said a word he sat down and said gaily to me: 'I have just spent a wonderful week in your country. In order to get to know myself better I have tried to make a list of all the people, things, and ideas that make me afraid. It is a fruitful mental exercise. I've filled up several notebooks; but one week isn't anything like long enough to compile a complete inventory.'

I shall never forget that visit. I am reminded of it every time one of these poor people defeated in life confides in me, as if it were a great secret, that he is afraid of this or that. I realize that his suffering is due in large part to a great misunderstanding. He thinks that the 'strong' are not afraid. He is ashamed of his fear,. as if it were an exceptional weakness, whereas my English friend talked about it quite simply.

Do not imagine that the fears I enumerated just now assail only the hearts of the weak, the defeated, the neurotic. The social successes, men before whom we all tremble, men in the highest political, economic, or military positions, men who have in particular circumstances given evidence of heroic courage, are nevertheless a prey to ridiculous fears which they are powerless to banish. How many of them are afraid of their wives—or of themselves!

The truth is that it is easier to hide one's fear, from others as well as from oneself, when one appears to be strong. In order to recognize it one needs, like my English friend, to withdraw from the world and take stock of oneself. When one is a social success one can save one's face and put a brave front on things. The fear which the weak feel in the presence of the strong prevents them from seeing the latter as they really are, and discerning in them also the fear they are concealing.

The pupil may fear the master, but the master also fears the pupil. No teacher will gainsay me in that. But the greater the master's fear, the more severe and even unjust he will be, the more he will resort to intimidation to cover up his own fear. The patient may fear the doctor, who is perhaps going to disclose some serious disease or put an awkward question, but the doctor is also afraid of the patient, afraid of disappointing him, of making a mistake, of not curing him; and the more afraid he is, the more prone he will be to failure. The workman may fear the employer who can at any moment deprive him of his livelihood, but the employer also fears the workman. And the more he fears him the more authoritarian and arrogant will his attitude be. Competitor fears competitor. It is when things are going badly and one is afraid of failure that one is most careful to display calm confidence —'so as not to appear to seem . . .', as one journalist has nicely put it.[1] One tries to frighten others because one is frightened oneself. The strong reactions which we have been studying are a screen behind which we hide our fears. Fear is as much the cause of them as it is of weak reactions.

All men are afraid, and all long to be reassured. The university degrees they take, the successes they turn to account, the esteem they seek and cultivate by means of honourable behaviour, the courage they show, the verve with which they defend their views, their tenacity in demonstrating that they are always right, the respect they claim from those weaker than themselves, the witticisms they come out with—all this is armour to cover up their weakness. But though it enhances our reputation and helps to give us some measure of assurance, we know well that death will strip it from us. That is one of the reasons for the universal fear of death, and in its turn the fear of death nourishes all our other fears.

Add to that the fear which men share with all other living creatures—of natural catastrophes, of those stronger than ourselves, that can hurt and crush us. Zuckerman, who has studied the social life of monkeys, tells us that within the group each animal seems to live under a constant threat of fear.[2]

But that is not all. There is the fear that comes from within,

---

[1] Samuel Chevallier, 'Mauvais signes', in *La Suisse*, Geneva, 24 Oct. 1947.
[2] S. Zuckerman, *The Social Life of Monkeys and Apes*, Kegan Paul, London, 1932.

the fear of oneself, the fear of the forces which we actually feel in ourselves, and which might at any moment burst out.

A patient comes at last to the culminating point of a long series of confidences: 'I am afraid of myself—I am afraid of what I am discovering inside myself—I am afraid of my impulses, afraid I shall let myself go, and do some act of vengeance, of hate, of jealousy—I am afraid of being carried away by my animal instincts and becoming involved in spite of myself in some vulgar adventure—I am afraid of my feelings, my temperament, of being so sensitive—I am afraid of taking rest, because I am afraid of my dreams—I had a call to become a nun and I refused, because I was falling in love with the chaplain—I am afraid of "transference": I am afraid of conceiving a sinful love for you.'

This all means one thing: I am afraid of committing sin. And fear creates what it fears. What we fight against is what we feel to have a hold over us. All these people who suppress their feelings for fear of getting sin mixed up with them, find themselves lost in an arid desert where such a thirst to love besets them that the most innocent affection is coloured with such overwhelming emotion that the door is opened wide to sin.

Do not imagine that these fears are confined to the sick who come to consult us. They hover around those who seem most self-confident. All of us know that we have certain failings over which we have never been victorious, in spite of all our efforts and resolutions, or over which our victories have only been fleeting and incomplete. The more we try to hide them, the more they sap our self-confidence and the more numerous are our weak reactions designed to cover them up, and these in their turn weaken our moral stamina. This is why confession is the necessary prerequisite of liberation. There are eminent men who suffer acutely on account of certain secret failings, and the more banal these failings are, the more humiliating they seem: absent-mindedness, sloth, carnal lust, untidiness, irritability, masturbation, faddiness, or some ingrained habit. The higher such men are in public esteem, the more powerful, well-known, or honoured, the greater is their shame and their reluctance to admit the failing. Such is the tragedy of the lives of many a teacher, industrialist, judge, doctor, or churchman; and sometimes they have a terrible feeling of hypocrisy as they continue the practice of their honourable profession as if they were play-acting. The most distinguished people have vulgar thoughts which they are unable to confess without a fierce struggle to overcome the resistance of their self-esteem. The most courageous are haunted by memories of astonishing cowardice; the most punctilious blush at the memory of certain of their acts or thoughts.

We shall understand this better if we turn from abstract enumeration to more concrete detail. One extremely active and busy man knows that at certain moments he childishly wastes his time and is unable to stop himself doing so, in spite of the mortification it causes him. A certain woman who has suffered from her mother's impulsiveness is distressed to discover the same failing in herself, and feels powerless to master the waves of irritability which suddenly submerge her—even to the extent of causing her to strike her child. A girl who has taken to stealing is horrified at how naturally skilful she is, so that it is like some irresistible game, and also how naïvely and unsuspectingly her best friends provide her with opportunities. A certain man, who in business is scrupulously honest, cannot resist perpetrating particular irregularities in his income-tax return, or cheating the customs of tiny sums, the loss of which he would never feel. Another, who always seems to have complete self-control, is aware that he is quite unable to resist the attraction of a cigarette, a cream bun, or a pornographic magazine. Yet another faces great financial difficulties and is always urging economy upon his wife, and yet does not dare to admit to her certain expenditure which he knows to be thoroughly foolish. He even avoids recording and totalling it in order to hide it from himself. Or else he weakly lends a large sum to a friend because he is afraid to tell him of his straitened circumstances, although he knows the loan to be injudicious. Indiscipline in spending is a never-ending source of feelings of weakness, as well as its no less constant symptom. One often finds that an exaggerated concern over incurring debts goes hand in hand with an absurd impulse towards extravagance as a compensation born of vanity.

What also humiliates and torments many people is the discovery of the inconstancy of their feelings. They tell us: 'I envy you your assured and constant faith; I am always going up and down between the heights and the depths!' Truly, we are all like that, for the motions of the mind and heart are indeed *movements*. If there were no movement, we should perceive nothing. Faith itself is a perpetual and determined return towards God, from whom we are constantly turning away. It is not like a direct current, which has no inductive capacity; it resembles an alternating current, with successive negative and positive phases. A similar alternation maintains the vibration proper to affectivity. True conviction of sin, for example, is extremely rare and fleeting. It is experienced for a few seconds; longer than that it would be unbearable. Thereafter for years, for the rest of one's life, the memory of it will from time to time revitalize the spiritual life. There will be many occasions on which we shall recognize our sin, more or less intellectually; but such illuminations will be nothing but a pale caricature of the blinding flash of enlightenment when we suddenly recognized our nothingness before the grandeur and the holiness of God.

And just as there are some clocks which need winding only once a week, while others must be wound daily, so the minds and hearts of men are subject to different rhythms, and this can lead the more unstable to a despairing lack of confidence in themselves.

In connection with this alternating rhythm there is a psychological law which is always a source of anxiety to the nervous. I refer to the delayed-action effect of repression. They have some serious worry—a conflict, a threat of failure, for example, or the unfaithfulness of husband or wife. While still in the grip of suspense they hold on. But when, later, lost and humiliated, they come and consult us, they exclaim: 'I just don't understand it— only now, when everything is settled, I am giving way under the strain.' That is what happens: as long as the conflict lasted, however painful it might be, it called forth in them an instinctive power of resistance, which fails as soon as its object is removed, and leaves them depressed.

In all these moral problems, what most saps one's strength is the consciousness of not being true to oneself. It lies at the origin of the most serious weak reactions. For example, a gifted artist gives up his artistic career because he fears he may not be able to earn his living, and becomes a bank-clerk or a civil servant. An inexpressible feeling of having betrayed himself remains with him for the rest of his life, and as a result his reactions in every circumstance are weak ones. The same is the case with the bright pupil who abandons his studies in a moment of despondency, or with the lover who does not dare to declare his love for fear of being turned down, or with the woman who gives herself to her fiancé before marriage because she is afraid of losing his love.

Thus we see that from the spiritual point of view the fear which is specifically human is always bound up with guilt. This is well expressed by the Bible when it shows us Adam and Eve fleeing from God and hiding immediately after having disobeyed him.[1] It is our intimate sense of guilt, even when it is partly repressed, unconscious and imprecise, which awakens in our hearts a fear which is unknown to the animals, and which we project on to external objects. And so we frighten ourselves with phantoms which we have, in a way, created ourselves in order to personify and localize an indeterminate and unbearable fear. It comes from our hearts, and that is what makes it so tenacious—let one phantom lose its power to frighten us, it is replaced at once by another.

The truth of this is eloquently demonstrated in the cure of certain cases of excessive shyness. It is true that shyness can be conquered by methodical exercises, as advocated by various books and institutes of practical psychology. The value of this course is not to be underestimated. But occasionally it falls to our lot to witness, in these cases of shyness, a quite different deliverance: one that is sudden—explosive, even—and which takes place when the patient makes a complete and concrete confession of his sins. It is true that such cases are rare, for confession of that sort is also

[1] Gen. 3.8.

rare. No one has the courage to make it unless he is led to it by God himself. But these cases are striking.

One such case is that of a singularly gifted girl whose life is paralysed by extreme shyness. She has already experienced conversion, and has found faith. But her faith is still uncertain, and her life is marked by bursts of enthusiasm and periods of gloomy despondency. She realizes clearly that her faith is basically sentimental, and of no help to her in conquering her shyness. Her teacher encourages her: 'You have possibilities,' he says, 'so have the courage to launch out. Don't be so timid.'

After a number of interviews she comes one day to see me in a state of considerable perturbation. Suddenly, one evening, she has thought about certain things in her life of which she has never spoken to anyone, and of which she is terribly ashamed; and she has decided to come and tell me about them. During the next few days I receive a series of letters from her. First there is the expression of the immense joy that has filled her following our last meeting, when she told me her tale, and we prayed together, and I was able to bring her the assurance of God's faithfulness to blot out the sins of all who confess them to him. Then a second dramatic letter. When we set out on the road of true confession it is as if a dammed up torrent had suddenly been released, bringing with it a flood of memories. This letter tells me of other things she has remembered—things of which she is even more ashamed. A terrible struggle is going on within her. This time she feels she is bound to forfeit my respect, and yet she cannot wait for her next visit to tell me all about them.

At last her faith has stopped being sentimental. It is founded now on an ineffaceable experience of the grace of God. It infuses her whole being, and her shyness melts away.

*   *   *

While we can always consider man from the spiritual point of view, we can still look at him from the technical and psychological point of view as well. There is no contradiction in this; in fact it helps us to avoid making false judgements and drawing facile conclusions. From the latter point of view all the strange types of behaviour of which I have spoken derive, as the psychoanalysts have shown, from inner conflicts. When two opposing forces clash within us we are paralysed and lapse into weak reactions. I have space for only a few examples in illustration of this immense and important aspect of our subject.

The child receives his moral code from his parents and teachers. He has not sufficient experience to form his own judgements. The adults around him—whom he looks upon as perfect, and who affect to be so—impose so many rules upon him that inevitably he accepts the code as a whole. Now, the first article in the code may well be legitimate: 'It is wrong to tell lies.' But the second article may be quite improper: 'It is wrong to have an opinion different from that of one's father.' The third article may be authentic: 'Keep your heart pure,' and the fourth false: 'The sex instinct is wicked and shameful.' Thus the child adopts wholesale a collection of rules, some of which correspond with revealed morality, while others are merely the expression of the personal problems of those who are bringing him up. Later on he will have to sort out all these rules, but the false and the true will have become so closely associated in his mind that the process of sorting will prove difficult. Even when he has in all honesty rejected a false rule, he will feel some qualms of conscience, and be left with a false sense of guilt, which is astonishingly like a true one. From then on he will be torn between the conviction he has acquired of what is right and false resistance which has been inculcated in him by his upbringing. Psychoanalysts give the name 'super-ego' to this false moral code, and Dr Odier rightly deplores[1] the fact that its importance is still underestimated today.

One of my patients constantly heaps upon herself reproaches which at heart she does not believe to be justified. She repeats strictures which her mother used to make upon her, and which she knows to be unjust. The result is a blocking which leaves her powerless. If she thought these strictures justified she would

[1] Charles Odier, *Les deux sources, consciente et inconsciente, de la vie morale,* La Baconnière, Neuchâtel, 1943.

88

submit to them; if she rejected them she would no longer make them. Another of my patients says to me: 'The trouble with me is that I am suggestible but not influenceable.' An odd way of putting it, but it expresses very well this feeling of inner divorce: she feels the power of suggestion over her, yet cannot submit to it without doing violence to her instinctive feeling that she has a right of self-determination. It is for this reason that suggestibility is generally seen as a sign of weakness. It is both a sign and a cause, in virtue of the inner conflict which it sets up.

Another woman has made a successful career for herself as head of an industrial undertaking. She criticizes the social prejudice which holds that that is not the proper place for a woman. To me she stresses, with satisfaction, the pleasure she also takes in running her household, as if she found it necessary to vindicate herself in face of the strictures of public opinion. But she soon realizes that both her criticisms and her assertions are a defence against a voice in her own heart which echoes the social prejudice and the criticisms of her neighbours.

Yet another woman has been brought up by an authoritarian father in a patriarchal and aristocratic environment. She never went to school, and never had any opportunity of mixing with the village children. Even the games she played were regulated by her governess. While she was still a child everything went well: it never occurred to her that things could be any different; there was no inner conflict. But now her extreme nervousness betrays the struggle that is going on between the docility that this upbringing has bred in her, and the need for moral autonomy, which she feels, without, however, daring to obey it. She would not be ill if, like her sister, she had been able to submit unreservedly to compliance with the family pattern. But her nature is too independent for her not to protest inwardly at injustices against which she has nevertheless been unable to defend herself.

So the weak blame themselves for not being themselves, for giving in to the strong even when they are in the right, for timidly concealing their good qualities and talents, and even denying them when they are pointed out by others, for appearing defeated and useless when all the time they know they possess hidden capabilities. It is always surprising to discover how courageous such people can show themselves in an emergency. They themselves are conscious of this potential strength and reproach themselves for hiding it in ordinary life. There is an inner conflict going on between their weak reactions and the strength which they conceal, and this conflict increases their tendency to weak reactions. Here is another woman who shows herself strong in her business relationships, but weak where love is concerned. In the struggle to make a living she has given proof of great energy, and yet she is unable to break off a liaison which is bringing her no happiness and which will probably prevent her ever finding it.

A man presents to the world the image of the 'good little boy'. I discover that he has the soul of an adventurer, which has never dared to assert itself, and fantastic longings to defy the social conventions. Another appears irresolute, pacific, and submissive in the extreme. In reality he is a fighter. In his heart he conducts tempestuous arguments with all those who trample upon him; he remains silent for fear that he would be too violent if he were to show his feelings. A woman appears to be timid, but in reality she is holding in check the audacious aspirations which were repressed in her childhood. So one observes a sort of inversion of the character, reminiscent of many other biological phenomena which answer to the law of 'all or nothing'. The headstrong child seems incapable simply of tempering his boldness with a modicum of prudence. Instead, influenced by the constraints of his upbringing, he swings over suddenly to the opposite extreme of pusillanimity. But the two tendencies, the suppressed natural one and the artificial, remain in collision.

Such is our human nature, infinitely complex and fragile, subject to all kinds of false suggestions, beset by innumerable fears, torn by incessant inner conflicts. Of course there are simple souls who are not aware of all that is going on within themselves; and there are others who are more discerning, and are able to contemplate, so to speak, the storms raging within. But the unconsciousness of the former has the appearance of a sort of instinctive defence against fear. There are not, therefore, as is commonly believed, two kinds of human beings, those who have inner conflicts and those who do not. If there is a distinction to be made among men, it is rather this: some hide their fears, while others admit them. Nevertheless, to recognize our fears and look them in the face, is frightening; but it is the only way of holding our own against them. Masson-Oursel remarks: 'There are some people who fear nothing and give in to everything. There are some who fear everything and give in to nothing.' The Great Condé's maxim is well known: 'You must fear the enemy at a distance so as not to be afraid of him when he is at hand.'

Strong reactions, with their bluster and swagger, lead more surely to defeat than does the recognition of one's weakness. Such recognition is the *sine qua non* of sincerity towards oneself, of all spiritual growth, of all creative endeavour.

I remember one evening I spent with some friends, among whom were two pastors. One of these, much admired and sought after as a preacher, confessed that he had an extraordinary fear of preaching. He told us of how he would spend hour after anxious hour during the week, preparing a sermon, and then on Saturday he would scrap his plan completely. He would climb trembling into his pulpit, and when he came down again he always felt as if he had betrayed his vocation. His colleague broke in, saying that preaching had never worried him. 'On Saturday evening,' he said, 'my text comes quite naturally into my mind, and I go to bed without worrying. When I am in the pulpit the words just seem to come of themselves.' Then he added: 'No, the really discouraging thing is to have to preach to empty pews. The people are neglecting their duty. The Church ought to take a strong line and really insist on attendance at public worship.'

No endeavour is fruitful without fear. There is no good actor who does not have to contend with stage-fright. There is no lecturer listened to who does not tremble. I am not ashamed to confess the fear in which I write this book, and which I know to be inevitable. Desire, fear, and sorrow, as St Augustine pointed out, may come from the love of good and of charity; they are not in themselves vices. 'Fear,' wrote Dubois, 'within certain limits, is an eminently useful emotion.'[1]

To reject the utopian idea of a life without fear, to accept our human condition, fear-ridden as it is, this is not merely resignation. It is to accept fear as a blessing from God, with its part to play in his purpose for mankind.

Fear is universal because it is an instinct; it is the instrument of the instinct of self-preservation. It has a providential significance. It is the source of all progress. It is the motive force of the whole of civilization; that of science, which seeks to pierce the terrifying mysteries of nature; that of philosophy and religion, whose quest is truth; that of labour, of agriculture and industry, by which men strive against their material insecurity; that of society, of social collaboration, by which they join forces and forget the things that divide them. This is clearly seen when a country threatened by danger from outside realizes the dedicated unity and social peace which has always eluded it in easier times. It is the fear of everything new which gives personal and social life its stability and the framework of habits without which all is confusion. It is also fear which—fortunately!—restrains men from blind obedience of their passions, whose fatal consequences they have learnt from experience.

I said just now that no one can love without experiencing the mysterious fear love awakens. A patient tells me of a dream he has had: he was in a boat, but every time he approached the landing-stage a menacing wild beast prevented him landing. At the third attempt he leaps ashore, grapples with the monster and throws it to the ground. He is suddenly aware that what he is embracing is a wondrously beautiful woman. This is the experience symbolized in all those legends in which a fairy palace is guarded by dragons.[2] Love would no longer be love if it did not involve fear and victory over that fear. All poetic emotion derives from the resonance of these fears which are the price of love and beauty.

But there is more to be said. Fear is also the narrow gate of

[1] Op. cit., p. 149.
[2] Leïa, *Le symbolisme des contes de fées*, Editions du Mont Blanc, Geneva, 1943.

which Christ speaks, and apart from which we cannot find God. Grace is promised to him who recognizes his weakness, and not to him who boasts of his strength. The Bible, with its realistic knowledge of the human heart, repeats 365 times the words 'Fear not.' It speaks also of 'the fear of God' as the beginning of wisdom. Christ, with his psychological insight, knows that there is no life without fear. He was not exempt from it himself, as Weatherhead points out:[1] 'his sweat became as it were great drops of blood'. He urges us to banish harmful fears in favour of a more fruitful fear: 'Be not afraid of them which kill the body, but are not able to kill the soul: but rather fear him which is able to destroy both soul and body in hell.'[2]

Thus fear is beneficial or harmful, according to whether or not it plays in our lives the part assigned to it in the purpose of God. The biblical perspective never suggests that we should pass over from the camp of the weak to that of the strong, but that we should recognize our weakness. If we find it so difficult to confess our fears, that is because we always want to seem strong. We are ashamed of our fear, and this shame consolidates the fear and renders it harmful. A woman patient of mine, suffering from a tumour in the breast, writes to me about her fear of cancer: 'A real Christian ought not to be afraid.' No, madam, the Christian is not exempt from fear, but he takes his fears to God. Faith does not suppress fear; what it does is to allow one to go forward in spite of it. When my English friend made his list of fears it was so as to face them—with God's grace. In God's presence we abandon the stoic's utopia of a life without fear, which is the source of so many repressions and so many lies. With him we can look our fear in the face and confess it to him, so that he can make fertile what is divine in it.

But this road is itself guarded by the dragon of fear. All men are afraid of God. Open the Bible and you will see that that is their first reaction whenever God speaks to them. They are afraid of God because they have a bad conscience and because they dread the sacrifices which he may ask of them.

[1] Op. cit.   [2] Matt. 10.28.

I often think that my vocation, both in the field of psychology and in the realm of the spirit, is nothing but the banishment of fear. Each in his turn, the strong and the weak, come and confess to me the fears that are standing in their way and falsifying their reactions. At the human level, I have no answer. Fear is not amenable to the will. We can repress it, but not liquidate it. We can compromise with it, restricting our lives so as not to expose ourselves to fear. But that is no victory. And I must be honest: all these fears beset me as well.

If, however, I can be of any help to others, it is only when I no longer seem to them to be a sort of inaccessible superman who does not share their struggles, when they feel me near them. It is because I have myself learnt to recognize my fears, and no longer lull myself with the illusion that I can escape from them. On the contrary, it is my experience that if we look them squarely in the face, if we bring them in faith to God, we can overcome them. This is no easy thing to do. Here as in war, he is not the strongest who thinks himself strong and underestimates the power of the adversary.

I am reminded of one of my patients who quite early on in our interviews told me she had a conscience about the ruling part that fear had played in her life and in her illness. We prayed together, and she felt relief. Optimistically, I believed that the problem was solved. Some years later, when all our therapeutic efforts had failed, she admitted that she had felt then that I had been too easily satisfied. She found herself alone with her fears, which she no longer dared to voice because I thought they had been overcome. What we must do, then, is realistically to accept the situation in which it has pleased God to place us as human beings, so that we may turn towards him. Day by day we must set aside what is sinful in our fear, but preserve its stimulus, in so far as God himself has put it in our hearts to make us aware of our wretchedness.

PART TWO

REACTIONS

4

WEAK REACTIONS

W E CAN NOW study in detail the two kinds of reaction—the weak and the strong—by which men manifest their common anxiety.

Weak reactions are those of inhibition; strong reactions, those of excitation.

Among weak reactions are depression, despondency, sadness, self-pity, self-reproach, weariness of life, exaggerated self-criticism, panic, escapism, withdrawal into one's shell, silence, and torpor.

Among strong reactions are exhilaration, euphoria, gaiety, condescension, self-satisfaction, optimism, exaggerated criticism of others, rashness, aggressiveness, buoyancy, glibness of tongue, and excitability.

I could lengthen these lists; but weak reactions are all connected with flight and inertia.

Of the various forms of flight I have already spoken in *Médecine de la personne*. I shall limit myself here to mentioning the many forms of flight represented by our little daily acts of cowardice: cleverly changing the subject of conversation when what is being said threatens to embarrass us or to provoke a disagreeable argument; discovering that we have something urgent to do in order to escape a less urgent but uncongenial task; protesting our incompetence or ignorance when we ought to speak out; taking refuge in prudent silence, in modesty, in theorizing, or in interminable and empty verbiage; invoking the opinion of a person whose authority will back up our own. The reason why so many conversations remain shallow is that the speakers are all running away from one another. They hide their vulnerable selves behind a screen of banal remarks, polite compliments, witticisms, or artificial extravagances.

An absolutely honest and direct intercourse, free from subterfuge, pretence, evasion and swank is difficult to maintain. As soon as it becomes dangerous we wrap ourselves like warships in a smoke-screen. With a little experience we are able to spot all the tiny signs of these constant movements of flight, even in the case of people who come into our consulting-rooms with the sincere intention of showing themselves to us in their true colours. But it is even more valuable to see these movements at work in ourselves. My colleagues often ask me: 'How is it that you manage to talk so intimately to everyone?' I think that the answer is never to let ourselves become accomplices in any of these attempts at evasion, never ourselves to fly off at a tangent when the conversation shows signs of turning down into the depths, to be ready ourselves at all times to face any problem, any question, however indiscreet.

One of the great virtues of setting a 'quiet time' aside for prayer is that it helps us to overcome these difficulties. When I place myself before God with my wife or with a friend, and silently note down all my thoughts, I am often obliged to write things which I should not like to talk about. That is why so many people are afraid of saying their prayers. I was chatting yesterday with one of my patients, a most likeable person, with whom I have already had a number of intimate and frank conversations. But when I suggested to him that we should pray together, he told me what was holding him back. 'I know very well,' he said, 'that if I try to pray, certain thoughts come into my mind which make me afraid!' All at once it seemed that our intimacy had increased tenfold. It was already great, but we both felt as if we had broken through into a deeper sanctuary.

It has also often happened that I have thought to myself: 'Now the moment has come for us to pray together,' and then I have taken refuge in the vain pursuit of conversation instead of suggesting it. Even in one's meditations it is hard to remain quite honest, not to banish any thought on any pretext of propriety or because it is inopportune. It is very much easier to flatter oneself by noting down a few high-minded but commonplace precepts, than to write simply what comes spontaneously into one's mind.

The other form of weak reaction is that state of inertia which physiologists and psychologists call inhibition. The untranslatable German word *Hemmung* admirably expresses this feeling of being obstructed by a strange invisible ligature, paralysed and petrified.

Take the case of a very emotional girl who had suffered greatly from the hostility of her parents. Her father had nothing for her but complaints and gestures of irritation. One day, when she was quite small, the father suddenly produced a trinket which he placed on the table in front of her. It was a little glass elephant. 'Look what I've brought you!' he said. Astounded, delighted, overwhelmed at receiving such an unexpected present, the child sat rooted to the spot, giving no sign of her feelings. The little elephant seemed to her to be shining as brightly as any Star of Bethlehem; she could not even tell what the little sparkling object was supposed to be. She could neither move nor speak. Then, like an automaton, she got up and went off into the next room, and when she came back she saw the little elephant hanging glittering from her sister's neck. 'Since you don't want it, I'm giving it to your sister,' her father explained quietly. That is the tragic thing about weak reactions: they lead other people into error. Highly emotional people are apt to be misunderstood. This girl was so intensely moved that it was as if she had been struck dumb, and her stupefaction was taken for indifference. In its turn the misunderstanding, which deprived her of her wonderful present, upset her so much that she remained incapable of explaining what had happened so as to clear it up.

This last is a fine point, but I insist on it because of the vitally important part it plays in the inner turmoil which afflicts emotional people. Take for example the case of another of my patients, a woman who is intelligent enough to be well aware of the complexes to which she is subject. A certain woman once did her serious harm, and now she cannot remember her without an acute feeling of distress. She is visiting some friends, when the name of this woman happens to come up in conversation. Our patient quite rightly feels that she ought to leave. She makes as if to go; her friends protest; her emotion prevents her from explaining; she stays, but from then on her confusion is complete. Added to the distress provoked by the subject of conversation is a kind of exasperation with herself at feeling incapable of explaining herself and going away.

Another source of misunderstanding is the persistent quality of an emotional upset. The weak person is unable quickly to throw off the effects of an annoyance, a disagreeable suggestion, or a failure. He is like a pupil who has to work out his algebra problem on a blackboard still covered with his comrade's equations, or a photographer who has forgotten to wind on the film, so that the pictures are mixed up together, one superimposed on the other. Other people do not understand him; they think that his distress is all over and done with; they take his numbness for inattention or indifference. The trouble is that, feeling himself thus misunderstood, the weak person finds it more difficult to regain his equanimity.

A similar mechanism is also often at work in the case of hesitation. The weak faced with a choice between alternatives, need more time and tranquillity than other people to make up their minds. Knowing their liability to emotion they are afraid that they will be rushed into evasion or into having their minds made up for them by others, and this fear makes matters worse. They say they do not know which course to choose—but that is not true: their choice is made already in their hearts. It is the expression of the choice which is paralysed. Then there arises that annoyance with themselves which occupies their minds to the exclusion of everything else, so that they cannot think, and are unable to formulate a decision or use their will-power.

Many sensitive people speak of an inner ferment which, once it is set in motion, aggravates their weak reactions and the consequent misunderstandings, a ferment which in its turn is fed by this feeling of not being understood. It is like a lamp that has the intensity of its light increased by the addition of a reflector. A blocking takes place, owing to the reflection upon himself of the subject's own emotion; and what inhibits him is precisely this irritation at not being able to express the sound intuitions, judgements, and choices which he has in his heart and which those about him believe he lacks. He is like a man in a hurry who has lost the key of the garage in which his car is. His very haste militates against his finding the missing key; and that deprives him of the car with which he could make up for lost time.

That car in the garage is like the feeling of impotence due to the blocking of one's powers. It gives an impression of fatigue, and lends colour to the conviction of the sensitive person that he is weak.

Fatigue is the characteristic sign of nervous prostration, and, as Dr Dubois pointed out,[1] it is the first symptom complained of by all such patients. In itself it is the weak reaction *par excellence*, the eclipse of a person's strength when he comes up against an insurmountable obstacle. But this very inhibition is itself the cause of many further weak reactions. The problem, therefore, is much more complex than a patient imagines when he thinks of fatigue as being merely passive, a simple lack of energy.

*   *   *

In ordinary practice, we can distinguish four chief causes of fatigue. We must beware of systematizing too rigidly, however, for these causes often overlap.

First there is genuine over-work. I believe this to be the rarest cause. It is due sometimes to external factors, to a concourse of circumstances—illness, poverty, social injustice, which imposes long hours of work, or does not allow proper holidays. But it is often due to an unregulated way of life, which one could remedy if one wanted to do so. One must adapt one's life to one's temperament. Those who are not gifted with boundless energy often over-work because they are afraid of being thought lazy or of being accused of mollycoddling themselves.

Many people take a particular pride in never admitting that

[1] Op. cit., p. 123.

they are tired. Christ himself experienced fatigue, and was able to rest. Many people too are ashamed of being ill. I am reminded of a young woman who suffered from a barely compensated cardiac lesion. Her friends, themselves bursting with health, told her not to be so afraid of exerting herself. It was a real moral victory for her to dare to use a lift when they were there.

Those who suffer from functional nervous complaints are especially ashamed of their illness. If some friend asks after their health they feel his kindly question as an affront. This false shame makes their condition worse, and this in turn increases their shame, for they do not know what to say to the friend when he shows his surprise that they are not better yet.

Another cause of overwork is our reluctance to give up some activity which we value, or to disappoint someone we love. I always find it hard to refuse a pressing request to give a lecture, or to tell a patient that I cannot see him before a certain date. If I am always in a fever of activity, how can I talk of peace to those who seek it? Thus one sees clergymen who preach the observance of Sunday as a day of rest, but who work late into the night seven days a week, and have no time left to devote to their own inner life; or politicians who wear themselves out honouring with their presence all sorts of futile ceremonial functions, and leave themselves with no leisure to think about the essential problems of those they govern.

Naturally, greed or financial worry is a frequent cause of overwork. One of the most important and difficult tasks of the doctor is to regulate his patients' activities in accordance with their physical powers. One receives many surprises: there are seeming weaklings who have unsuspected reserves to draw upon, and giants who have no powers of resistance at all.

But without actual overwork, fatigue is often the result of bad organization. I was at one time very tired as a result of the free consultations which I used to give three times a week in the early afternoon, because it worried me when they went on so long that they interfered with the appointments I had arranged to follow them, and this was detrimental to both the free consultations and the private appointments. The quite simple solution, which came to us only when we prayed about the matter, was to keep one whole day a week for free consultations, so as to be able to work peacefully on the private appointments on the other days.

Particularly difficult is the regulation of the lives of convalescents. After a physical illness or a nervous breakdown, a slow and progressive resumption of activity is essential. One comes up against many snags: impatience on the part of the convalescent, who wants to run before he can walk, or do straight away whatever he likes; lack of confidence on his part, or discouragement at feeling his limitations so soon; lack of understanding on the part of employers who do not like part-time arrangements, or who promise special consideration which does not last three days.

This is the place to mention the law of training, which is so simple and yet so little understood. Those doctors who were concerned with the planning and control of physical training in our armed forces during the war demonstrated quite clearly that rest is as important as exercise.[1] An athlete does not reach his best form by making superhuman efforts, but by gradually increasing his effort, little by little, and especially by taking a proper rest after each effort. The same is true of intellectual work. As Father Sertillanges says: 'There is no real work without real rest.'[2]

I have written elsewhere of the misuse by large numbers of people of their Sunday rest or their holidays. They tire themselves more than when at work, to say nothing of the accompanying abuse of food and alcohol. We may recall, in this connection, the fatigue-effects of intoxication, the importance of which was pointed out by Dr Paul Carton.[3]

A second cause of fatigue is excess of zeal. One young man suffering from the effects of overwork was a commercial traveller

[1] A. Delachaux, 'L'homme et ses facultés d'adaptation', in *Revue médicale de la Suisse romande*, 25 Oct. 1944, p. 744.

[2] A. D. Sertillanges, *La vie intellectuelle*, Editions de la Revue des Jeunes, Paris, 1921.

[3] P. Carton, *Traité de médecine, d'alimentation et d'hygiène naturistes*, Maloine, Paris, 1920.

who spent himself immoderately and doggedly at his work. As a matter of fact this relentless toil was the expression of a deep-seated need to rehabilitate himself in life, because of a feeling of inferiority implanted in him by undeserved criticism during his childhood. A young domestic servant was actually sent to me by her employer because she never seemed able to relax. It became clear that she was trying by means of hard work to dull the pain of a serious conflict with her family. Many people thus indulge in a ceaseless whirl of fevered activity because they are afraid to be left alone with themselves and their thoughts; or because they are afraid of 'cracking up' if they stop—as they themselves not infrequently admit.

Work like this is fatiguing not only by reason of the bodily strain it involves, but also because of the mental strain which accompanies it. The same task can in fact either be a game, if accomplished with a light heart, or lead to exhaustion when it sets up a moral tension in us, due for example to jealousy (the jealousy of each other's zeal, so frequent in those who are working on a task together; the jealousy of a wife who wants to get through as much work as her more robust husband); or it may be due to pride, as in the case of some hospital nurses who are so proud of their vocation that they will never acknowledge their fatigue; or to the fear of not being equal to the task in hand; or, lastly, the tension may be due to an overwhelming sense of duty, which becomes a burden to anyone who has not had the experience of God's grace.

But what fatigues us most of all—and this is our third cause—is our rebellion. A disabled woman who had always suffered from a feeling of intense fatigue came to tell me that she had suddenly been liberated from it. It happened when she had learnt to accept her infirmity through meditating upon a remark made by an old doctor: 'What matters in this world is not the amount of one's strength, but the use one makes of what one has.'

'Fatigue,' writes Dr Pierre Ponsoye,[1] 'is largely an encephalic

[1] Pierre Ponsoye, *L'esprit, force biologique fondamentale*, Causse, Graille & Castelneau, Montpellier, 1942.

and cortical phenomenon.' We do indeed feel it in our members, but it often has its seat in the mind.

A man who is discontented in his work, who does it only with a continual inner irritation, who blames circumstances or other people for having unjustly imposed on him a task that is beyond his strength or that has no relation to his capabilities and interests, who is always harking back in his mind to the disappointments he has had, who reckons that his employer is taking advantage of him and exploiting him, who longs for a holiday and is afraid of a breakdown in health as a result of overwork and persecution —such a man is worn out with fatigue. All this mental book-keeping makes him see his work and the injustices he suffers as worse than they are, and this alarming mental picture of them makes his fatigue—and consequently his rebellion—still greater. In such a case real acceptance can cause the fatigue to fall away like a cloak cast aside. Or else the man must summon up the courage either to demand equitable working conditions or to give in his notice.

Many people describe as fatigue what is really only irritation. 'I am exhausted,' they say, by which they mean: 'My nerves are all on edge.'

Such people are suffering from 'false fatigue'. False, not because they are lying, for they have a real sensation of fatigue, but because their fatigue has not weakened them. On the contrary, they are capable of extremely lively reactions. They are often fatigued by inaction, and this is our fourth cause. I have seen many people brimming with vitality, who ought to have been spending themselves in some absorbing and useful activity, but who have lapsed into a kind of sterile exhaustion simply because the energy bubbling inside them is not being used. Nothing is more fatiguing than a perpetual inner battle. Psychological complexes, mistakes in upbringing, conflicts or fears lie behind the nervous state of such people. Instead of looking after them, helping them to triumph over their condition, people have over-simplified their problem with the remark: 'If you're feeling nervy, take a rest.' A young man, engaged to be married and up to then very active, becomes suddenly depressed, because he is secretly fighting the temptation to possess his fiancée, and the anguished fear of succumbing to it. He is made to stay away from work. The resulting void in his life is now filled completely with his secret struggle. His health is endangered, and there will be no improvement until he is able to unburden himself of what is troubling him and take up his work again.

Another case is that of a very able man who found his capacity for work gradually diminishing. He was granted extended leave in order to have a complete rest. On returning to his office he is disappointed to find no improvement. He begins to lose confidence in himself, and to fear that he is becoming prematurely old. But when we carefully examine his case, we see that on the contrary he is aware of his own worth; he knows himself to be capable of undertaking great responsibilities, whereas he is still entrusted with only minor tasks. There had been a chance of promotion for him, but string-pulling and nepotism behind the scenes had caused him to be passed over. His lassitude is really a nervous state, betraying a secret impatience. His condition will only get worse so long as its real significance remains unrecognized, and so long as he is afraid, quite wrongly, that he is losing his faculties.

Another man, of an enterprising and lively disposition, needs to exert himself. A serious disappointment brought on a fit of depression, and he was sent away on a rest cure. There the meticulous care taken to see that he did not over-exert himself helped to attach to his own person and his health the emotion due in reality to his disappointment. The result is that he is in constant fear of over-taxing his strength. When he goes to play tennis, instead of throwing himself into the game he wonders whether it is not going to last too long and tire him. If he were really exhausted this life measured in driblets would be just the thing for him, but it is contrary to his vigorous nature. It only makes him feel worse.

There are people who are made to rest like this for years. Their lives are so restricted that anyone in their place would be turned into an invalid, deprived of everything that builds up strength: joy, work, hope, love. And the more ill they are, the more strictly are they forbidden all activity, and the more deeply implanted in their minds is the fear of fatigue and that 'conviction of lack of power' the tremendous importance of which in nervous fatigue has been pointed out by Dubois.[1] As they feel the gulf separating them from normal life getting deeper and deeper, they become more and more despairing of ever having the strength to cross it, and look to the nursing-home as the only refuge for their impoverished lives.

*   *   *

Fatigue, the weak reaction *par excellence*, is therefore frequently due to emotional blocking. It paralyses the powers of the subject, just as a labour strike paralyses a country's economy. Like the strike, it is a weapon of the weak. A person who does not feel himself strong enough to dominate another in conversation becomes the victim of a strike by his brain and his organs of speech. He is assailed by mental catatonia: he can no longer think; or else, if he does think, the words are arrested at his larynx, thronging there like a crowd of strikers. This is the mechanism of chagrin and sulkiness. Understandably, those around him are irritated by the victim's sulks, and set on him in an effort to break his strike. Their efforts, however, only make matters worse. This is the explanation of certain instances of dumbness in children whose development has been hindered or whose sensitivity has been injured. They withdraw into unsociable solitude. Similarly, a passion for animals may be a way of holding aloof from human society.

This strike reaction is very common. Dr Allendy has shown very definitely[2] that, apart from certain cases that are pathological in origin, a lazy child is one who is on strike, and that what is needed is to find out what has injured him rather than to rebuke him. The passivity shown by many people is another form of strike reaction, while petty time-wasting and much of our

[1] Op. cit., pp. 123-4.   [2] *L'enfance méconnue.*

forgetfulness is to be seen as a sort of go-slow strike. Sometimes, in spite of my having set my heart on writing this book, in order to pass on to my readers what I can see of the human problem from my privileged observation-post, I find myself sitting stultified in front of my writing-paper. I turn some sentence over and over in my mind to find the right wording, and yet if I were merely writing a letter it would come to me at once. I seem to have forgotten how to think. A weak reaction. Then I waste time doodling, or carving thumb-indexes in my dictionary; and when I am proud of having hit upon an ingenious method of spacing them out regularly, the tiny satisfaction it gives me is some consolation for all the trouble I am having in expressing my ideas. I realize that at bottom what I am doing is wasting time in order to give myself a twinge of conscience, from which to draw the necessary energy to overcome the obstructive effect of my weak reactions.

Many functional disorders are strike-symbols—one example is an overwhelming desire to sleep. An office-worker is attacked by writer's cramp. He is the willing horse, to whom his fellow-clerks leave all the most unpleasant tasks, and who has not the courage to protest. He nurses a feeling of sullen rebellion against them, but represses it beneath an obliging exterior. The illness interrupting his work is nothing but a strike fomented by his unconscious. In the same way frigidity in women and impotence in men more often than not represent a sexual strike against a husband or wife against whom unexpressed grievances are being harboured. Further examples of strikes may be found in escape into religious piety or into disease in an attempt to find shelter from the hurly-burly of life. I refrain from repeating what I have already said in *Médecine de la personne* about many other maladies, such as constipation, migraine, asthma, paraplegia, and asthenia. Most cases of bed-wetting in children are to be explained as an unconscious way of going on strike.

Excessive thinness often seems to me to be the expression of a strike against life. Such was the case of a young woman who suffered from mental anorexia. Meals were a veritable nightmare to her. Seeking to understand her I found that she was haunted by a feeling of having missed her opportunities in life. She was conscious of having great talents, which circumstances had not permitted her to put to use. She felt as if she had been left standing alone on the station platform while the others went off on a wonderful journey. Subconsciously her chagrin had provoked a hunger-strike in her.

Bad writing and a sullen appearance represent a strike with regard to social relationships.

Sometimes a strike is accompanied by sabotage. Without wishing it a man does just those things which will make him fail to attain what he most ardently desires. His unconscious is thus making him demonstrate to his parents, to whom he has not dared to complain openly, the catastrophic results of the upbringing to which they have subjected him. If he were to succeed in life, his complaints would be proved groundless, and his unconscious is unwilling to give them up. I once had a woman patient who could not stand the singing of birds, so great was the resentment it aroused in her.

I do not wish to disparage these reactions, which often have a useful function as a defence instinctively put up by the personality against a suffering so keen that it could not be endured without doing even greater damage. It is like stopping up the chinks in the armour. Many people blanket themselves in daydreams or woolly sentimentality in order to deaden the harsh blows of reality. A young woman says to me: 'My father goes away whenever the conversation takes a serious turn.' 'I don't like hearing people talk about war,' says another. It is 'ostrichism', as a third remarked, the art of shutting one's eyes to the things that are frightening or unpleasant. Many of my patients suffering from nerves confide in me their fears that they are becoming indifferent to everything, that nothing matters to them any more. It is a protective indifference, which bears witness to their sensitiveness, whereas they think they have become insensitive. I am told that this is one of the effects of repeated aerial bombardment. A similar feeling of general indifference often makes its appearance as a premonitory sign of recovery after a period of depression.

The systematic scepticism of certain people is often merely a way of showing their chagrin at being unable to attain the absolute certainty to which they aspire. 'I couldn't care less' means, as in the fable of the fox and the grapes, 'I am mortified at not getting what I long for.'

These protection-reactions are like the safety curtain which is lowered in the theatre when there is a fire on the stage, or the drawbridge that is raised to defend a fortress from attack. Every weak person, in fact, looks for a shield. It may be the tone of banter or levity under which he hides his distress, or the continual flood of complaints with which the neurotic seems to be warning those around him that his cup is full and that he cannot stand being crossed any more.

But though many weak reactions seem thus to be in certain respects attempts at a cure, they are always false remedies. Thus, recourse to stimulants, notably alcohol, to which vast numbers of the weak resort in order to fortify themselves, saps their real powers; and they themselves see in it the proof of their weakness. A quarrelsome, irascible man once admitted to me that in his perpetual arguments he was really seeking an artificial stimulant to overcome his timidity. A sensitive, intelligent, and gifted man, he realized that his weakness of character veiled from view his good qualities. His violence was a vain attempt to tear aside the veil; but all it did was to add a mask to the veil. Or else he drifted into daydreams to console himself for the failure of his efforts.

Another of my patients told me that he used to go over the events of his life in his mind like a play, in order to imagine a different dénouement for them. Many people repeat over and over to themselves certain phrases or clichés. The true explanation of fads and mechanical gestures—the lighting of a cigarette, for example—is often that they are also a way of mustering courage. The state of mind of one of my patients was like a gramophone with only two records: one described an idyllic land in which all was perfectly beautiful and marvellous; the other was all ugliness and horror. He played the second only rarely, merely to set off the splendour of the first.

Some men with a passion for intellectual culture are hindered in their studies by feelings of inferiority. They shut themselves up in their rooms at night and pursue their studies in secret, sometimes attaining a really expert knowledge of their subject. But this very secrecy cuts them off from society and aggravates their feeling of inferiority. They have contact neither with their colleagues in the office, whose commonplace conversation holds no interest for them, nor with the intellectuals, whom they avoid, naïvely thinking them more erudite than themselves.

Daydreams, detaching the mind as they always do from reality, make the dreamer still weaker and less capable of coping with the real world.

Many emotionally unstable people put a brake on their lives—they turn the lights low, as it were—in order to lessen the emotions aroused in them. At the end of a conversation which has remained entirely on a superficial level, they admit that they have not had the courage to talk to me about the things they have really come to see me about, for fear of becoming too emotional, and they go away disheartened—and overwrought with emotion, too, for when we block our lives we isolate ourselves in a fume of bottled-up despair. I often think that these people are like whistling kettles—except that they have stopped up the whistle in order to conceal the tell-tale sign of their inner tension. Eventually, an explosion is inevitable. When we bottle up our emotions they only become more violent, and our fear of showing them is the greater, so that we redouble our efforts to hide them, and the vicious circle is complete. Every woman, for example, feels with intense emotion the desire to get married. Those who are ashamed of the desire and try to hide the emotion it causes, increase their distress, so making it unlikely that anyone will fall in love with them. One girl I knew actually gave up learning the piano, in spite of having considerable musical talent, because she was obsessed by the fear of becoming too attached to her tutor.

Thus the weak tend to cut themselves off from social contacts. But when they have scarcely any friends left the emotion aroused in them by some rare friendship becomes so intense that it spoils the friendship by making it forced and unnatural. All their pent-up need to love is concentrated on a single person, and the relationship is spoilt. They are afraid, too, of wearying their friend by the very excessiveness of their affection. When a liquid is poured into a very narrow vessel, it rises much higher than it would in a wide one. Emotional people keep on restricting the base of their lives, and their emotion rises ever higher. Or else they hide their affection for fear of becoming too attached, and this secret unavowed affection grows until it enslaves them.

Their exclusiveness sometimes makes them look upon the friend as a god, imagining him to be perfect. Inevitably the time comes when they are disillusioned; the friend tumbles down from his pedestal, to become the object of equally violent obloquy. The emotion is as strong as ever, owing to the inner conflict between repressed affection and resentment.

Self-depreciation may also be seen as a vain attempt to diminish emotion. A man sends me his poems, which are remarkable. He adds: 'I am quite aware that they are valueless.' In saying this he is insuring himself against the emotion he will feel in face of my praise or criticism. Another says: 'I have never had a religious experience.' The remark is an insurance against the emotion the recognition of such an experience would cause in him, involving as it would the drawing of certain conclusions about his life, and the adoption of a particular course of conduct in consequence. A young communist has joined the party in order to force himself into action, in an attempt to cure himself, for he is strong in ideas but weak in practice. So I suggest that he should become a really active member of the party. To this he replies that his decision was a 'false remedy'. His answer is one more way of providing intellectual cover for his flight from action. A student who postpones his examinations from fear of the emotional anxiety they cause him is much more nervous when he does eventually have to sit them, and perhaps he will never do so. People who say: 'I am no good at anything; I am stupid; I am ugly', are unconsciously trying to lessen the risk of having to put their capabilities to the proof. A woman, new to business and still nervous, proposes the cheapest article to her customer, in order to reduce the emotion she feels at making a profit.

*　　　　*　　　　*

A man is afraid of being deceived by his feelings. In his anxiety he is suspicious when he ought to be trustful, and trustful when he ought to be suspicious. As a result of his frequent mistakes he loses confidence in himself and his anxiety is increased. Montaigne wrote of fear: 'There is no passion which so quickly unhinges our judgement.' But the feeling that one is lacking in judgement is itself a potent source of fear.

The wife who is afraid of her husband's angry outbursts only provokes them by her dissimulation and embarrassment. The weak husband, afraid of quarrels between his wife and his mother, tries to humour them both. His indecision only provokes the quarrels, and draws them on to himself, as each brings pressure to bear on him in an effort to tear him away from the influence of the other.

There is, then, a strict chain of cause and effect which increases weak reactions, snowball fashion.

As Dr Allendy points out,[1] the child who is persecuted at home shows himself diffident at school, and soon becomes the butt of the class. I myself recall with deep regret the refined cruelty with which at school we used to treat classmates who were sensitive to mockery and unable to defend themselves. Children, like adults, respect those who are self-assured, and torment those who are nervous. The master who is afraid of not being able to keep order is the one who is played up. The father who feels his authority crumbling reminds his son of the respect due to him in a tone of voice which completes the collapse of his influence. The timorous give way to the strong, because their painful memories of parental squabbles have given them a terror of all argument. But the strong then use them as pawns in their own conflicts, letting them take all the raps.

'All my life,' a woman writes to me, 'I have been afraid of

[1] *L'enfance méconnue.*

suffering, and my fear has led me into endless suffering.' The child who is afraid of his father only irritates him by his shrinking attitude, and brings down his father's anger upon himself. Or else his fear drives him to seek his mother's protection; but he fares no better, since he now falls foul of his offended father's jealousy. The mother herself often makes matters worse by giving him a distorted and terrifying picture of what his father is like. I was for a long time concerned with the case of a young girl to whom this had happened. She was eventually cured only after a course of psychoanalysis. She was reconciled with her father, and wrote me a letter in which she said: 'I know now that I have a father I can be proud of.' A widowed father is afraid of upsetting his daughter by telling her of his plan to marry again; he even denies it when, having heard of it through friends, she challenges him on the subject. The shock is irremediable when, a short time afterwards, he presents to her her 'new mother'.

The person who feels weak has a great need of affection. This very need makes him more dependent upon those who show him affection; and this feeling of dependence makes him more keenly aware of his weakness. A person who, from weakness, puts off an urgent task—a difficult letter that has to be written, for instance—has a bad conscience about it. The longer the delay, the worse this feeling, and the more it paralyses him, making him put off still further the painful moment when he will have to make excuses for his delay.

The person who finds it hard to go to sleep is afraid of insomnia when he goes to bed, and this preoccupation keeps him awake. A nervous man with an obsessive fear of cancer came to see me, worried about intestinal troubles in which he already saw the onset of the disease. He admitted to me that he had for years taken a daily purgative because he had read somewhere that purgation prevented cancer!

An emotional young woman suffered from mild functional disturbances. Worried about her health, she gave up her missionary vocation, and following upon this abandonment of her calling, her troubles were aggravated.

A person who lacks confidence in himself consults everybody and in face of the contradictory advice he receives, is left in a state of even worse indecision. A young woman, crushed by a domineering mother, seeks refuge in one religion after another. Brought up as a Moslem, she has tried the Roman Catholic Church, she has immersed herself in the writings of Indian sages, and attended Christian Science meetings. If in my turn I talk to her about my Calvinist faith, I shall only make her more unsettled.

Similarly, a woman consults one doctor after another about her nerves. Too often they undermine her confidence in medicine by criticizing their colleagues who have treated her hitherto. Or else, full of enthusiasm for her latest doctor she irritates her friends with her constant eulogies of him, so that they are goaded into telling her of cases in which he has failed. Or worse still, they accuse her of being in love with him. Such an insinuation disturbs her and makes it impossible for her really to trust herself to his care.

And then, one of the results of much consulting of doctors is the depressing feeling of being a 'case'. Always asking their advice makes one incapable of standing on one's own feet. One of my patients was a woman who had undergone a long and unsuccessful course of treatment by a psychoanalyst, followed by the equally unsuccessful intervention of a Christian healer. Both had been full of zeal and good intentions.

But the trouble was that she felt so ignorant beside the learned psychologist, and so unbelieving beside the believer! Her village doctor sent her to me. One more humiliating attempt to seek help. If I do not succeed in convincing her that I am essentially as weak as she is, everything I have to say to her, especially if it is right, true, and good, will be only one more crushing lecture for her.

How many sensitive people have finally lost all confidence in themselves through being sent to a nursing-home, a mental hospital, or an approved school 'in order to be helped'! How many hesitant souls have been crushed under the weight of the good advice they have had showered upon them! A woman confesses to me that as a result of prayer she has seen that she must leave her sister alone, and not go on trying to help her run her home, because her offers of help only humiliate and discourage the sister, and make her neglect her house-work all the more. A wife tells her husband he ought not to worry so much about his health. It is true, but the remark makes him worry about himself all the more.

One man who came to see me had had psychological troubles, aggravated by the exigencies of communal life in the army during his period of military service. His medical officer considered that the best thing for him would be to have him discharged, and had sent him before a medical board for this purpose. But since then his feeling of being incapable even of serving his country had become a veritable obsession. I sent him back before the medical board, which ordered his reinstatement in the army. Several years later he came back to see me. He had extended his period of service, and all his troubles had vanished.

Sometimes a doctor allows himself to be influenced against his better judgement by over-anxious parents. A girl wants to become a nurse, but her parents see her picking up all sorts of dread diseases if she takes up such a career. They send her to see her doctor, furnishing him with a wealth of detail concerning the uncertain state of her health, and the practitioner allows himself to play their game by telling her that she is not strong enough to become a nurse. Disappointed of her vocation, the girl lacks the driving force—essential to health—which comes of having an aim in life. She goes from one illness to another, from failure to failure, so that in the end her life is a far harder one than it would have been had she become a nurse. I have seen many 'false weaklings' who have asserted roundly that they were 'delicate', but who on examination have proved to be endowed with an excellent physique. They were ill because they were not using their strength. A man who is perfectly well only needs to meet a friend in the street who says to him: 'You do look ill!' and he will at once feel less well. Some people are always telling others they look ill, because they have an unconscious urge to pity other people so as to persuade themselves that they are kind-hearted.

Let us recall here the distinction we have made between true weakness and weak reactions. We doctors often confuse the two. When an emotional patient finds that every effort at adaptation has physiological consequences which can amount to serious functional disorders, we are too ready to advise him to give up the attempt. And thereafter the man who has interrupted his studies, the woman who has resigned an interesting post, will harbour in their hearts the feeling that they have been cowards, and this feeling will still further weaken their defences against their weak reactions. Nor will they be able to banish from their minds the memory of the doctor's words, which will sap their confidence in their ability. One of my patients got through a tremendous amount of work; she rose at four o'clock in the morning to do a big wash, and quite unnecessarily went round each room in the house with a polishing-cloth every day, because she still had imprinted on her memory a summary verdict pronounced by a doctor: 'Your output in life will never be more than fifty per cent.' Apparently the excess of work she imposed on herself answered an instinctive need to demonstrate that the doctor was mistaken. But nothing succeeded in ridding her mind of the suggestion she had received.

One of my friends, a paediatrician, expressed to me his views in this connection. They are of the greatest interest. There is a tendency in children's dietetics to avoid the necessity for difficult efforts at physiological adaptation on the part of the child. If he finds it hard to tolerate a certain food, it is cut out of his diet. He is given predigested baby-foods, so that his stomach does not have to make an effort which is necessary to it. The same applies in every department of the child's physical and moral welfare. Childhood, however, is the age of greatest adaptive capacity. Advantage should be taken of these early years to train the child in physical and moral endurance. By the time he is adult his adaptive capacity will have reached its limits, beyond which it cannot be further stretched. Digestive intolerance, after all, would appear to be a sign of vigour in the organism, rather than of weakness—unco-ordinated vigour, it is true, but it represents the lively reaction of the subject to a new stimulus.

Dr Arnault Tzanck has suggested[1] a new and tempting classification of diseases. He groups them into three fundamental categories: those of the intoxication type, in which the organism passively suffers the lesions caused in it by the harmful agent; those of the intolerance type, the symptoms of which on the contrary represent a vigorous defensive reaction on the part of the organism; and lastly those of the dystrophic type. He points out that doctors have instinctively given to the first type names ending in '-itis', to the second, names ending in '-osis', while the third group have names ending in '-oma'. The author has brilliantly demonstrated that these three types are found in all branches of medicine, in dermatology as well as in haematology, in cardiology as well as in urology. Even in psychiatry there are passive diseases, which derive from lesions, and active diseases, which are intense responses of the nervous system or even of the entire organism to psychological stimuli—to emotional shocks and to conflicts; and lastly, dystrophias.

Dr Tzanck says that all the diseases of the second category are largely referable to the medicine of the person. Whether it be an allergic dermatosis or a neurosis, the local lesions are secondary; it is the whole person, mind, body, and soul, which is reacting. The reaction is excessive and disordered, it is true, but what is required is to assist the reaction rather than to shelter the person from the external stimulus. It is, in short, very much an internal reaction, but it is being translated into an external weak reaction.

It is in fact in those whom we classify as weak that we find all those symptoms which are connected with physiological and psychological intolerance: anaphylaxy, heightened metabolism, functional disturbances, emotionalism, obsessions, and so on. The importance of the problem is clear. When, because they are ill in season and out of season, because their ills are severe and unusual, and disproportionate to the cause that provokes them, we tell these subjects that they are weak; when in order to spare them

[1] Arnault Tzanck, *Immunité, intolérance, biophylaxie*, Masson, Paris, 1932.

these ills we keep them away from everything that may provoke them—the foods they find hard to tolerate or the difficulties of social life—we are enclosing them in a vicious circle. They continue to suffer, and their troubles are aroused by even weaker stimuli; the slightest deviation in diet, or the mildest argument, upsets them. Their lives become increasingly impoverished, and they become more and more firmly convinced that they are weak.

Of course, the treatment of such patients is no easy matter. The mere prescription of a bottle of medicine is no use. They need constant encouragement to persevere in their efforts to live and to face difficulties in spite of the painful reactions they arouse. But the reward of these efforts will be the attenuation of those reactions, although it must be recognized that they will never disappear altogether. We must teach them not to be afraid of their reactions, and not to give way to their fear.

Going back to the paediatrician's example, the doctor who intends to follow this out in the treatment of a sensitive child who cannot tolerate certain foods, must fight hard against the parents. Instinctively, parents the world over wish to save their children from suffering, difficulties, and obstacles. They would like to keep them from food which hurts them, books which may upset them, and from friends who may have a bad influence upon them. But it is just this contagious fear, which the children feel with unerring perspicacity behind their parents' defences, which aggravates their sensitiveness and increases their vulnerability.

*   *   *

Another vicious circle in which the weak are caught is due to what one might call their maladroitness. After a long period of self-effacement they suddenly wish to assert themselves. But they set about it in the wrong way. They adopt an aggressive manner which earns them a crushing riposte. 'I am incapable of framing a reproof in a way that does not sound disagreeable. I always make things sound worse than I intend to,' writes a young woman. Hence their feeling of never being able to make themselves understood. The strong need to make no such effort. They expect to be listened to, and so are able to express their views calmly and with assurance. The weak, on the other hand, nullify their authority through their exaggerated effort. When the loaf is hard one has to press so hard on the bread-knife that it goes too far and cuts one's finger.

Moreover, the members of a family become accustomed to the balance of forces which has gradually become fixed among them. One daughter gets from her parents everything she asks for. Her sister never dares ask for anything. If one day she does take it into her head to put forward some timid request, she upsets the established order of things. Everyone comes down on her for what they describe as her selfishness.

In their fear of not being listened to, the weak exaggerate their arguments to absurdity, so that a curt 'Don't be silly!' puts an end to the discussion. They get their way only by making a scene, and to this they are inevitably driven. They are then ashamed of their behaviour, and their feeling of inferiority is correspondingly increased. They are rebuked for making a fuss; they are stigmatized as spoilt children, when the truth is that they act as they do simply and only because they are not spoilt.

They talk too much of their difficulties, so that people take for serious failings what are no more than conscientious scruples; or else real mental torment is dismissed as empty scruple, and they are left alone. They drop so many bricks that they conclude that it is never safe to tell the truth. Instead of allowing themselves to be guided by their intuition and their feeling as to what is best to say or to leave unsaid, they become entangled in their own attempts at diplomacy, and commit one blunder after another.

Everything they do is undertaken hesitantly, and their failures multiply. The thought of their failures increases their distress. A young man has to overcome serious complexes in order to associate with girls, and yet he longs to do so. At last he meets one, and takes her out for a walk. They chance upon a mutual friend, who joins them. From that moment on our young man is unable to control his behaviour. He adopts a rude and waspish demeanour which discredits him in the girl's eyes. As he tells me about this a childhood memory comes back to him: he was playing with friends in a park, and was hurt already that the girls paid less attention to him than to another boy. He reacted by playing the clown, which gained him some attention, but not the esteem and affection he sought.

All this brings down on the weak not only failure but also unjust and wounding criticism, which saps their self-confidence and provokes fresh weak reactions.

A little girl of four had the greatest admiration and affection for her seven-year-old sister. It happened that the elder girl died. The little girl realized how grieved her mother was when a few days later she spoke of her dead sister and saw her mother sadly turn away her head and leave her. This made the child feel that she must never speak of her sister again. Now the older girl, before she died, had made the younger promise that she would write to her in heaven. She must keep her promise, but she did not know how to write. She took a piece of paper and with a pencil she made marks on it, whispering as she did so the text of her message. On her mother's desk she found an envelope which happened to have the mother's address on it. She put her letter inside it, and took it to the post. Next morning when the postman brought the letter there was a surcharge to be paid, as the envelope was not stamped. When her mother opened it and saw the little girl's scribblings she thought she had done it as a joke, and gave her a thorough scolding. The little girl was dumbfounded, and not daring to explain, she shut her secret up in her heart.

Another girl, emotionally upset by the death of her mother and the remarriage of her father, reacts in her distress in a way that is taken for perverse indiscipline and earns her a series of solemn lectures from her headmistress, which gives the final touch to her revolt.

These poor souls are constantly rebuked, lectured, exhorted and unjustly punished. Appeal is made to their will, when their trouble is really an emotional one, lying right outside their will. They end up continually blaming themselves, with a silent 'I detest myself.'

Much of the misbehaviour that is severely condemned by teachers and by society at large is seen on closer examination to be explicable as a weak reaction to an unresolved problem. One child takes to lying through fear of being scolded; another to stealing to make up for the presents he does not receive, or the maternal affection which is denied him. One man lies to his wife from chagrin at not having been able to establish with her the completely frank and intimate relationship he had dreamed of; another lapses into adultery as a haven of refuge from the tyranny of his wife.

One man, criticized on account of his conceited airs, is in fact suffering from sexual impotence; another, from some sort of perversion. A woman buys one luxurious fur coat after another, at the cost of heavy debts and bitter reproaches on the part of her mother: she lacks confidence in her good looks. A nurse who irritates her companions with her naïve exuberance, lacks confidence in herself. They accuse her of trying to attract attention to herself, and their criticism increases her want of confidence, from which her extravagant behaviour does not succeed in delivering her.

The domain of sex is a particularly fertile field for false judgements. I know many men and women who are looked upon as sensual Don Juans or adventuresses, but who are really the victims of psycho-sexual inhibitions. They seem always to be in search of fresh conquests, when in reality they make none at all; they are really seeking to overcome their inhibitions in their impulsive career from one liaison to another, each of which they abandon because they are incapable of really loving.

A woman is accused of wantonly indulging in vulgar adventures, when the truth is that she is driven by an imperative urge to seek an intellectual and spiritual communion which none of her lovers has ever offered her. A man apparently refuses stubbornly to break off an illicit love-affair; in reality the woman who has managed to seduce him in a moment of weakness is simply holding him by the threat of 'doing herself some mischief' if he leaves her.

A woman throws herself impulsively into some crude liaison in her mortification at not having been able to give herself to the man she really loved. A man's adultery breaks up his home: the truth is that a puritan upbringing has instilled in him a contempt for sex, and that is why in marriage he has been unable to bring about the coalescence of affection and erotic love. A refined woman has allowed herself to give way, in a moment of distress, to the advances of a man whom she despises. Disgust with herself saps her powers of resistance and prevents her breaking with him. This is a phenomenon frequently encountered. It is those who set the greatest store by purity who are the most mortified, exaggeratedly mortified, when they transgress against it. They angrily fling themselves into impurity as if to make real the degradation of which they accuse themselves. A man has remained attached for years to a mistress because from her he has been able to derive moral strength, because she has sustained him and prevented him, better than his wife was able to do, from going 'on the loose' and taking to drink.

A young woman is powerless to break off a guilty association which irks her, because she is afraid of returning to the awful solitude in which she has in the past experienced much more serious defeats than this.

When one sees behind the scenes in people's lives in this way, one realizes how unfair are the hasty and hypocritical judgements that are the common coin of conversation in drawing-rooms and cafés.

This feeling of always being unfairly judged plays a most important part in the crushing of the weak and the binding of them in the chain of their weak reactions. I do not pretend that they are without sin. Of course there is pride, egoism, rancour, envy, impurity, touchiness in them, as there is in me, and in everyone else. It is just this very fact that they intuitively recognize, that at heart all men are really alike, but that they themselves, the weak, are always censured because their reactions betray these ills of the heart, whereas the strong are able to screen them from sight.

The grinding vicious circle of weak reactions and criticism takes on the appearance of a 'war of nerves', which provokes its victims to do the very thing that brings about the evil they are afraid of. The desire of the weak to rehabilitate themselves, to be understood at last, is a constant torment to them, and this emotion triggers off their weak reactions, which doom them to further misunderstandings. Flying from Scylla they fall into Charybdis. One might say that they suffer from a 'he who gets slapped' complex. Their lives seem to go from one disaster to another.

*   *   *

The doctor who seeks to be objective contemplates these lives with intense sympathy. It seems to him as if their course were directed by some clever hidden force. He speaks of masochism, or, with Dr Allendy,[1] of inner justice. It seems that these people draw misfortune upon themselves as if to punish themselves interminably for their long-repressed passions and rebellions— legitimate though they were—against parents or teachers.

Such a doctor is then tempted to counsel them to adopt the method of the strong: to turn against others the keen-edged weapon they are constantly using against themselves, to defend themselves, to make use of the aggressiveness they are repressing, and the sadism hidden behind their masochism. Sometimes this is successful. But sometimes also these sensitive people are far too kind-hearted to be able to follow such advice. When they strike a blow it hurts them far more than the person against whom it is directed.

It is then that another solution is necessary, a solution that goes much deeper—the solution of faith.

In the last analysis, all these weak reactions are only symbols of despair. 'Why was I born?' cries one of my patients, and the cry sums up all her distress. This despair can go so deep that the sufferer no longer believes in happiness, and thrusts it away by his awkward reactions when it does appear. Coué once said that in order to be happy one must believe in happiness.[2] The weak

[1] René Allendy, *La justice intérieure*, Denoel, Paris, 1931.
[2] Emile Coué, *La maîtrise de soi-même*, J. Oliven, Paris, 1929.

have an unhealthy taste for drama; they dramatize any and every situation, and even in the course of a consultation they will hide their emotion behind some silly remark which they do not really mean, but which would be likely to break the confidence between us if I did not know their true thoughts behind this screen. It is as if their subconscious were still trying to cut the last thread of hope on which they hang. One patient wrote to me: 'I spoil everything in my life myself; and it is that that makes me despair.' 'What is the point of coming to see you again?' they say, 'It does no good and only wastes your time.' What they really mean is, 'I am frightened you will weary of me and abandon me.' They say: 'Don't talk to me any more about God. I hate him.' They mean, 'I no longer have any hope except in him.'

This is in fact the supreme consequence of being caught in the toils which hold them, namely, that the road to faith is closed to them, though it would be the true solution for them. 'I cannot pray any more,' an emotional woman remarked to me, 'I've lost God's address.' It was only after many talks together that she told me of the circumstances under which she had lost it. One day she had wanted courageously and faithfully to witness to her faith in God. She has been criticized for doing so by her superiors, and had beaten a retreat. It had seemed to her that God had let her down and was abandoning her to her weak reactions.

One of my patients sees in her neurosis a proof that she has been rejected by God, and that his forgiveness, of which I speak to her, and which would break the vicious circle of her weak reactions, is not for her. Another is ashamed of not having sufficient courage to break off an improper association. She thinks she no longer has any right to pray, and so does not try. She is thus depriving herself of the very communion which would give her the strength she needs.

These people also often hide their despair behind cynical theories, fatalistic philosophies, so-called biological concepts of the inexorable laws of heredity, or belief in the transmigration of souls, the last resort of those who have given up the struggle in this life. And then they use their unbelief as one more reason for despair: 'God will not come to my aid; he can't love me, since I don't believe in him.'

All these reactions, however,—fear, emotion, despair—belong to the domain of affectivity. Neither will nor reason can control our affectivity, which has a much stronger hold over us than we like to admit to ourselves. My son failed an examination. I thought I had really accepted the fact. But on graduation day the procession went past my windows, headed by the band. It only needed that rousing music with its physical effect on my sensitivity, for my eyes to fill with tears. I had repressed my affectivity; I had not overcome it.

Only a feeling can be opposed to a feeling. In this our unbelieving colleagues are in full agreement with us: the feeling we need is confidence, which is reborn when we feel ourselves to be loved. We call it faith.

As their confidence grows, the weak begin once again to show their emotions, the repression of which has been paralysing them more and more. 'Impression without expression produces depression,' an Englishman once said to me. Everyone knows that an emotion held in check, a bereavement in which one 'has not been able to weep', a secret disappointment in love, produces disorders. The sensitive are ashamed of their sensitiveness and try to conceal it. It then finds an outlet in false reactions, for which they are taken to task, and this makes them still more ashamed of their sensitivity—and so the vicious circle is closed. Often their upbringing has aimed above all at teaching them to hide their feelings; and that is precisely what has made them over-sensitive. A woman suffering from eczema came to see me. She underwent a religious experience, after which her eczema disappeared. But suddenly one day there was a recurrence. My patient wrote to me that she had at once realized what had caused it. She had had to suffer a grievous injustice; in order to appear generous, or from weakness, she had restrained her indignation. This was not true self-sacrifice, but repression, which set up an internal conflict; and the eczema reappeared.

These false reactions in which a repressed emotion is finding an outlet often have the effect of reviving another complex, like a spark falling on a powder-barrel. A mother reproaches herself for striking her children, whom she nevertheless tenderly loves. She makes great efforts to control herself; she is afraid of beginning again: she is in a state of unstable equilibrium. Should she encounter, in some quite different sphere, an annoyance to which she cannot give vent, we shall find her raising her hand again to her children at the slightest misdemeanour on their part.

The weak need to unburden themselves concerning everything that hurts them, without being at once accused of mischief-making or of constantly insisting on their rights. A sensitive woman says: 'My husband irritates me; I can't stand the sight of him.' If we rebuke her, telling her she ought to love him, she feels misunderstood, for in reality she wants to show him her love. Why she expresses the repressed irritation which prevents her doing so is simply in order to liberate herself from it. The over-sensitive do not talk in order to formulate their ideas, but in order to give vent to their feelings. That is why they come back again and again to the same complaint, to the annoyance of those around them, who have nothing more to say than what has already been said. It is necessary to understand that the sensitive go on repeating the same thing until their emotive discharge is completed. I remember that when I realized this distinction between the two meanings of speech I felt I was making a discovery that was the key to many of my mistakes. When a man speaks in order to express an idea, discussion is legitimate—not to discuss the idea he puts forward would be not to take him seriously. Such discussion is fruitful, and throws new light on the subject for all concerned. But when a man speaks in order to give vent to his feelings, it is necessary to listen and not discuss, for in such a case discussion leads to misapprehensions, and gives the man the feeling that he is not being understood.

The weak need to unburden themselves at length for another reason. Fears, as I have said, are connected one to another like the links in an endless chain. It is only after expressing the most obvious and conscious fears that the over-sensitive dare to penetrate, little by little, more deeply into their hearts, to discover there fears that are less conscious, but still more highly charged with repressed emotion. They stand in need of still more understanding and confidence in order to have the courage to express them. Going back in this way along the chain they see the tremendous part that has been played by fear in their lives, and come thus of their own accord to the threshold of the problem of faith.

The weak need affection. They need to find in our hearts a reflection and a witness of the love of Christ. Then they are able to win victories over themselves which they have despaired of winning, and which will break the bonds of their despair. The first concrete victory—rising as soon as the alarm-clock rings, having the courage to make a clean breast of something to their parents, asking forgiveness of someone they hated, speaking to husband or wife about debts contracted and kept secret—can have incalculable consequences. It is like the opening of a second front in a war that has reached a position of stalemate, transforming the strategic situation.

But in this it is important that our faith and our love for them be genuine. Nothing so surely destroys the chances of success as overdoing one's feelings, uttering fine words which do not spring from the heart, showing an artificial benevolence. There are two kinds of gentleness, confidence, sympathy, or fervour: those which are spontaneous—they alone are efficacious; they blossom quite naturally in us when we are 'in good form' spiritually; and there are those which we invent when we are not, but wish to appear so. It is when we have no hope of seeing a tree break into blossom that we hang artificial flowers on it.

5

STRONG REACTIONS

WE HAVE CALLED the active reactions strong reactions. The phenomenon is not only psychological; it concerns the entire person, manifesting itself in the body, in the feelings and imagination, in ideas and the mind. In a manner contrary to weak reactions, which immobilize the person and paralyse thought, strong reactions stimulate motive energy and open the sluice-gates of the imagination and the intellect to an abundant flood of apt mental pictures, interesting concepts, and pertinent arguments. They even have their echo in the spiritual life: whereas love and faith seem distant and inaccessible to the weak, they seem easy and natural to the strong.

These are automatic, spontaneous, and immediate reactions; a response of the natural temperament to every physical or psychic challenge. Faced with the physical danger represented by an invasion of microbes, a toxic food, or excessive fatigue, the biological defences are stimulated, the white blood corpuscles are mobilized, the vaso-motor reactions are brought into play, the chemical metabolism is accelerated, all the functions which Dr Tzanck[1] groups under the heading of biophylaxis are set in motion. Faced with the danger represented by a conflict with another person, a trial of strength, a heavy responsibility, or an association of ideas (conscious or not) calculated to arouse the deep and undefinable malaise which haunts every human being, the psychological defences of the strong are similarly stimulated. A reassuring thought comes to blot out the unease, a spurt of courage comes to cover up fear, confidence of victory comes to stimulate ardour. The words needed to save the situation are on

[1] Op. cit.

the lips, the gesture already made which will impose upon the adversary, the will to power is in evidence in the person's whole attitude.

Now, no one can develop his personality indefinitely without coming into collision with others, so that their strong reactions soon draw the strong into innumerable conflicts in which they clash with the strong and crush the weak. But struggle and risk act as a stimulus to the reactions of the strong, amplifying them in the same way as we have seen weak reactions aggravated in a vicious circle. What is more, the strong need struggle and risk, they seek them and provoke them for the euphoria they provide, in order to nourish the living flood of reactions which cover up an inner torment as acute as that of the weak.

But strong reactions lead to conflicts only indirectly, in so far as resistance is encountered. We must be careful, therefore, not to confuse them with mere pugnacity. In all sincerity the strong claim to be pacific: it is not their fault, but other people's, that they are in conflict with them; all they want is to get on well with people—and they get on very well with everyone so long as no one resists them! It is not people they are fighting, they say, but people's mistakes. They are quite ready to hold out the hand of friendship to them provided they are prepared to recognize and abandon the error of their ways.

So, for example, a mother-in-law can subject her daughter-in-law to atrocious persecution, and at the same time tell us ingenuously that she cherishes for her a love without blemish. It is because of her love for her, and for her son, and her desire for their happiness, that the mother-in-law combats so fiercely everything that seems to her to be wrong in her daughter-in-law's conduct. 'I know my son; I know how he needs to be managed and what needs to be done to make him happy. Isn't that what you want as well—and what will make you happy, too? Act then as I have always acted, instead of forcing him into these new and stupid habits that come from your own bad upbringing!'

But strong reactions also bear peaceful fruits. They stimulate zeal for work, self-control, the practice of virtue, the creative imagination, and the play of mind and heart; all of which also help the strong to forget the anxieties which they become aware of once more when they are no longer borne up on the wings of success.

Psychological analysis thus reveals that much that is good and valuable, many noble acts and generous efforts, are in reality compensations for those same secret anxieties which overwhelm the weak. They are not for that reason to be despised; but it is useful to be aware of this compensatory mechanism if one wishes to know oneself and to understand others.

I realize now how much my own intellectual activity was stimulated by unconscious complexes when I was a student. Though I never admitted it to myself I was terribly lonely; I was afraid of other people. Then I perceived that my aptitude for handling, formulating, and defending ideas could be used as an admission-ticket to society. I could thus win the affection and esteem for which I craved in order to bolster up my self-confidence. I played the card. I wrote plays, I mugged up mathematics, studied law, made long speeches, became president of my students' union, threw myself into work for the Red Cross, and then for the Church, and passed my medical examinations with flying colours.

None of this delivered me from my secret complex, but it helped me to hide it. In my heart, compromise and defeat still went on, but at least I was able to some extent to forget them. I do not now repudiate those youthful enthusiasms, nor the intellectual and religious truths for which I fought. Later on I underwent spiritual crises, in which I felt how much there was of artificiality in the zeal with which I used to defend doctrines too often belied by my real life. The discovery, far from undermining my convictions, fortified and renewed them, requiring of me more conformity between theory and practice.

There came to see me one day a woman who until then had thought herself a pure intellectual, and who had had a brilliant career at the university. Suddenly, on coming into contact with the thought of India, she had undergone a religious experience which had thrown a quite new light on her inner life. In this light, she said, she understood at last that what she once sought in knowledge, in intellectual research and argument, was an answer to her soul's religious nostalgia. She had never been able to find this answer on the intellectual level. She had in fact always had an uncomfortable feeling that she was in some way going against her true nature in acting like a cold intellectual. But now, she added, she would be able to put her intelligence at the service of her faith and thus achieve a real inner harmony.

In so far as our activity, however generous and useful it may be, constitutes a psychological compensation for feelings of inferiority or repressed problems, it carries with it a certain tension, an intransigence and exaggeration which corrode it. Thus I was fired with enthusiasm for theological verities; I had a passion for argument, barricading myself in the positions I had adopted. But one day I realized that all this resulted more in conflicts than in blessings, that it was religious activity rather than a spiritual ministry. I felt, so to speak, that my partial successes amounted in the end to general failure.

Therefore, just as we have not overlooked the fact that there may be something useful in certain weak reactions, it is not my intention here to condemn strong reactions outright. I am simply attempting to throw light on the secret springs which impel human beings to act, after examining those which impede them.

*   *   *

First, there is the desire to 'get one's own back'. Many black sheep are simply exacting compensation for an upbringing that has been too strict. A young woman, after an adventure that has ended in disillusionment, exclaims: 'I thought I was asserting myself; but I see that I was only reacting against my environment.'

Often, after some costly act of obedience, I catch myself indulging, as a sort of requital, in some act of disobedience which I affect to believe to be harmless. A woman who had lost her mother in adolescence, and had laboured hard to bring up her brothers and sisters, took little trouble over the upbringing of her own children, to get her own back for the sacrifice of her youth to duty. A man who had once willingly, and for love of his wife, given up certain pleasures which she did not share, now comes back to them, pretending that in this way he is rediscovering his personality; but the frenzied way he throws himself into them clearly reveals a vindictive impulse. A girl who has long been dominated by her father, accepting as her own all his opinions, now takes her revenge on him by contradicting him at every opportunity; another forces her ideas in turn on her own daughters. Similarly, a man is obsessed with the idea of taking up some course of study, which represents in his eyes a way of compensating himself for everything of which his parents have deprived him in the past.

A man tyrannizes over his wife by incessantly reminding her of all the sacrifices he has imposed upon himself in the past for her sake, and which he now intends to make her pay for in servile obedience. So we come to the second degree of recompense, namely vengeance. An enormous number of our acts, impulses and feelings really represent vengeance for wounds we have failed to accept. 'Money disgusts me, so I spend it in order to avenge myself on it,' writes a young woman. 'I behave towards men,' writes another, 'as if I were trying to get my revenge on my father and my brother.' A weak husband is henpecked by a wife who is really taking it out on him for the vexations imposed on her by her first husband. Similarly, another wife who subjects her husband to incessant and intolerable jealous suspicions, is taking her revenge on him for a fiancé who once jilted her. A man, in spite of all his resolutions, finds himself in constant conflict with his mother. He discovers the underlying meaning of these impulses—a desire to avenge his father for suffering inflicted on him by his mother in the past. In the sick these impulses can grow to enormous proportions, in the form of an obsession with vengeance, or persecution mania. Even the refusal to believe represents in many people a sort of vengeance against God, whom they blame for their ills.

Impulses of this nature can take on the character of a noble crusade. A girl has lost her mother. Thereafter she is very much attached to her father, and suffers cruelly when he remarries. She sincerely believes she has forgiven the new wife for having taken first place in her father's heart. She would never permit herself, she tells me, to be carried away by vulgar jealousy: it is a question of justice: really her father is a weak personality, and she feels called upon to protect him against undue domination by his wife. A man sets himself up as an apostle of tolerance and freedom of conscience in order to avenge himself for the dogmatic intransigence with which his father treated him in his youth. And he himself is somewhat intolerant in the way he defends liberalism against orthodoxy. Another, who attacks hypocritical conventionalism by means of eccentric behaviour and tart remarks, is taking his revenge for the constraint amid which he has been brought up. Not without eloquence, he always argues on the side of grace as against law; but it is not just by condemning law that one obtains grace, and his criticisms, justified though they may be, remain bitter. Another man is an ardent upholder of public morality. He campaigns against everything that might pervert the young, in order to avenge himself on the harmful influences which in the past have led him into moral lapses of which he is ashamed.

It is appropriate to recall here the shrewd comments of Dr Baruk,[1] when he showed that the severest censures of public morality come from those who hide a bad conscience behind their indictments. He emphasizes the great dynamic energy which the mechanism of repression gives to such champions of society and justice.

Criticism is, in fact, the commonest form of strong reaction. Since reading Dr Baruk's book I readily recognize that whenever some criticism, however justifiable, comes into my mind—and especially when the criticisms come in a flood, to the exclusion of other considerations—it is because of wounded pride, or else it is a reaction aimed at covering up a bad conscience with regard to

[1] Op. cit.

the person I am criticizing. It was in recognizing this fact that Peter Howard[1] underwent one day the religious experience which changed the whole course of his life. Like all journalists, he had until then exercised his critical talent on men, on society, and on the government of the day. On the day in question, at a luncheon, he was once again regaling his neighbour at the table with one of his brilliant diatribes, when this person suddenly interrupted him: 'You know, criticism is not much good by itself. Any fool can do it, and most fools do.' Then he went on, adds Howard: '"I believe the men of the future are those who match their criticism with cure. . . . Everybody says the world ought to be different, but only a few people know how it can happen."'

Among strong reactions must be counted also stubbornness, obstinacy, the grim determination to have the last word, to defend the position one has taken up—even in spite of secret doubts— for fear of seeming weak. I ought perhaps to write *because of* secret doubts, and not *in spite of* them. In my book *Désharmonie de la vie moderne* I quoted, from Dr Maeder,[2] a case of defiance neurosis. This concerned an adolescent who defied his father, his teacher, his headmaster, and even the doctor. The doctor was in fact able to show that the source of the boy's defiance was a troubled conscience which he was attempting to hide under his bluster. I pointed out how frequently a scoffing, revolutionary, or extremist attitude on the part of individuals and nations can be attributed to these compensation mechanisms. Thus, I knew one young man, intelligent, refined, and sensitive, who was well aware that the excessive ardour and assurance with which he upheld his extremist political views was only an attempt to escape from the hesitations of his scrupulous nature, and from a certain bourgeois docility which still persisted in him.

But compensation mechanisms of this sort are not by any means found only in revolutionaries. They are at work, if I may put it so, among the silks and satins of the drawing-room as well

[1] P. Howard, *Ideas have Legs*, Frederick Muller, London, 1945, p. 71.
[2] Op. cit., pp. 88-103.

as the kid gloves of the learned society. The scientist propounds his theories with all the more assurance for knowing, better than his opponents, the objections to which they are open. The society woman gives her opinion on the latest book with the more conviction the less confident she feels of her literary competence, or the more hastily she has skimmed through its pages. I am reminded here of a woman, full of feelings of inferiority, who admitted to me that she had to read a book in order to have something to talk about to her society friends! Do not let us smile at this: it is a method which at bottom we all adopt to some extent. We all find it difficult to be open and frank in conversation, to express our thoughts and convictions simply as we feel them. We are afraid of not being taken seriously as we are, of not appearing sufficiently authoritative. So we invoke the opinion of others, quoting this scientist or that writer, or drawing upon the mass of anonymous material provided by the University, the newspaper, or common gossip, so as to cut a better figure in our conversations. This display of often very superficial knowledge serves us for culture, and we use it to impress others. An adroitly gauged allusion to some event in our lives which shows us in a good light, or to some occasion on which we met an important personage, procures for us a success which is both flattering and reassuring.

This is a slippery slope which very quickly takes us across the frontier of deception, and that is a territory into which it is easy to go deeper and deeper. And of course the supreme deception is to indulge in deception judiciously, so that we never allow it to grate on those upon whom we practise it, and thus we retain an air of modesty, while at the same time winning flattering social successes for ourselves.

Peter Howard, in the book I quoted,[1] gives an amusing account of the advice given to him by his chief at the outset of his brilliant journalistic career under Lord Beaverbrook: ' "Peter, pour the soft oil of flattery down their backs. You will find men cannot have too much of it, however much they protest

[1] Op. cit., p. 22.

they do not like it." ' The method was successful. He gives a lively description of the whole society of the inter-war period, when everyone was chasing success: 'Success was my aim. I sought it through power. And I sought it through money . . . most young men like myself believed that our first duty to ourselves, our families and our nation was to get ourselves along in the world. . . . I, for one, never stopped to think what sort of nation would be produced by millions of individuals all selfishly elbowing, manœuvring and tearing each other's throats to obtain for themselves a larger cut off the national joint.'

It is a fact that success is the implicit aim of every strong reaction. In order to achieve it one must show oneself to be strong physically, psychologically, intellectually—and even spiritually. In some respects the excessive modern addiction to sport and to physical culture, the passionate devotion to the idea of the development of bodily vigour, have as their goal the success which physical strength will assure. This too lies behind the idea, so widespread today, that health is the sovereign good, and that when one is ill health must be recovered at all costs. It is appropriate to quote here a penetrating remark made by Dr Biot at the last Abolitionist Congress: 'Morality before health.'

Among the strong reactions also must be counted all the manifestations of vanity: a certain coquettishness, in men as well as in women—an exaggerated concern over the choice of a tie or a fancy handkerchief, or over the setting of the hair, and the servile following of fashion, are always seen by the psychologist as compensations for feelings of inferiority. Of course I do not mean to condemn all coquetry, especially in women, in whom it represents a proper instinct. But the moment this concern takes on an obsessive character, the moment one becomes a slave to it, one is no longer acting from self-respect, but indulging in a strong reaction.

At the other end of the scale, moreover, a certain irreverent originality of dress, a careless bohemianism, an affectation of non-conformity, or even a certain disdain in regard to one's personal appearance or cleanliness, paraded as a sign of moral superiority—

all these, too, are nothing other than compensatory strong reactions.

The same can be said of an air of bravado. I have received a letter from a woman who is just now discovering the baneful consequences to her life of the weak reactions to which she has for too long given way. 'A few days ago,' she writes, 'I was with a childhood friend who is a keen sportswoman, healthily egoistic, living openly in adultery, criticized by everybody but not caring what people say; and when I was with her I experienced an odd sensation of well-being. . . . And all at once I find that I like women who are cynical, bold, untrammelled by prejudices, who have been able to get something out of life. I should have liked to be like that if I could, if I dared—to hold my own with men and not be afraid or be at their beck and call. . . .' The distinction between strong and weak reactions could hardly be put more clearly. My correspondent, who has so often given way to weak reactions, hankers secretly after strong reactions. Her friend, however, is not so different from her as she thinks: cynicism is never more than a façade behind which suffering and anxiety lie hidden.

Strong reactions, too, are anger, the thump of the fist on the table, the door slammed behind one, the noisy outburst, or the dishonest argument calculated to wound an opponent at his weakest point, the temperamental scene, the fit of hysterics. One of my patients told me of how once, when her son had done something wrong, she was trying to make him own up and had been met with dogged obstinacy on his part. Suddenly the boy snatched up some flowers from the table and tore them to pieces— a strong reaction! 'Why did you do that?' his mother asked him. 'Because they were looking at me,' the child replied.

Of course, these violent reactions are often set in motion by unconscious factors. But in the same way the threat of nervous reactions can be used by one member of a family as a means of imposing his wishes on all the others. Such reactions do not need to be noisy. Thus a mother makes sure of the servile obedience of her daughter by cultivating in her a desperate fear of hurting her.

Here again a terrible vicious circle is quickly set up. For in giving way for the sake of peace to all their whims one makes such people more and more the slaves of their reactions.

I feel I must add a word of warning to what I have just written: I am afraid of some reader in such a family showing this with a faint air of triumph to some one whom he already in his heart accuses of exercising this sort of nervous tyranny. Let him not imagine that he will thus help the sick person to control himself. He will make him worse. So true is it that each of us must inquire into his own problems instead of judging his neighbour.

Among the strong reactions must also be counted loquacity, a glib tongue, and high spirits. But also we must often include the prudent silence, the impenetrable air of mystery. Strong reactions may also take the form of humour and wit, which allow a person to extricate himself from an embarrassing situation by means of some clever remark. Here again, I am not condemning good humour and spontaneous flashes of wit, but rather that bitter and artificial wit which is used as a weapon of defence and attack. In an article in *Culture humaine*,[1] Dr René Lacroix has made a shrewd analysis of humour in which he distinguishes carefully between 'positive' and 'negative' laughter.

*　　　*　　　*

Obviously we can make the same distinction in every other field. Every one of our characteristics, both physical and mental, can be seen in its positive form when it shows itself spontaneously, without ulterior motive; but each can take on a negative quality when it becomes the instrument of a more or less conscious attempt to win in the battle of life. Even our moral qualities, our witness to our religious experiences, and our professions of faith, can be used as a means of exercising greater influence.

Genuine authority is the antithesis of authoritarianism. Only today a shy young woman, perplexed by the problems she faces in life, was telling me some of her childhood memories. She came from the country to the town in order to enter a secondary school.

[1] René Lacroix, 'Le rire, l'humour et l'ironie', in *Culture humaine*, Paris, Feb. 1948, p. 108.

Hungry to learn, she began impatiently exploring this wonder-land of knowledge. Her heart beat faster when in her first lesson the master said that the earth is not subject only to two motions, but to seven. Our little girl boldly put up her hand to ask what were the five other motions. This took the master by surprise; he could not remember them, and was covered with confusion in front of his class. So our schoolgirl found herself kept in on the following Saturday afternoon as a punishment for having put an impertinent question. And when she returned home she was punished again by her father for having misbehaved in school.

Such incidents are more frequent than is generally supposed; but we often have better success in hiding our strong reactions, which themselves hide our shortcomings. Each of us wears a mask, even in our own families. Each strives in a thousand small ways to safeguard the flattering appearance we have given our-selves, or which has been given us by others. We try to play the role we like to play. To lower the mask and admit the weaknesses it conceals is always extremely humiliating, and none of us can do it without a miracle of the Spirit.

Furthermore, we help each other in the game of hide-and-seek which is social life. We pretend to take other people's masks seriously, for fear that they in their turn will unmask us as well; just as when a little child amuses himself by hiding behind a tree-trunk that is too thin, we enter into the game and pretend that we cannot see him and do not know where he has gone to. As Bergson wrote: 'The evil is so well screened, the secret so univer-sally kept, that in this case each individual is the dupe of all: however severely we may profess to judge other men, at bottom we think them better than ourselves.'[1]

When we look closely at any case of tyranny, in a family, in an association or commercial firm, or in a State, we observe that its establishment has involved the complicity of all. The doctor cannot be surprised at what happens in politics when he

[1] Henri Bergson, *The Two Sources of Morality and Religion*, translated by R. Ashley Audra and Cloudesley Brereton, Macmillan and Co., London, 1935, p. 3.

sees what happens in countless families. 'Ask yourself,' writes Dr Frank Buchman,[1] 'is your home governed by a democracy or a dictatorship?' The doctor is quick to observe that most families live under a tyrannical régime, and that even men who are sincerely attached in politics to a liberal and democratic ideal act like despots at home. 'When two people live together,' writes Emile Coué, 'the so-called mutual concessions almost always come from the same person.'

A husband drives his wife to desperation by calmly expecting her not only to tolerate his adultery, but even to take kindly to welcoming his mistress into the home. He tells me, with the utmost sincerity, that everything would be all right if only his wife would fall in with his plan. He puts down his wife's resistance to nerves, and asks me to treat her. A wife is surprised that her husband spends so much of his time in the public house. The truth is that she compels him not only to live in her parents' house, to eat at their table and to work with her in their business, but even to accompany them every Sunday on the walks that they have chosen.

But most dangerous of all is a religious tyranny. I once knew a woman whose life had been ruined by the hold exercised over her by a religious fanatic who claimed that he alone possessed the Holy Spirit. In so doing he was, no doubt quite unconsciously, satisfying an unhealthy urge to dominate others. He terrified her with the threat of divine punishment. She felt intuitively that her only hope of salvation lay in flight, but he assured her with such authority that it was God's will that she should remain with him, that she gave way.

This was only the exaggeration to a pathological degree of a spiritual perversion which lies in wait for every one of us. I do not believe that any one of us can entirely escape it. However sincere our zeal for a person's conversion, there slips into it an insidious satisfaction at exercising a prophetic role in his life, at being able to dominate him. When one man saves another, the

[1] F. N. D. Buchman, *Remaking the World*, Blandford Press, London, 1953, p. 77.

weaker of the two is not always the one we imagine. And how great is the temptation, when there is a divergence of views, to claim that God is on our side! To increase one's strength by claiming to be the interpreter of God's will—this is a strong reaction. It is also a concealment reaction, since our greatest spiritual anxiety comes from the difficulty we all experience in truly discerning God's will, and from the uncertainty which, despite our sincerity, still persists in our heart of hearts; and nothing brings us greater consolation than seeing others coming to us as to divine oracles.

It has often happened that a husband, a wife, or parents, themselves believers, have come to me to tell me of their ardent desire to bring to faith their wife, husband, or children. Their motives are always quite pure and disinterested. Nevertheless I have sometimes felt that the resistance they have encountered is a sort of defence mechanism on the part of the unbeliever, prompted by his fear of having to knuckle under if he acknowledges himself to be a believer. Sometimes, ingenuously, they have admitted as much to me: 'I am sure my husband would be much kinder to me if he became converted, and would give up the bad habits which are so painful to me.' There are some husbands who are interested in religion, and have their own convictions; they talk about them to their friends or with a spiritual director—interviewed in secret—but they are careful not to raise the subject with their wives, who, being keen believers, may then want to take over the control of their religious life. This is often also the case with an adolescent who avoids admitting to having religious beliefs, for fear that his parents will use the fact as a handle to force him into greater conformity with their wishes or their own theological views.

Thus it is sometimes the very proselytizing spirit of religious people which obstructs the conversion of those who are in contact with them. In some sects one finds that one member of a family holds in complete spiritual tutelage all those around him, who have been led by him to accept his beliefs.

One day a kindly woman sent to see me a young orphan girl

in whom she had taken a benevolent interest, without, however, succeeding in exercising any real moral influence over her. The girl had been made rebellious by the death of her parents and various other misfortunes. She had adopted a distrustful and defensive attitude towards all authority. My own efforts were no more successful. I spent an hour with her, but was unable to break through her discontent. To all my questions I obtained no response other than brief monosyllables. She had been made to come and see me; in her eyes I was merely an extension of the moral authority she rejected. I heard no more about her for two years; and then one day I saw her again. This time she came freely, of her own accord, to ask for my help and advice. She began by apologizing for her stubborn silence on her earlier visit, and then confidently opened her heart to me. Since then we have had many fruitful discussions.

Of course we are able sometimes to furnish useful advice—but that never leads anyone to the experience of the grace of God. I am reminded of a woman whom I saw only once. Rarely have I been so warmly thanked after a consultation: she went away, she said, quite transformed. As a matter of fact I had scarcely said anything to her at all. But for months previously she had wrestled with herself, and when she at last decided to come and see me, that determination was the sign of a decisive victory within herself. I really had nothing to do with it. The spiritual event had already taken place in secret in her heart even before she came to my consulting-room.

One can never foresee the means that God will use to touch a man's heart, the roads along which he will drive him, nor the moment at which he will intervene in his life. It may be at the height of happiness, or in the midst of a painful crisis. It may be within a fervent religious community, or in utter solitude. It may be by means of a slow process of evolution, or quite suddenly and unexpectedly. But it is always through the free intervention of the Spirit. Edward Howell, who served with the R.A.F. in Crete, tells[1] how when he had been terribly wounded, taken

[1] E. Howell, *Escape to Live*, Longmans Green, London, 1947, p. 101.

prisoner and transferred to Greece, God suddenly broke into his despair during one sleepless night, without the possibility of any human influence having foreshadowed such an experience. All at once there arose in his mind certain quite simple questions: 'What if there was a God? Who could make me different? Who could set me free? Who could bring me home? Or bring home to me? At that moment, God spoke to me . . . Later, I lay in utter peace and quiet. I was sure and secure in the belief that now I knew the secret of living.' Then came his escape, miraculously successful, in which he followed God's inspiration step by step.

Constraint is the negation of all spiritual life. We can help others by telling them of our experiences and convictions. But let us have the honesty to tell them of our failures and doubts as well. Above all, we must beware of the natural inclination which makes us think that others must come to faith by the same road as ourselves. If we exert any sort of pressure upon them, we shall inevitably harm them. Pressure of that kind will either force their decision, in which case we shall be usurping God's place; or else it will arouse their resistance, and we shall have become for them an obstacle to faith.

What is often hidden behind the subtle strong reaction of proselytism is a certain sense of superiority, a certain disdain of those who do not possess the truth or who are still 'living in sin', as some believers say, alas! Here again we see at work the phenomena described by Dr Baruk.[1] A wife torments her husband with her suspicions concerning his infidelity. But I perceive that she herself is assailed by adulterous desires. She is so ashamed of them that she has repressed them and now projects her remorse upon her husband, representing him to herself as inconstant in order to be able to picture herself as irreproachable.

A husband, in a fit of conscience, decides to put an end to the double life he has been leading, and to confess his past to his wife. This confession is a God-given opportunity for the couple to rebuild their married life and to attain the true spiritual communion which the wife has assured me she ardently desires. But,

[1] Op. cit.

on the contrary, the wife's attitude hardens into one of contempt; she refuses to pray with a husband who has deceived her, calls in doubt the sincerity of his change of heart, and never stops humiliating him with her allusions to the wrong he has confessed.

*   *   *   *   *

This brings us to the form of strong reaction which we may call the reaction of the 'righteous', to use the biblical term. I have heard people declare without hesitation: 'I have never told a lie,' or 'I am not afraid of anything,' or 'Since I handed over my life to God, I have no problems,' or 'No one has any secrets in our family; we are always completely frank with one another.' I have heard believers say: 'The true Christian does not sin any more.' If I answer them by talking about my own sins, they will stubbornly refuse to believe me: 'You aren't going to make me believe that a man like you can tell a lie.'

These people are sincere, of course, but all real human contact with them is impossible. And they crush the weak whom they try to convert. The latter are keenly conscious of their own failings. In their weakness they allow themselves to be impressed by this claim to perfection. Some have even told me: 'I shall never be able to be a Christian; I shall never be able to be without sin like those people!' One only needs to open the Bible to see that they are nearer to Christ than the people who preach to them.

I do not deny, however, that there is a certain grandeur in the moral austerity which some believers impose upon themselves. They abstain from drink, smoking, gambling, theatre-going, and dancing; they impose upon themselves a religious discipline which I, alas, am far from attaining. All this, it is true, is done for the love of God—and that is what really counts in his eyes, so that it is I who would be the Pharisee if I cast a stone at them.

One sees how complex the problem is. I limit myself here to looking at it from the psychological point of view. Moral perfection often looks like a strong reaction, in the sense that it is a means of reassuring oneself through one's pride in observing a strict discipline, a means of appearing strong and impressing others with one's reputation for virtue.

But if, on the other hand, in these pages I confess the sins which I discover daily in myself, I know very well that this may conceal a desire to impress the reader with my sincerity.

Be that as it may, an appearance of virtue is dangerous. It incites the subject to safeguard the reputation whose prisoner he is, at the price of repression rather than liberation. We sometimes see patients who have the reputation of being angels, who have no failings, but who curse this armour of saintliness, which they have put on in order to protect their anxiety. Everybody praises them, everybody thinks them strong; but in the privacy of my study they confess in tears how weak they feel.

The same is often the case with a reputation for courage—the strong reaction *par excellence*. Here too there is a vicious circle. A plucky person is expected never to weaken. Everyone depends on him and pushes him out to the front: he it is who must take the blow, not only for himself, but for all those who have attached themselves to him, and that without admitting what it costs him in worry and in fear of giving way.

Here again we must be careful not to generalize. Our present system of education does not do enough to develop pluck. It is not my intention to condemn all strong reactions. If one does not react strongly, one reacts weakly, and that is no better. What matters is that we should be the slave of neither, and that freedom is found through the Spirit.

The same can be said of every other quality. Zeal for hard work is an excellent thing. But in the case of one girl a fierce determination to come top in her class is only a strong reaction against the secret torment caused by her sex instinct and her frequent lapses. Later in life she will tell me this, when after doing extremely well she finds that in spite of all her frenzied hard work she has found no relief for her disquiet. A man has devoted all his energies to achieving success in life; his all-absorbing interest has been his professional advancement. He is conscious that the secret spring of this relentless urge has been his need to rehabilitate himself in the eyes of his family, who when he was a child considered him a good-for-nothing. Yet another falls ill just when he has been appointed to the important post which has been his sole ambition for years. A sickly student is so industrious that he carries off all the prizes. But his hard work is a strong reaction against his feelings of physical inferiority, and once he has passed his school-leaving examination he confesses himself incapable of facing everyday life. A certain man astonished everyone by his prodigious capacity for work, but he admits to me that he is seeking in it a compensation for his sexual impotence.

The same is true of idealism. 'The idealist,' writes Dr Maeder, 'tends to deceive himself, whereas a living faith looks at things with a realistic eye.' In fact we often meet an aggressive, stubborn kind of idealism which is only a strong reaction, a means of holding reality at arm's length, with all its problems and difficulties. Idealism of this sort leads only to disasters, especially in a person's professional or married life. One man throws himself naïvely into an undertaking the financial basis of which is unsound. He does not recognize the dangers inherent in it, and the deeper he gets into debt, the more readily he imagines that some miracle will save him, and the less willing he is to admit to himself the gravity of the situation. Another pictures the woman he marries as the image of all perfection, and when difficulties crop up between them, he finds himself incapable of solving them, because he is quite unprepared for them.

Finally, there are many women who marry from an idealistic feeling of pity, to save a man from alcoholism, from some sexual complex, from running into debt, or from the effects of his lack of will-power. And simply because they have not weighed up the difficulties, thinking that love will work miracles, they sink with him into one disaster after another.

The same can often be said of generosity. Extravagant gifts, risky and unjustifiable loans, guarantees too trustingly entered into, exaggerated benefactions—all these may be weak reactions, as I have shown. But they can also be strong reactions, motivated by a desire to gain power through money. Thus, in a moment of great trouble a woman has aroused in a friend a lively response of pity. Thereafter she ruins herself through plying her with extravagant presents, which are the expression, as it were, of an obsessive desire to preserve her friendship. Such acts of generosity awaken in the beneficiary a sense of guilt which shows itself in ingratitude and often in hostility.

Impulses of a similar nature sometimes take on the appearance of a veritable complex of self-immolation. A strong woman, for instance, wears herself out working to pay off the debts incurred by an idle husband.

While a sacrifice can bear much fruit when it is a free response to the inner call of the spirit, it can also be sterile and destructive when it is merely a psychological reaction.

So we are led in everything to distinguish what is authentic from what is only a psychological reflex; what proceeds from inspired conviction from what is merely a strong or weak reaction.

Psychoanalysis has revealed the importance of the phenomenon of rationalization—the invention, that is to say, of idealistic reasons for behaviour which is motivated unconsciously by our instincts, and the belief that we are then acting from loyalty to these ideals. But whereas the psychoanalysts have chiefly had in view rationalization of the instincts, it is now clear that rationalization also covers the disquiet caused within us by our weaknesses and our sins of omission and commission. I shall be told perhaps that this is an aspect of our instinctive 'will to power'. In some respects this is true. But such an interpretation seems to me to be too restrictive. In the disquiet of which I am speaking here, especially when it is a question of moral disquiet—remorse— there is much more than the instinct of power. One might even put it the other way round, and look upon the instinct of power rather as a psychological compensation for remorse of conscience. This is Dr Baruk's interpretation of it,[1] and his analysis goes much deeper than that of the Freudians. But I recognize that we choose this or that interpretation not so much for objective

[1] Op. cit.

reasons, but in virtue of our conception of the nature of man. As in all other fields, science reveals only the existence of a relationship: a link between the disquiet of the moral conscience and power-reactions. Science does not furnish the grounds for adopting one interpretation of this connection rather than another —for looking upon the moral conscience as the projection of an unsatisfied power instinct, as the Freudians do, or for seeing, with Dr Baruk, power-reactions as the projection of a repressed remorse of conscience. The mistake the Freudians make is to claim that their interpretation has a scientific basis, whereas in fact it derives from their metaphysic.

On the other hand, we can all agree if instead of setting one interpretation over against another we distinguish the phenomena of compensation, projection, and rationalization—whatever their mechanism—from genuine moral and spiritual phenomena, simple automatic psychic reactions from the spontaneous motions of the Spirit.

The line of demarcation, admittedly, is not easy to draw. If we try to draw it for others, we run a grave risk of doing so in a self-righteous spirit of criticism, for each of us must search out the mechanisms of his own behaviour. We only need to try it on ourselves to see at once how easy it is to delude oneself.

In any case, I am not setting up here the utopian ideal of a life exempt from psychological reactions. The rewarding thing about introspection of this sort is not so much what one discovers as the fact that one discovers it. In fact, as we perceive, time and time again, that we are more bankrupt than we imagined, that the things we thought we could put down on the credit side must often rather be put down as debits, that weakness hides even under our strong reactions, we undergo the most fruitful of human experiences. We abandon our futile attempts to save ourselves from our inner disquiet by means of victories in the social struggle, by drawing comfort from our reputation and all that we do to fortify it. Rather do we turn at last towards God, the only true answer to human distress.

That is the only way to get the insight which will enable us to discriminate in our own lives between genuine acts of will and mere automatic reactions—we must turn towards God in prayer. I have written this many times before, and many of my readers have written to me, saying: 'Yes, of course that is the answer, but how do we get it?'

'How to get it' is also the title of one of the concluding chapters of Peter Howard's book.[1] Like him, I can only answer from my own personal experience. How do we get it? It is enough faithfully to try. In the silence before God we soon see that this action or that remark was not in conformity with his will, that they were weak or strong reactions, cowardly flight or proud bravado, the aim of which in either case was to preserve us from our uneasy conscience.

In the silence before God we thus come gradually to a better knowledge of ourselves; we come to know more clearly, at one and the same time, what are our weaknesses and sins and the quite new road we must follow in order to overcome them—that we must confess them in order to receive the divine pardon, instead of hiding them in order to receive the praises of men.

Prayer will not deliver us from our natural reactions, whether weak or strong; but it will bring us to recognize them for what they are, and thus continually to fresh experiences of grace.

[1] *Ideas have Legs.*

6

MUTUAL REACTIONS

IN A THOUGHTFUL study entitled 'Fear, Panic, and Politics', Dr Oscar Forel[1] asserts that men teach their children 'the art of living, which is the art of dissimulating one's own basic fear, and at the same time exploiting the fear of others.' For my part I believe that every man can at all times act freely, through individual inspiration, and that that is the true art of living and the source of every fertile movement in history. But I agree that this is very rare, and that the play of forces in society is ruled, in its broad lines, by the mechanism described by Dr Forel. Fear is the invisible conductor controlling the symphony—sometimes more harmonious, sometimes less—of strong and weak reactions between human beings. 'A particular fear,' writes Abauzit,[2] 'produces in us, according to the circumstances, either an inferior form of tolerance, or the most vehement intolerance.' What he describes as 'an inferior form of tolerance' is what we have called a weak reaction, giving way through weakness, submission without conviction, clenching one's fist in one's pocket. What he calls 'intolerance' is what we have described as the strong reaction, the spirit of contradiction, the stubbornness of mind which makes us impose our ideas on others for fear that they will impose theirs on us.

In this respect human society differs little from that of monkeys. Zuckerman describes[3] the more or less peaceful equilibrium which controls the life of a group of monkeys as soon as a hierarchy of

[1] Oscar Forel, 'Peur, panique et politique', in *Revue suisse de psychologie*, 1942, No. 1-2.

[2] Frank Abauzit, *Le problème de la tolérance*, Delachaux and Niestlé, Neuchâtel, 1939.

[3] Op. cit.

forces, or if you like, of fears, is established among all the individuals. At the apex of this hierarchy is the strongest male, whose sovereignty depends on the fear of all the rest. The arrival of a new individual in this society is followed by a period of disturbance, of sharper conflicts, until, sooner or later, a new balance of forces is established.

These two phases are found also in human society. In any grouping—family, firm, association, international organization—there are periods of instability during which the interplay of forces takes a violent form: angry scenes, attempts at intimidation, resort to force, war, flight, panic, bewilderment. But the interrelationship of forces tends to become crystallized in an apparent state of peace which is made up of a pattern of strong and weak reactions. There is then a sort of mutual acquiescence; each individual plays his role, giving way to those he accepts as being stronger, and taking advantage of those who are weaker. There are coalitions, alliances, intrigues, a battle going on beneath the surface at every stage, in which it is always the same ones who suffer.

We learn to distinguish at a glance the strong from the weak—by their way of sitting in an armchair, for instance, reclining at ease, while the weak, on the contrary, perch forward on the edge. The strong spread themselves, get themselves looked after, talk easily, know how to hide their weaknesses and emphasize their strong points, and have to hand for use at need a subtle form of bluff. But even when he is expounding some academic point, it is easy to see that the strong personality is laying down the law for others, that his aim is to consolidate his own prestige. The weaker man is retiring, as if he had no right to his place in the sun. He is silent or self-deprecatory, admiring others and unsure of his own worth. When I am in a shop I often allow customers who have come in after me to be served first if the shopkeeper does not himself come and ask me what I want. Last year I was at a conference abroad, and one day my car failed to start. After much hesitation I made up my mind to ask a friend who had a car to give me a tow in order to get it going. But I had to overcome a strong inner resistance: my heart beat faster at the thought of disturbing my friend in what he was doing. Next day during my quiet time I saw how great a part this repugnance against asking for help played in my life, distorting it and preventing my being free and straightforward, and in the last analysis how much it sprang from fear and pride. There was a friend with me, and I confessed all this to him. We prayed to God together that I might give up this fear and pride.

So our weak reactions are as likely to spring from pride as our strong reactions are. One of my patients once gave me an allegorical description of her feelings, giving each a particular character: those noisy, violent guests, rebellion, animosity, and doubt; activity, given to overwork; faith, a sickly creature who just managed to survive the diseases to which one expected her to succumb. And then there were the twins, shyness and pride, so alike that it was easy to mistake one for the other. 'And because Miss Pride is always repulsed and disdained, she tries to cheat by dressing herself in the same clothes as her sister Shyness.'

We can understand, then, the strange harmony that is established in every society in the interplay of the mutual reactions of all its members. In reality we all have in our hearts, simultaneously and with regard to the same persons, contradictory feelings. Under the appearance of an ardent love may be hidden a desire to dominate and possess, which is in fact a form of aggressiveness. Submissiveness may be a means of laying a trap—of pushing one's partner into showing the authoritarianism one complains of, in order to feed the rancour that lies beneath the submissiveness.

This also explains the curious and sudden about-turns we often observe in people's behaviour towards one another. Thus, a man chooses a woman very different from himself, prompted by an intuitive desire to find what he lacks. He is drawn to her because of the unknown treasures she reveals to him. There is no fiancé more delighted, more tenderly attentive. He marries her; but then his self-esteem as a husband can no longer bear her thinking and acting differently from him. He has married her for her spirit, say, and now her vigour irritates him, because it puts him in the shade. The enthusiastic lover has given place to the peevish and tyrannical husband.

The school of Pavlov has shown that in the nervous system every focus of excitation creates around it a zone of inhibition. On this score society behaves like an organism: the strong reactions of some sustain the weak reactions of others, and *vice versa*; but the whole organism is governed by the same factors and tends towards the same end. As long as our ascendancy is great enough and the fears of others encourage us, we pursue our little diplomatic enterprises by means of strong reactions; but let the social pattern change, and we seek to attain the same ends by means of weak reactions.

A constant reciprocity is established between the strong and the weak, between the policeman and the burglar. It was not without surprise that one heard recently that during a strike of French customs officers in the St Gingolph region, the smugglers had decided to suspend their operations. Doubtless they were put out by the absence of their adversaries, who are also the justification for their existence. The weak need the strong; if the person who dominates them disappears, he is promptly replaced by another, whom they accuse in his turn of preventing them from manifesting their personality. The strong also need the weak; if the daughter of a domineering mother marries a husband who removes her from her mother's influence, the mother transfers her tyranny to her own husband, whom she manages like a pawn in the game she thereafter plays against her son-in-law.

We are so used to taking our reactions for the genuine expression of the life-force in us that we need to cultivate the mechanism in order to give ourselves the illusion of life. True action would demand a much greater effort of creative imagination. So true is this that in certain families one stereotyped pattern is reproduced with unbelievable regularity. The husband, for example, always voices the same protests about meals not being ready on time. As for the wife, she remains true to her part in the pattern: in spite of praiseworthy efforts she is never ready in time. She always gives the same reply, reproaching her husband for the extra work he causes her through his negligence. After this uncertain beginning the husband invariably loses his temper at these complaints —though he is quite accustomed to them—and the wife takes refuge in weak reactions, declaring herself to be misunderstood and unhappy, and talking of leaving home. Thereupon follows a series of old attacks and old insinuations, with the same precision as if it had been recorded on a gramophone record, until, like a secret weapon in an undecided war, the final argument appears, to reduce the wife to tears. But the weapon is less secret than victor and vanquished seem to think, since it is always brought out, and right from the start both have expected the argument to end in this way.

One sees this gradual crystallization of pairs of domination-submission relationships in many families and social groups. But let some new element intervene, and we have the unstable phase once more. Many plays are built on this principle: into a society which is set in its ways, in which each member plays the conventional role laid down for him by custom, there breaks an unexpected event or an innocent actor, completely upsetting the established order. Each character is shown up in a new light, his true nature suddenly revealed. True human nature, too, is revealed in its violence and cowardice, together with all the falsehoods which have underlain the apparent social stability. In the ensuing chaos those who seemed accomplices are seen to be rivals.

So in life we see the weapons of the strong turned against those who have wielded them: the same nervous reactions by which a wife has maintained her hold over her husband turn out to be of no avail when she is really old and ill; the same complaints which have procured her husband's compliance now exasperate him, and the only response she gets is a string of rebukes which precipitate her defeat. The same arguments as to his authority by means of which a father always silenced his son's impertinences while the latter was still young, provoke rebellion when he reaches adolescence.

If one thinks about it, one sees that from the start the strong have a presentiment that their strength will not last for ever, and that it is in order to delay its collapse as long as possible that they dig themselves in ever more deeply behind the defences of their strong reactions, until the day comes when they bring about their downfall. Such is the history of every dictator—and they are to be found everywhere. Moreover, like dictators, such people declare their intentions to be sincerely peaceful. And indeed, as long as they rule unopposed over those around them they ensure peace, as in the society of monkeys we were considering just now. Ingenuously, they assert that peace would have lasted longer still if some instigator of disorder had not come along and set himself up against their sovereign will.

Intimidation, however, is far from being the only weapon used by the strong. Their domination often rests on the admiration they arouse, on the prestige of their reputation for perfection. But here too the same chain of events can be seen: nothing fortifies them so much as seeing themselves thus taken as models. Even our finest religious experiences can be used as weapons to dominate others, if we do not take care. Even when recounting our faults and God's mercies towards us we can savour the flattering pleasure of using ourselves as examples. But submission born of admiration is sterile. Thus we often see a wife who is loved and admired by her husband deserted by him in the end, because he does not feel himself to be her equal.

It is possible to classify people according to their mentality, on a scale running from the simplest to the most complex. The simple are usually strong, and the complex weak. For instance, the doctor whose mental make-up is simple, who tends to see things in black and white, is full of self-assurance; he pronounces his diagnosis promptly and unhesitatingly, prescribes his treatment with authority, has no doubts about its success, and does his patient a lot of good by communicating his confidence to him, even if he is wrong. On the other hand the doctor whose mental make-up is complicated, who sees many sides to every question, hesitates; he is aware of all the objections that could be made against every diagnosis; he constantly puts off having to make a decision, to see how things will turn out; he says prudently: 'We might try such-and-such a treatment, but it is extremely doubtful whether it will do any good!' This doctor may also do good, because of his sincerity. There are patients who look to their doctor above all for the assurance and support of the strong. There are others who look for the comfort and understanding of the weak.

In spiritual matters, too, we find the same two types of person, the simple and the complex. For the first, there is no mystery at all. He confidently expounds everything concerning God and theology; there is only one truth, which he blandly demonstrates; he lectures the more complex person, and with the praiseworthy intention of saving him he urges him to accept his own ideas and beliefs. But the second is too sensitive to the impenetrable mystery of the divine to be able to acquiesce, so that he comes to doubt whether he has any faith at all.

In this way the relationships between people tend to weaken the weak and strengthen the strong. The poorer and more wretched they feel, the more the weak go to others for help and advice. The strong are only too ready to give it to them, for it is always flattering to be able to tell a person what is the right thing to do. What the strong have is a natural optimism which gives them confidence; they have found the road to happiness, and they readily impart the secret to others. But when the weak try to apply the recipe, with their natural disposition to doubt, they fail. This failure in its turn aggravates their doubt, their dismay, and their feeling of being weak where others are strong. This is what Dr Pierre Buffière complains of in Drs Pauchet and Morche: 'Their happiness,' he writes, 'is due to their inborn disposition, but they boast of it as if it were the virtue of the philosophic system they advocate.'[1]

This, too, is why doctors who are vigorous characters, bursting with health, can provoke, if they are not careful, two kinds of reactions in their patients: either excessive dependence, an eager desire to live in the comforting glow of their vitality; or utter

[1] P. Buffière, *L'avenir médical*, Paris, July-August, 1942.

discouragement, a feeling of being overwhelmed by the contrast, and finally defensive hostility.

It is curious to observe, however, how frequently feelings of inferiority are reciprocal. When I admitted to one of my closest friends that I had such feelings towards him, he burst out laughing and said: 'If you only knew how often I feel exactly the same about you!'

This reciprocity often exists between husband and wife. The wife feels small beside the husband with his logical mind, explaining and proving everything; and the husband envies his wife her intuition and sensitiveness, which give her the key to spiritual domains in which the husband feels utterly ill at ease. As a result he withdraws into the shell of his logical system. He professes such contempt of the weak that his wife wears herself out with overwork, not perceiving that her husband's stoic philosophy hides a guilty conscience because in secret he gives way to his passions.

One often sees what on the stock-market would be called a 'bearish tendency' in the mutual effect of weak reactions. A married couple, both weak, try to outbid one another, so to speak, in weak reactions. Each disparages the other. The distress of each is increased by the reflection of that of the other, and each complains of not finding in the other the support that both are seeking. It is like a man with both his legs sinking deeper and deeper into a quicksand.

But I have shown, too, that strong reactions are always a form of armour behind which we hide our weaknesses. And so, after the 'bearish tendency', I must turn to the 'bullish tendency'. Although apparently opposite, they are equally so alike that it is not always possible to tell the one from the other. Husband and wife cover up their own failings by lecturing each other on those points on which each feels strongest. Also, each attacks and wounds the other at his or her weakest point, so that the other hits back in the same way. Even without apparent conflict, this drives married couples to counterbalance each other, to their mutual distress: if the wife shows timidity, the husband affects boldness; and the more the latter hides his own worries, the more fearful his wife becomes. If the husband talks about economy, his wife has a wild desire to be extravagant, and the more she spends, the more her husband preaches economy to her. The more talkative the wife, the more silent the husband—and the more silent he is the more she talks to fill the horrible silence. The more loudly the wife proclaims her religious belief, the more the husband hides his own convictions—and the more he hides them, the keener her desire to convert him. The more eager the wife to help her husband in his work, the more humiliated the husband feels, so that he abdicates his responsibilities, and the wife has to take all the more into her own hands in order to save them from ruin. Each sees and takes his stand by what is right in his own attitude, in order to reassure himself; each denounces the errors in the attitude of the other. This perpetuates and aggravates the counter-balancing effect, and reduces the chances of any reversal of their respective attitudes. Sometimes a tragic event like the death of a child is the only thing that will break the vicious circle and bring the couple together again.

Otherwise the situation can lead to real mutual cruelty, even between a husband and wife who love each other.

This competition for supremacy can take many different and more or less subtle forms. Sooner or later it brings the strong into conflict with each other. It takes place at all levels, from the tall stories and petty bluff that form the basis of 'oneupmanship' to the arms race between the great nations.

*   *   *

What we have just seen throws a particular light on the processes of history. Let us go back to the example of Professor Zuckerman's monkey society. The balance of forces in the group is determined by fear. The power of the strongest is based on the fear he inspires in all the others. Fear also ensures the cohesion of the group, each member of which seeks protection in the shadow of this collective power, incarnated in the strongest individual. In human society we find fear performing the same double function, promoting a tendency towards concentration and centralization, and constituting a pattern of ever greater and more powerful groups, which become gradually smaller in number, until finally, and inevitably, they engage each other in titanic conflicts.

Thus the countless lordlings of medieval times have gradually given way to the great centralized nation-states of our own day. The state tends to become that supreme power of the group, under whose wing each individual in his weakness seeks refuge. This I believe to be the explanation of modern statism. At the same time as he grumbles about the state, each individual contributes to the reinforcement of its power, for in that power he seeks protection against fear. But each individual also feels intuitively that the power-race must end in catastrophe. In fact, since the process produces fewer and fewer yet stronger and stronger power-blocs, conflict between them becomes more and more inevitable. Moreover, the movement is augmented and precipitated by fear. Unless some spiritual intervention takes place, humanity tends to separate out into two great coalitions, fated to collide.

This movement can be traced periodically throughout history. I am not competent to analyse its outcome in every case, but sometimes, as in the break-up of the gigantic Roman Empire, it leads to a fresh splintering of power.

In virtue of the phenomenon of rationalization, each age tends to construct a philosophy to account for what it thus experiences under the impulsion of its own unconscious urges.

The actions of peoples, like those of individuals, are dictated by these urges. Fear is the great driving-force behind politics, economics, and culture. It plays the same role in the evolution of society as in that of the individual; and yet society and history are constantly presented to us as determined by material and objective realities.

The modern myth of power, of which Nietzsche is the chief prophet, and with which I dealt in *Désharmonie de la vie moderne*, is the philosophical expression of this process of power-concentration, the emotional origin of which we are studying here. The very formulation of the doctrine, however, accentuates the movement, persuading mankind as it does that power is the supreme value. For the respect for the human person, the protection of the weak, charity and the necessity of salvation by God, professed by Christianity, our age has substituted the cult of the State, the veneration of force, the crushing of the weak in the struggle for life, and confidence in the greatness of man, 'ceaselessly climbing the ladder of progress and power'.

It is this that makes the problem of the strong and the weak so acute today. We live amid a lying philosophy which flatters the strong and despises the weak; which affects to believe that salvation lies in the victory of the strong over the weak; which denies the awful distress of man; which encourages the strong in their perilous strong reactions; which plunges the weak into their fatal weak reactions.

The modern world is hard on the weak. The doctor is well placed to observe this. But the spectacle of their unjust oppression becomes so common that even he comes to look upon it as an inexorable law, instead of seeing it as a terrible condemnation of our age. He finally gives up being outraged, protesting, denouncing the iniquity of our times, and defending the weak. He ends up saying to them: 'What do you expect? The world is unjust. Become strong yourself and defend yourself by striking back at others.'

In the very essence of his vocation the doctor is the defender of the weak. I was thinking of this recently while listening to Professor Eichrodt, of Basle. In the course of a lecture on the political and social message of the Old Testament he was showing that the fundamental principle of the divinely-inspired legislation of the Israelites was the protection of the weak against the threat of the strong. Such was the aim of the laws concerning property, designed to prevent the concentration of property in a few powerful hands, and of the institution of a jubilee year, and so on. This ought always to be the prime function of all human political, juridical, economic, and social organization, as also of traditions, manners, and the dominant currents of public opinion. Each of us can gauge for himself how far we have strayed today from this ideal.

Through our consulting-rooms pass all the victims of modern society. It is often those with the richest personalities, the artists, the sensitive, the generous-hearted, and those with the most fertile imaginations, who come to us as men defeated. 'Among those with nervous troubles,' writes Dr Georges Liengme, 'one finds truly creative personalities.'[1] But they are ashamed of their weakness, because our society despises weakness. And on the appearance of the functional troubles which are increasingly prevalent in our time, they are ashamed of them as well, because they feel them to be a sign of weakness, and this false shame aggravates their condition. The doctor says: 'It's nothing; just nerves.' The husband says: 'I get headaches, too, but I don't make such a fuss.' Sometimes nobody says anything, for the patient is afraid of talking to anyone about the fact that he feels there is something wrong with him, and wears himself out imagining in secret all sorts of fantastic causes, especially in the case of quite ordinary erotic sensations. Sometimes functional disorders of the most varied kind succeed one another in an apparently inexhaustible series. All this causes humiliation, lack of self-confidence, and monstrous fears, which in their turn provoke and nourish the weak reactions, which is what these functional disorders really are.

Then again, the man who has in childhood been the victim of injustice or disease, and so has had no chance in life, who has failed when still young to get his foot on the ladder of success—success, that is, as society understands it—finds bolted and barred all the doors behind which we each defend our little place in the sun. 'Our society,' writes Eric de Montmollin, 'does not exactly despise the poor, but it has no consideration for those who have no regular employment, for those who have not succeeded.'[2]

*　　　*　　　*

Is this respect for the strong and contempt for the weak legitimate? Is it, from the purely practical point of view, even profitable to society? Does man's value lie in his strength, in his aptitude for

[1] G. Liengme, *Pour apprendre à mieux vivre*, La Baconnière, Neuchâtel, 1947.
[2] E. de Montmollin, *La tâche sociale de l'Eglise*, an unpublished lecture, 1946.

elbowing his way through life, for extricating himself from difficulties, for defending himself and imposing his will on others? Such are the questions which crowd in on our minds.

A man's true value consists in his likeness to God. What gives value to his thoughts, his feelings and his actions, is the extent to which they are inspired by God, the extent to which they express the thought, the will, and the acts of God. Sometimes, it is God's power which is manifested in a man's courage, in the authority with which he speaks and the strength with which he acts. But sometimes, also, it is God's tenderness which we observe in the heart of one who is weak, his creative suffering that we discover in a tormented soul. Remember the experience of Elijah, that giant of action, when, broken and discouraged in the desert, he understood that God was speaking to him in the still, small voice, rather than in the storm.

The fact is that our whole civilization suggests to us a false scale of values. It accords positive value to all that is strong, and negative value to all that is weak. It is shameful to be weak, sensitive, pitiable, or affectionate.

Only today I have heard from one of my patients the poignant account of the battle she has to fight day after day within herself against the temptation to run away and commit suicide. Again and again this tragic dialogue starts up between her and the Tempter. He points out to her how empty and useless her life is, limited by sickness as it is. She replies: 'Yes, I haven't much strength, but on the other hand I have lots of love. It was God who gave me that; and so I have a job to do, small though it may be.'—'What an idea!' answers the Tempter. 'Today, in these modern times, sentiment doesn't count any more. What matters is the amount of work you do and the strength you have. The age of feelings and tenderness has passed. Being strong, throwing your weight about, being tough: that's what's called living. The weak aren't needed any more; the world wants to be rid of them.'

I am reminded of a man whom I held in the highest esteem. An ordained minister, and of a sensitive nature, he was tortured by complex and powerful psychological difficulties which made him a prey to morbid impulses. He was always haunted by the idea that these symptoms were the mark of God's disapproval of him. To avoid sinking into despair he had to hold fast to the promises of the Bible and constantly turn his eyes towards Christ. Struck down by disease, he had been prevented for a long time from exercising his ministry. He had courageously taken it up again without waiting for the cure which none of the doctors he had consulted had been able to bring about. Oh, how awful it was to feel powerless to bring him relief, to be able to give him no other consolation but my affection, my spiritual companionship, and the certainty that Jesus Christ is nearest to those who suffer!

But the greatness of this man, as of all men, lay in what did not come from him. It lay in the fact that this man, whose secret troubles I knew, was bringing with incomparable power the message of Grace to innumerable people who flocked to him. I myself, in the course of our consultations, upset as I was at my failure as a doctor to help him, received much more than I gave. There was an astonishing contrast between the distress of his human nature—his body so weak, his psychological make-up so fragile—and the spiritual power he had received from God, made the more striking by this contrast. Moreover, the trials of his physical and mental health, and of the constant war he had to wage against the doubts that assailed him, seemed to be the burning crucible in which, day by day, his faith was purified. Such strength crushes no-one.

He once confided his worries to a colleague whose solid and simple theology was the reflection of an optimistic and uncomplicated personality. His colleague's answer was that genuine faith is unshakeable, and that since the day of his conversion he had never doubted! One can well imagine the effect on our patient of these words, which could hardly fail to sow in his mind a doubt of his divine vocation. But though his psychological reactions swept down on him like a storm, his faith held firm.

In my consulting-room I am able to observe that the believers are not always those one thinks; that those who talk most about their doubts are often those on whom Jesus Christ has laid hold, never to let them go, in spite of all their failures; and that there are strong personalities, admired or feared by all, who in private admit their distress, while there are weak personalities— people who, it seems, must collapse at the first breath of adversity —who have a strength of mind that is beyond compare.

That is what Alfred de Musset meant when he wrote his well-known lines:

> *L'homme est un apprenti . . . la douleur est son maître,*
> *Et nul ne se connaît tant qu'il n'a pas souffert.*
> *C'est une dure loi, mais une loi suprême,*
> *Vieille comme le monde, et la fatalité*
> *Qu'il nous faut du malheur recevoir le baptême*
> *Et qu'à ce triste prix tout doit être acheté.*

> ('Man is an apprentice . . . pain is his master,
> And none knows himself until he has suffered.
> It is a hard law, but a supreme law,
> Old as the world, and fate
> That we must receive the baptism of misfortune,
> And that at this sad price everything must be bought.')

One of my colleagues, a refugee in Switzerland, and in poor health, after escaping from the concentration-camps, has written me a remarkably interesting letter about the benefits of illness and misfortune. He recalls that in history those who have given most to the world have not been the powerful, but the weak, the sick— a Pascal, a St Francis, and many more.

What mankind needs in our day, if it is to escape the catastrophe towards which it is being led by our rationalist and technical civilization, is just these qualities of kindness, conscience, emotion, sensitiveness, beauty, and intuition, which lie repressed and asleep deep in the hearts of those whom that civilization despises.

These are real 'frozen assets'. Instead of being mobilized as a matter of urgency, they are locked up in broken lives, which are discarded because they are labelled 'weak'. No one knows what these people might be capable of if only they were trusted; men are measured only by what appears on the surface. In this connection Sartre's words are truly significant: 'There is no love apart from the deeds of love; no potentiality of love other than that which is manifested in loving; there is no genius other than that which is expressed in works of art . . . ; the genius of Racine is the series of his tragedies, outside of which there is nothing.'[1]

There has been no more open denial of the inner reality, as yet formless and mysterious, from which springs everything fruitful that we can create. Before writing anything at all we hear it painfully within ourselves, like an elusive dream which cannot be embodied. The emotion that accompanies this tempest within us is paralysing, but still necessary. Bergson wrote: 'Creation signifies, above all, emotion.'[2]

We need confidence if we are to master this emotion and put it to good use. But confidence is the very thing we are denying to emotional people when we rebuke them for their emotivity because it is a sign of weakness.

And the affection we are capable of giving is but a pale reflection of our gnawing need to love which is unable to find expression. I shall always remember the tone of voice in which one of my colleagues once said to me: 'I long to express my affection for my mother, but never succeed in doing so. When I am with her I am paralysed. I could kick myself when I leave her. It is such a torture to me that I hesitate to go and see her.'

In this rationalist century of ours, Bergson has reminded us that intuition is the most fertile form of intelligence; it is in fact among our 'weak' patients that we find people richly endowed with this faculty. And the striking thing is that instead of being proud of it, they look upon their gift as a curse; instead of using it, they are ashamed of it and repress it.

It is true that intuitiveness makes social relationships more difficult. It makes a person aware, in those with whom he con-

[1] J.-P. Sartre, *Existentialism and Humanism*, translated by Philip Mairet, Methuen and Co., London, 1948, pp. 41-2.
[2] Op. cit., p. 33.

verses, of the slightest movement of defence, criticism, irony, or contempt in regard to himself, even when it is unconscious. That is what makes the treatment of nervous cases such a marvellous training in sincerity. If I feel the slightest impatience with such a person, even though I automatically repress it because of the conscious solicitude I have for him, he notices it, and everything is spoilt. If he has sufficient confidence in me, he will be able to bring himself to tell me what it is in my attitude that has hurt him; and if I examine myself honestly, I recognize that the rebuke is deserved. This admission on my part re-establishes the fellowship between us. But if out of chagrin at being caught in the wrong I try to defend myself by denying my secret irritation, having not even noticed it, everything is compromised.

This applies to all the social relationships of intuitive people. But the world defends itself against this irksome perspicacity, and such people are accused of being touchy, critical, and suspicious. In order to defend ourselves, we attack them. The other members of their families tell them that they are 'imagining things'. They are accused of being too fussy, with all their psychological subtleties which nobody can make head or tail of. And when events prove them to have been right, those around them, annoyed at being mistaken themselves, grumble at them all the more.

It is true that intuition sometimes makes mistakes. Nor is it susceptible either of analysis or of logical demonstration. It is often indefinite, and we find our patients troubled because they feel that something momentous is going on inside them, but they are unable to put it into words. This only makes them feel worse, increasing their lack of confidence and their suffering; and so they hide their intuition, and suffer still more at not being able to use it. 'If I were a university professor,' a young woman once said to me, 'people would take what I say seriously, even though it were prompted by my intuition, and my learning had nothing to do with it; but because I am only a sick woman, people pay no attention.'

Our civilization is rationalistic, so that intuitive people constantly try to act in accordance with logic like everyone else, setting their intuition on one side; and they fail. It is like a traveller who has an innate sense of direction, so that he could easily find his way if he trusted his instinct, without asking whether it were right. But he loses his way because he tries to use map and compass, which a man with a practical mind can use with complete success.

Intuition can express itself only in symbols. For the person who is endowed with it, 'everything that happens is but a symbol', as Goethe wrote—and he at any rate was able to make use of the fact. That is why intuitive people are usually so intensely artistic. Art, which in others is an occasional distraction, penetrates their very souls. I understood this clearly one day when one of my patients, a musician, confessed to me that there was a melody running through her mind all the time we were talking, claiming a part of her attention. So they feel themselves to be misunderstood, because other people, even those who are sensitive to beauty, have no idea of what art means to them.

They also have an extremely vivid imagination—so vivid that the fictitious world of art becomes as real to them as reality itself. This presents them with countless problems which they are unable to resolve, for one can no more resolve a fictitious problem than one can strike down a ghost. Thus, there are women who worry themselves about what attitude they ought to adopt towards men they suppose to be in love with them, but who in fact never give them a thought.

Think of the extent to which our whole conception of the world, however scientific it may be, depends in the last analysis on the subjective evidence of our senses and our intuition, so that we have no final proof of its reality. We can gauge, then, how great must be the constant and disturbing doubt in which imaginative people live, since for them all the contours of reality are blurred and indistinct. They believe what they fear and what they want. They say what they believe, and are then accused of lying; and that increases their distress.

The slightest constraint in the atmosphere of their social relationships upsets their inner equilibrium. 'It is not my fault,' a woman writes, 'if I am like a precision balance which reacts to the slightest breath of air.' Precision balances are extremely useful to those who know how to use them. What I am aiming to show here is that our civilization, a veritable battlefield of clashing forces, puts sensitive people in a position where their valuable gifts are nothing but a source of useless suffering and distress both to them and to society.

'To us men of the West,' writes Dr Carrel, 'reason seems very superior to intuition. We much prefer intelligence to feeling. Science shines out, while religion is flickering. We follow Descartes and forsake Pascal.

'Also we seek first of all to develop intelligence in ourselves. As to the non-intellectual activities of the spirit, such as the moral sense, the sense of beauty, and above all the sense of the holy, they are almost completely neglected.'[1]

This false scale of values which serves as the norm of our rationalist and realist civilization is no less a danger to the strong. They, in order to remain strong, repress everything which might betray the weakness inherent in their human nature: their need for affection, their metaphysical anguish, their artistic sensibility, their remorse of conscience, and their nostalgia for God. 'I have a horror of weakness,' writes a young woman, 'because I am so weak myself.'

The strong have learned how to play their hand so as to win in the game of life, and they become prisoners of the game.

If we are to be strong we must also simplify life, shutting our eyes to its disturbing complexity. Thus the strong quickly become the prisoners of a systematizing habit of mind and a simplistic philosophy which ends by drying them up and cutting them off from true life.

Their repeated success soon leads them to believe that they are better than other people—above all, better than the weak, who think that God disapproves of them. Their success, even when it is unjust, they easily take to be a flattering sign of divine blessing;

[1] Alexis Carrel, *Prayer*, translated by D. de St Croix Wright, Hodder and Stoughton, London, 1947, p. 15.

and this deprives them of the most fruitful experience this world affords, namely the experience of God's grace, to which the only road is repentance. I could cite here a great number of my patients who, after years of happiness and success, have nevertheless lived to bless the day when some affliction has allowed them to find a living faith. One of these writes to me of how much nearer salvation she feels now that she is fully aware of the disorder of her life, than when she thought everything was in order. Another realizes that in the happiness of the early years of her married life she had forsaken God. Her husband was taking his place, and it required a painful marital conflict to bring her back to God.

Here is another most interesting case: the good little girl, always held up as an example to her comrades. She succeeded in everything she undertook, as if it were child's play. She went up to university, where she found it extremely difficult to choose between the various courses: she was good at everything. And now she begins to have doubts about herself: what, at bottom, is her true personality? What is her bent? What is her aim in life? She has no idea. It seems that through never having had to surmount any obstacle she has never been able to get to know herself.

How quickly we become intoxicated with illusions about ourselves when everything is going well! That is what happened to the world in the nineteenth century. In the euphoria of that facile age of scientific and technical progress a wind of optimism blew on mankind. Men came to believe not only that they were richer and more knowledgeable, but also that they were better, and safe thenceforth from vulgar barbarism. Alas, we have had to take ourselves down a peg or two since then! We have been shocked to discover once more of what crimes we are capable in circumstances where the salutary constraint of society is withdrawn. But how quick we are to forget it, to shut our eyes to human iniquity, and to our own. The respect in which we are held when we are strong has taken the place of a good conscience.

*   *   *

This physical strength which earns the respect of others—what is it worth in itself? It is the old story of the soldier who killed Archimedes, recalled, aptly enough in this day and age, by René Gillouin.[1] But is our psychic or intellectual strength—even our moral strength—any more valuable in the perspective of our true destiny?

I do not wish to let my pen run away with me into paradox and exaggeration. Though I was trying just now to rehabilitate the weak, I do not want also to calumniate the strong. Indeed, they hardly need me to defend them! But strength may also be a gift vouchsafed to certain people for the defence of goodness and justice. The vigour of their bodies, the power of their intelligence and imagination, their moral authority and self-mastery, like the intuition and sensitivity of the weak, have tremendous value when they are directed by God.

What I am maintaining here is only that the dignity of man derives neither from his strength nor from his weakness, in themselves, but from the use to which he puts them in God's service; that strength and weakness are merely natural facts, and are therefore neutral like everything else that comes from nature. They involve each its own dangers and privileges, its potential for good or evil.

The trouble is that these natural differences divide men and are a source of discord among them. We are generally strong in regard to one person and weak for another; and these differences alter our relationships with them. He who becomes the strongest of all in a community runs the greatest danger. His strength cuts him off from all. He is terribly alone.

I have seen men to whom everyone defers, men covered with honour and esteem, break down and weep in my consulting-room as they tell me of the spiritual solitide to which this universal deference condemns them. Strength and weakness are suits of armour which disguise the person and prevent fellowship. That is the tragic aspect of the great problem of the strong and the

[1] René Gillouin, *Problèmes français, problèmes humains,* Editions du Milieu du Monde, Geneva, 1944.

weak: one can be isolated by admiration as surely as by scorn, by the fear one inspires as surely as by the fear one feels. 'On the one hand envy, and on the other fear, dry up all human intercourse,' writes Gustave Thibon.[1] And Jean de Rougemont: 'Man . . . seeks his fellow-man who flees from him, and flees without knowing it from the man who also seeks him.'[2]

There can be no true fellowship between men so long as they see each other as weak or strong. There may be an apparent, though false, fellowship due to the blind submission of one to the other. But this false fellowship, whose cost is the suppression of the personality of the weak, leads sooner or later to disaster for both.

There is no human fellowship except within the concept of the equality of persons. While it is true that the person is the same in every man, it is hidden behind the screen of our strong and weak reactions. In order, therefore, to reopen the way of fellowship to our modern society we must denounce the great aberration of our time, which is that men are judged according to their strong or weak appearance.

We must help the strong to understand the weak, which is very difficult. Among nations, too, relationships founded on force give rise to offensive and defensive attitudes which put serious obstacles in the way of mutual understanding. In order to know men, we must go behind this curtain of appearances and discover the person, which is the same in each, neither strong nor weak, or rather both strong and weak at the same time, torn as it constantly is between the aspirations and resistances of each.

This has been strikingly expressed by Jean de Rougemont: 'If my neighbour is stronger than I, I fear him; if he is weaker, I despise him; if we are equal, I resort to subterfuge. What motive could I have for obeying him, what reason for loving him?'[3]

The medicine of the person, the education of the person, the politics of the person, all involve the re-establishment of a true relationship of man to man beyond external appearances. In

[1] Gustave Thibon, *Diagnostics*, Librairie de Médicis, Paris, 1940.
[2] Op. cit.   [3] Op. cit.

virtue of their functions, the doctor before his patient, the master before the pupil, the leader before the people, are all clothed with a certain power which separates them from those with whom they have to deal. They may welcome the fact, and use it to hide their own weaknesses, indulging in a one-way traffic of prescription, teaching, and government, comfortably sheltered behind the screen of their authority. But then they are merely functions and not persons; they may render technical services, but not win men's hearts.

The sick, the sensitive, children, and those big children we call nations, long to find humble men who will come out to meet them, who will confess to them that in spite of the authority with which they are clothed they are no stronger than they are them-selves. 'The one thing that hinders the patient from talking openly,' writes Dr Maeder, 'is the fear of being condemned.'[1]

We can of course help our patients with our scientific know-ledge. But there are moments when we can help others, the healthy as well as the sick, only by being frank with them, and confessing our own weaknesses. I am reminded of a patient who suffered from the well-known condition in which there is a constriction of the throat which patients describe as 'like a lump going up and down'. One day as she came into my consulting-room she said: 'Thank you for talking to me yesterday as you did about some of your own difficulties. At that very moment my lump suddenly disappeared.' A true personal relationship had been established between us, and that is the foundation of all effective psychotherapy.

Naturally we must not turn this self-revelation into a system. If we practised it as a system, it could become one more method of conceited self-display, more likely to crush a person than to gain his confidence. This is a matter of life, but of *free* life, freed from the strong or weak reactions which so often veil it in our human relationships.

To a patient who was painfully confessing her shame at having burnt the notebook she used for her prayers, I had to admit that

[1] Op. cit., p. 137.

I too, in a moment of revolt, had once torn up mine. And I reminded her that Moses did the same thing when he smashed the Tables of the Law.

'The physician as a person,' writes Dr Maeder, 'is drawn into the treatment of the patient; he does not merely observe the "case" . . . A new approach which introduces a profound transformation of the field of medicine!' It is this 'personalist' attitude which needs today to be restored in every sphere of human relationships.

Let us make no mistake: this new attitude will not be found without the intervention of God's grace. It is only before God that we can realize the full depth of our poverty, and see ourselves as truly brothers to all men. Then we shall be enabled to bring them the help they need most, because day after day we have to seek it for ourselves: the grace of God. Without that grace I give way to my weakness by means of weak reactions, or hide it under strong reactions. But neither the one nor the other gives life. Living is acting, not reacting; it is acting freely from conviction, and not from submission or in a spirit of contradiction.

The optimism of the strong is as tenacious as the pessimism of the weak. But one is as false as the other. One of my patients, a woman overwhelmed by the difficulties she has to face in life, has become distrustful of everything. I tell her that there is both good and evil in the world, white stones and black stones. 'When you see a black stone, you take it to be genuine, whereas if you are shown a white one you think it is a black one painted white.' Similarly, a strong person takes the white ones to be genuine, and considers the black to be white ones painted black.

The spiritual perspective is neither optimistic nor pessimistic. In this perspective one sees stones neither exclusively white nor exclusively black. One sees the world as it is, and man himself, whether he be strong or weak, as marked with both black and white. It is as difficult to help a strong man to see his weakness as it is to assist a weak man to regain confidence in the secret strength that lies asleep in him. The remarkable thing about grace is that it produces this apparently contradictory two-way movement.

And since we are at one and the same time both strong and weak, grace also at one and the same time convinces us of our wretchedness and saves us from despair—it breaks us and restores us.

Thus, though weak and strong reactions seem to be poles apart, they are nevertheless alike in that they are both natural mechanisms. What is quite different is the religious experience which liberates us from these mechanisms. 'The answer lies in . . . a change of heart,' writes Peter Howard.[1]

In truth, we are all weak and wretched. We are all 'down and out'. Whether we are optimistic or pessimistic, intuitive or rational, confident or distressed, if one looks into the heart and not at the appearance, we are all alike. That is in fact the message of the Bible. It is the message which can cure the over-sensitive of the feelings of inferiority which overwhelm them.

We are all equal in sin and in moral wretchedness. It is conventionalism which judges men by their social façade, whereas the Gospel looks into the heart. This misleading classification is in fact propagated and cultivated by all those who wish to appear strong, in order to hide from themselves and others their secret weakness. We can take pride in retailing our victories and experiences, vaunt our social successes, proclaim the perfection of our philosophic, theological, or sociological system, and claim to teach others the secret of happiness and virtue. We do it all in order to reassure ourselves. A system the solidity of which one takes pleasure in demonstrating is like a shelter in which one seeks security.

But we are well aware that along with our successes we have known defeat, and that no doctrine and no experience has been able to preserve us from it. And the further we advance in the Christian life the more we become aware of our sin. It is as if weights were continually being added to one of the pans of a balance; and each time this happens we need more of God's grace in the other pan in order to re-establish the equilibrium. But this equilibrium is always unstable, so that the very slightest weight is enough to upset it: discouragement and doubt are at

[1] Op. cit., pp. 153-4.

our door. It is then that we are tempted to shut our eyes to our defeats, to go back to the old method of covering up by means of strong reactions—and the temptation is the greater the further we think we have advanced along the road of the spiritual life. But to do so would be at the same time to deprive ourselves of the grace which alone can redress the balance.

So, then, there are not, as the world thinks, weak persons on the one hand, and on the other the strong. There are, on the one hand, weak persons who are aware of their weakness, who know the vanity of all psychological compensations, and who in the last resort count only on the grace of God. And there are on the other hand weak persons who believe in the value of their strong reactions, of their doctrines, their successes, and their virtues.

PART THREE

PSYCHOLOGY AND FAITH

7

LEGITIMATE DEFENCE

No DOUBT THE important question has been raised in the reader's mind as to whether it is legitimate to set the Christian attitude, as I have done, not only over against strong reactions, but also over against weak reactions; not only over against hate, aggressiveness, and vengeance, but also against self-sacrifice, abnegation, and forgiveness. Does not Christianity, with its doctrine of non-resistance, provide the apologia for weak reactions? Conflicts between individuals are inevitable in life; and we can either return blow for blow, or let ourselves be struck; we can claim justice upon those who treat us unjustly, or give way to them; we can resist those who try to impose their will upon us, or obey them. Is this not precisely what is meant by strong and weak reactions? Does not Jesus Christ in fact call on us to choose the weak reaction every time?

Is not the Sermon on the Mount quite explicit on the point? 'I say unto you, That ye resist not evil: but whosoever shall smite thee on thy right cheek, turn to him the other also. And if any man will sue thee at the law, and take away thy coat, let him have thy cloke also. And whosoever shall compel thee to go a mile, go with him twain' (Matt. 5.39-41).

We cannot shirk these grave questions. They lie at the root of the argument which divides the Freudian psychoanalysts from the Christian. The Freudians have formulated a doctrine of aggressiveness and set it up in opposition to Christianity. All the symptoms shown by neurotics, all that we have called weak reactions, they believe to stem from the repression of their natural aggressiveness, of the will to live, of the individual's need to expand, of his libido. Furthermore, it is social constraint,

traditional morality—especially that of the Christian Church—
which is responsible for this repression.

The reader will remember the illustration of the domineering
mother's two daughters which I gave in the first chapter. One is
submissive, the other rebellious. The first seems Christian, the
second anti-Christian. In actual fact it is quite probable that the
first does profess the Christian faith, finding in Christianity
the justification of her conduct and even some consolation for her
sufferings; while the second, no doubt, violently attacks Christianity and its morality, in order to assuage the remorse she feels
as a result of her harsh behaviour towards her mother.

Psychoanalysts, it is true, have found an enormous proportion
of neurotics in Christian families. They have been brought up by
pious parents, in a rigid and austere moral atmosphere; they have
been taught from infancy to keep quiet and to obey, to put up
uncomplainingly with injustice, to curb their desires and their
questions, to serve without claiming anything in return; trained
to repress their tears, their laughter, and their hunger for affection,
to hide their worries and their fears, to conform with the habits,
and adopt in all things the tastes, ambitions, and opinions of their
parents. And these parents, in order to obtain this blind submission, constantly appeal to the demands of the Christian faith;
they threaten them with hell-fire; they force them to bow before
God and ask his forgiveness when they have disobeyed; later,
when the children reach adolescence, the parents instruct their
priest or pastor to reprimand them severely if they have taken it
upon themselves to choose their own career, or have taken up
with a girl-friend from a different social class. If, when still quite
young, they innocently ask how babies come into the world,
their parents reply with considerable irritation that Christian
children do not ask such wicked questions.

Later, the victims of such an upbringing sink into neurosis. A
prey to anxiety, obsessions, scruples, inhibitions, sexual perversions or feelings of inferiority, they come as patients to the
psychoanalyst. Can we complain that he urges them to adopt a
different attitude? 'Learn to defend yourself,' he says, 'give

expression to the complaints you are bottling up inside yourself, dare to assert yourself, win your independence. Open your eyes and look at your parents: they do not practise themselves the self-denial they demand from you; they are touchy, authoritarian, vindictive, and egotistical. The religion they have taught you is only a human invention, an instrument of domination, a bogy that they use to frighten and crush you. Every man is endowed with an aggressive instinct, to defend his right to live his own life. If you lack self-confidence, it is because you have repressed that instinct. Give it free play and you will begin to enjoy life again. You will realize that the divine curses with which your parents threatened you are nothing but a myth. On the contrary, you will be happy. Along with your aggressiveness you have also repressed your sex instinct; you have believed it to be wicked and shameful, instead of being proud of it.'

I shall be told that not all neurotics come from religious families. Let us be honest in this argument. Let us recognize that the psychoanalysts are not mistaken when they claim that even in circles which have no connection with the Church, an upbringing like that which I have just described has its roots in some of the ideas with which the Church has impregnated society. Like the psychoanalysts, I too have seen such cases—many such, since religious patients come willingly to consult me. Religious parents, especially, willingly send me their children. As with the priest or pastor I mentioned just now, I have had such parents appeal to me to quell their children's rebelliousness. They have sometimes been surprised and outraged that a Christian doctor should take their children's part, willing to listen to the tale of their grievances, and inviting them to assert themselves and express their own likes and opinions.

The argument, then, is a serious one. Most Christians avoid it by taking refuge in compromise. They think that the non-resistance taught by their Church is a fine ideal, but that it cannot be applied in practice. So they try to be as gentle, as honest, as disinterested, as kind as possible, but acting in all these things with a proper moderation. When necessary, they defend themselves;

they tell the lies that are indispensable to life in society. When asked if they are Christians, their conscience will not let them say 'Yes'; they say: 'I try to be.' They avoid too much church-going for fear that people will accuse them of pretending hypocritically to beliefs which they do not apply in all their rigour.

It is clear that the way of compromise offers no solution. It leaves the malaise untouched. The argument put forward by the psychoanalysts is a serious one, and we cannot run away from it. Obviously, too, its application goes beyond medicine and the particular problem of the neurotic; it concerns our whole day-by-day attitude in society. It requires a reply that is coherent, faithful to the Bible, capable of inspiring an explicit social ethic.

This is what I am attempting to do here in denouncing the dangerous error of confusing weak reactions with Christian morality. It is a confusion constantly made by both Christians and non-Christians.

There is in the Bible the call to non-resistance which I quoted just now. But the Bible also contains a personalist doctrine of man, which we cannot evade. Everywhere in the Bible we see men who, made strong by the inner call God addresses to them, dare to assert themselves, to stand up to those in power, to proclaim their message, and defend their convictions. Christ himself once used a whip. And when in Gethsemane he accepted the Cross, he did so because it was God's will, and not because he did not dare to defend himself.

There lies the whole difference. The victory of Gethsemane is obedience to God and not submission to men, an act of courage, not a weak reaction.

When Christ preached the Sermon on the Mount, he was speaking to a world that was subject to the law of retaliation, in which it was inconceivable that a strong man, capable of returning blow for blow, should forgo the opportunity of doing so. The non-resistance proposed to such a man by Christ is a victory over his own strength, and not cowardice. There is all the difference in the world between the strong man, capable of defending himself, who renounces that power in order to follow

Christ and obey God, and the man who does not dare to defend himself, who is afraid, and who weakly gives way. The first is a case of spiritual victory, the second one of psychological defeat.

The ethic I am seeking to define here, therefore, has nothing whatever to do with a compromise between resistance and non-resistance, casuistically adopting the one or the other at the dictate of expediency, defending ourselves when we can do so with impunity, and giving in when we dare not defend ourselves. It means discriminating between the underlying motives of our behaviour; asking ourselves whether we are acting in obedience to God or because we are frightened.

People often delude themselves in this matter. When they are afraid of asserting themselves, they persuade themselves that their silence is the result of Christian self-sacrifice. But if we pray honestly to God about it, each of us will be enabled to see whether the generosity he is showing is a victory or a defeat. By the light of the same biblical revelation, one man, able and ready to defend himself, sees that God is calling him to forgive; another, about to give way from cowardice, sees that he is being called to stand firm.

Thus, the spiritual life rises above the level of biological reactions. It breaks the strength of the strong, and stengthens the weak. It is always fertile. Defeat-generosity (which is false generosity) harms the vanquished as much as the vanquisher, whom it encourages in wrong-doing. Victory-generosity, on the contrary, adds to the stature of the one who gives in, and earns the respect of the one who would have won an unjust triumph.

Through having too often identified Christian morality with weak reactions, the Church has given us a watered-down image of Christianity. There are in our day many weak people who feel at home in our churches simply because of this confusion. That is hardly 'to the greater glory of God'. For their humble self-effacement and their gentleness are in fact determined much more by their psychological weakness than by their faith; and their faith is a justification for their weak behaviour rather than a victory over their psychological make-up. And so we find them to be sad, anxious, and inhibited. In their turn they contribute to the spread of this fatal confusion. 'People who do not feel quite strong enough to face the struggle of life,' writes Eric de Mont-mollin, 'have, so to speak, retreated into the Church, as being a society in which temptations are not so strong.'[1] I am reminded of one anxiety-ridden patient of mine who was obsessed by the desire to enter a religious community, which she looked upon as a haven in which she might find shelter from the storms of life. It was not without reason that she hesitated to take the final step, doubting whether God was really calling her to do so. She sensed that her longing had more to do with a temptation to run away than true vocation. We know too how carefully our Catholic brethren seek to guard against this sort of confusion in the minds of those who wish to enter a monastic order.

*　　*　　*

All this throws light on the problem of aggressiveness as it has been presented by the psychoanalysts. There is some truth in what they have shown us. The crushing of the person, as we see it in neurosis, the vicious circle of weak reactions which paralyses and sterilizes the person, is a disease, and not a normal state in accordance with God's will.

It would be best to avoid the word 'aggressiveness', which has unfortunate overtones implying a whole false philosophy. Let us say rather that there is a legitimate defence of the person, founded on the biblical revelation, and that to repress this legitimate defence is to disobey God and not to practise Christian non-resistance.

In the light of the Bible our life is seen as a gift from God, an incomparable treasure entrusted by him to us, a talent which we must put to use and protect, so that it may bear fruit. To let ourselves be crushed, to allow the aspirations which God has put in our hearts to be stifled, to keep our convictions to ourselves, to abdicate our own personality, to allow someone else to sub-stitute his tastes, his will, and his ideas for ours—that would be to bury our talent in the ground like the servant in the parable. That

[1] Op. cit.

would be to disobey God for fear of men; and disease, the inevitable witness to every disturbance of the divine order, comes to remind us of this.

So we may perfectly well accept the psychological doctrine of repression; and the analytic technique can help us to track down the false self-sacrifice which brings disease instead of new life. 'Unacknowledged, repressed, hatred towards another person,' writes Dr Maeder, 'can unconsciously transform itself into a destructive hatred against the self. Out of a certain decency one hates one's own life instead of the person who has been insulting.'[1]

This is indeed the mechanism we can see in operation. At bottom, every external weak reaction is compensated for by an internal strong reaction. The repressed counterstroke is turned back upon the self. There lies the whole difference between repression and spiritual cancellation. In the process described by Dr Maeder, the subject appears to have liquidated his hate, but in reality he has repressed it, and is engulfed in a complex of self-immolation. True spiritual liquidation sets us free; repression leads to disease.

Thus when the weak, who never retaliate, and appear content to allow themselves to be trampled upon, come to us and open their hearts, we find there an immense accumulation of grievances encumbering and poisoning them. It is only with difficulty that they bring themselves to put these things into words. They are afraid that we too will rebuke them for keeping this secret account of all the injuries, affronts, and prohibitions they have suffered. They fear that we shall call them selfish and vindictive, and think them too critical of their parents, their teachers, their friends, and their husbands or wives.

The truth is that they are no more vindictive than anybody else. All they have done is to repress the natural reflexes of defence which come into play quite normally whenever a person is injured. Every attempt at domination of any living being arouses at once a legitimate movement of defence. In man a further movement, inspired by grace, may enable him to forgive. But

[1] Op. cit., p. 34.

185

this real forgiveness, always difficult, always miraculous, always productive of good, is one thing, whereas the premature suppression of the first movement of legitimate defence is quite another. Genuine forgiveness is a spiritual victory which frees the heart of all resentment. Suppression is but a weak reaction, liquidating nothing, and laying up in the heart a store of fierce grievances. 'Rancour,' writes Dr Maeder, 'resolves nothing. It only makes matters worse.'

It is with a view to this incomparable liberation brought about by true forgiveness that we must first help the weak to unburden their hearts of all the complaints that they have never dared to put into words. There is no forgiveness without that. In order to be able once more to love parents, husband, or wife, they must first express without false shame the animosity which they nourish in secret towards them. Otherwise they will remain imprisoned in the vicious circle of their weak reactions. When the strong man strikes back, he not only discharges his sense of grievance, he imposes respect and protects himself from further attack. On the other hand the weak man by his passive attitude draws fresh affronts and constraints upon himself. To these he replies with further weak reactions, in an apparent submission which is in singular contrast with the violent passions of his heart. And this tension between his external and internal attitudes bars the way to any experience of grace.

For fear of appearing to be wicked, the weak man represses his legitimate reflex of defence, and then reproaches himself for harbouring in his heart so much bitter resentment against those who have injured him. He begins to think that he is more wicked than other people, and this leads him to further repression in order to hide his wickedness. Repression leads to depression—and then he thinks that his ill-health is a punishment for his wickedness in not being able to 'forget' the injuries he has suffered!

I am reminded of a woman who had adopted such a magnanimous attitude in the face of her husband's adultery that I congratulated her on such great-hearted forgiveness, and told her she would surely be blessed for it. It was only much later that she admitted to me that her distress had become worse after my departure, and that she had had to undergo a regular course of psychoanalytical treatment in order to rid herself of it. After that, she had experienced a newfound fellowship with her husband, whereas formerly what I might call her premature forgiveness had raised a barrier between them.

Another patient came to me, troubled by acute obsessions. I found that she had always sacrificed herself to those around her and effaced herself within her family. She believed she was doing so willingly. Even when her intuition told her—rightly—that her husband was acting improperly in his business affairs, she took care not to mention the fact to him, for she considered that a weak woman should not meddle in such matters. And then illness had come, showing that the price of stifling her personality in this way was a serious inner conflict—a sort of unconscious feeling of having betrayed her purpose in life, of having buried the treasures of intuition and sound judgement which had been entrusted to her.

A very intelligent woman came to see me in the throes of deep depression. She had undergone the negative upbringing of which we have spoken, and this had trained her to react weakly. As a result, when she became the victim of certain vile machinations and calumnies, she repressed her legitimate reaction of defence, and allowed herself to lose her job without a word of protest. Worse still, the vicious circle of weak reactions was so powerful that it prevented her being objective: in her depression she almost came to the point of declaring that those who had so unjustly treated her were in the right. She blamed herself for being stupid, useless, and unsuited to the important responsibilities she had taken upon herself. But behind this façade of self-denigration her legitimate indignation lay hidden. We had to study in detail the circumstances of her conflict so that she might look at it objectively, and be able to give me an accurate account of the scandalous facts which had broken her life. Then she was able once more to regain her self-confidence. It was not long before she found a new employment, more rewarding than that from which she had been dismissed; and then she underwent a genuine religious experience: one day while at prayer she felt herself invaded by an immense peace. All her resentment melted away, and she was able truly to forgive those who had wronged her. At the same time she found strength to overcome certain faults of character, from which her strict upbringing had never delivered her. This victory, in its turn, contributed to her return to health.

A complex of self-immolation distorts reality. The subject sees others as better than they are—while secretly criticizing them —and sees himself as worse than he is, while nourishing a secret pride. He must correct all his impressions and judgements, just as I should have to add six inches to every measurement I took with a yard-stick from which the first six inches were missing.

These psychological mechanisms are merely natural reactions, which must never be confused with supernatural experiences and Christian non-resistance. They resolve nothing; they build nothing; they create nothing. They are destructive of the personality and of fellowship. They lead sometimes to depression and obsession, as we have just seen; sometimes to violent outbursts which act as a safety-valve to release the pressure of accumulated grievances; and sometimes to frigid indifference: 'I do not love my wife any more,' a man says to me. 'I have even stopped hating her; she means absolutely nothing to me. One can't love to order.' In reality he has for a long time been repressing in silence his resentment of her attitude; and his present pretended indifference towards her is but one more turn of the key to make the repression more certain.

Strong and weak reactions both tend to annihilate the person, by shutting it off from the free inspiration of the spirit and dragging it down into the blind determinism of their mechanisms. Our reply, therefore, to the questions raised at the beginning of this chapter is this vision of a life directed by the Spirit, set over against the automatic mechanisms of the psyche—whether they be strong or weak, stimulating or paralysing.

It would not be difficult to apply these considerations to the sphere of international relations, and thus to throw light on the problem of national defence which so exercises Christians today.

The strong reaction of militarism sooner or later leads the country which gives way to it into the very calamity which it hoped to avoid by engaging in an arms race. The fear of being over-whelmed by rival nations leads it to look to arms for salvation; and its provocative attitude drags it into the war which it thought to avoid by applying the well-known but unsound maxim, *si vis pacem, para bellum*.

But a systematic doctrine of non-resistance and disarmament at any price more often than not represents a weak reaction of public opinion, an escapist policy, which also brings on the catastrophe to which it has closed its eyes. I use the word 'doctrine' advisedly, for it is not my intention to criticize the attitude of real conscientious objectors, who show more moral courage than their conformist critics.

In face of a distorted conception of Christianity, which reduces Christ's insistence on magnanimity and forgiveness to a stifling moralism, turning it into a rigid, soul-destroying system of self-abnegation; in face of a doctrine of aggressiveness which puts first the development and defence at all costs of the individual, which represses the voice of the Spirit, and is in the end equally soul-destroying, we put forward a third attitude, which is neither an ethos nor a system; it is incapable of being confined to any inflexible line of conduct; but neither is it a compromise that hovers between the two other systems. It is the attitude of the man who seeks at all times to be directed, not by principles and doctrines, but by the living God. In the Bible he finds God's call to self-sacrifice and forgiveness; but he also finds there God's call to be bold and courageous, to stand unshakeably by his convictions. And in meditation before God he learns to distinguish whether the passion that has carried him away is no more than a strong reaction which it is God's will that he should overcome; or whether the renunciation which he has in mind is no more than a weak reaction which God is calling him to overcome; whether the forgiveness he has offered is genuine or not; whether his readiness to fight is legitimate or not. It is, then, neither a morality of false sacrifices nor a morality without sacrifice.

I am reminded of one of my patients, a most religious woman, who had always sacrificed herself to help others. In her depression she was complaining against herself. A nurse had said to her: 'If you thought more about other people and less about yourself, you would not be ill!'

'I am much more inclined,' I told her, 'to preach egoism to you—Christian egoism. God wants us to love in ourselves the person created by him in his image, worthy of being tended with care, of being protected so that it may grow properly. It must indeed be pruned, but so that it may bring forth fruit, not so as to destroy it.'

So there is a legitimate defence of the person, willed by God for the fulfilment of the task to which he calls us. Employing the terms used by his teacher Charles Secrétan, the philosopher Frank Abauzit[1] contrasts the individual and the person, natural man and man regenerated by the Spirit. From the one to the other, he says, 'there is a profound evolution—a conversion, in the sense that the direction of the individual and the direction of the moral person are diametrically opposed . . . [nevertheless, in practice] the individual and the moral person are one. . . . Each of us being first an individual must remain an individual in order to realize the moral person. I might almost say that he must remain egotistical.'

Thus the moral person may be likened to a branch grafted on to the individual. Its vitality cannot be preserved at the price of the destruction of the stock. When the stock has been crushed and starved, far from preaching systematic self-abnegation, we must, like good 'gardeners of men',[2] nourish it. God created it; he wills it to live and grow.

Another of my patients had, as a result of numerous repressions, become arrested in an infantile attitude, and I was trying to reawaken her to life and growth. I found her one day quite distraught. 'I am becoming selfish and jealous,' she told me. 'I received a letter from a friend who is expecting a baby, and I

[1] Op. cit.

[2] Armand Vincent, *Le jardinier des hommes*, Editions du Seuil, Paris, 1945.

began to cry. I've never had such wicked feelings before. When my sisters or my friends have got married or had babies, I have always been genuinely pleased!' 'That is a real sign of improvement,' I said. 'You were wholeheartedly glad in the past, in the way a little girl of twelve is glad that her big sister is getting married, because she is not yet of an age to compare herself with her. But you were no longer a child, and if you felt no trace of jealousy, that was a sign that you were repressing it, because you lacked confidence in yourself and in the possibility of getting married yourself. Every unmarried woman, if she is normal, feels some slight stab of jealousy when one of her friends marries or becomes a mother. I do not say that she ought to give way to the jealousy. But it is one thing to recognize it, to take it to God, to fight the battle we all must fight against the selfishness in our hearts, and quite another to run away from the fight, to hide our jealousy from ourselves and think that we are exempt from feeling it, and to fall ill as a result of the ravages that jealousy can work in our hearts when it is repressed, unheeded, and unconscious.'

*   *   *

Let us now try to clarify this notion of the legitimate defence of the person. I am not going to advocate any sort of casuistry. As I have said, when a man sincerely seeks to be led by God, he gets better and better at seeing in which circumstances he ought to give way and in which he ought to stand firm. Doubtless he will often be mistaken. That is why he ought not to stand alone in the search. I can understand that a minister of religion, whose vocation it is to speak in God's name, should practise the direction of conscience, that is to say that he should prescribe a line of conduct for the faithful who consult him. But the more I practise 'soul-healing' the more convinced I become that a doctor such as myself—usually a layman—must carefully avoid taking the place of priest or pastor. He must, by means of the questions he asks, help his brother to listen to the voice of God, and not claim to lay down what that voice is saying. Many people come to me expecting me to act as the arbiter of the divine will. Generally I avoid satisfying their expectations, except when I can point out to them some biblical passage which settles the question. In the main, I give very little in the way of advice; I try to help people to have the courage to do what they already know they ought to do.

Take the case of a young woman who has formed an attachment for a married man. Not only is this liaison contrary to her religious faith, but also the man does not in any way represent her ideal—she has no real respect for him. 'What do you think,' she asks me, 'ought I to break it off?' I need not answer. All that is necessary is to put another question: 'What do you think yourself?' Most often the real problem is not to see what is God's will, but just to obey it.

Nevertheless, the doctor can help his patients in their search, not only by offering his fellowship to them, and prayer to God for them, but also by means of his professional knowledge. Every violation of the legitimate defence of the person brings in its train psychological disturbances because of the repression involved. It is therefore the part of the doctor to reveal them, to lay bare their mechanisms, and by tracking them down to show his patient that he has taken the wrong road, that he has given in to his weak reactions when he thought he was acting from charity.

This is particularly true, as I have shown, in the case of a child, especially an adolescent, who has allowed himself to be dominated by an authoritarian father or mother to the point of entirely abdicating his own will and personal tastes.

It is also true of the young woman who sacrifices all her friends to her fiancé's jealousy, along with all the pastimes which enriched her life—sport, art, and intellectual pursuits—because they make him feel inferior to her, and so he will not tolerate them. I have seen several such cases. And when the engagement is broken off the girl suffers doubly: not only because she has been abandoned, but also because of the great void left in her life by the removal of a servile attachment which had hitherto fully occupied it.

It is true, again, of the wife who suffers the tyranny of a neuropathic husband, and who thinks to appease him by giving up little by little everything she holds dear. What demonstrates the error of all these lines of conduct is that they fail in their object: the victimized child sees his father or mother becoming more and more authoritarian, and heaping him with abuse; the jealous fiancé, when he has robbed his betrothed of all her personality, tires of her and leaves her; the weak wife only feeds her husband's neurosis.

It is true in the case of the adolescent who renounces the career to which he feels called, especially an artistic career, under pressure from his father, either because the latter thinks it right that he should follow him in the family business or because he thinks that, in spite of him, he is safeguarding his son's material security by pushing him into an office employment. It is also true, for example, of a man who takes up theological studies at the behest of a mother who has a sentimental aspiration to see him occupying a pulpit.

But, to a less degree, it is true every time anyone renounces a personal conviction or a legitimate desire for fear of 'what the neighbours will say'. One girl gives up dancing, another gives up a close friend who is in less fortunate circumstances, a third always comes docilely home for the holidays, when a holiday tour would do her good: all are giving in to the prejudice of others.

It is worth pointing out here how few parents love their children for themselves alone. Generally they consider themselves slighted as soon as the children give evidence of having different personal tastes from their own, and rebuke them for it as if it were an act of indiscipline.

But the most serious violations of the legitimate defence of the person are those connected with moral or religious constraint. Such is the case of the confirmation-candidate who declares to his parents and his pastor that he cannot conscientiously go forward to confirmation, and who finally, against his will, gives way in the face of the storm that breaks on his head. Such, too, is the case of the person who lets himself be pushed by some fanatic into a sect whose convictions he does not share, for fear of the divine curses with which his mentor threatens him if he resists. And such is the case of the woman who in order to keep her husband allows him to bring his mistress into the home; or who lends herself to the abnormal practices of a sexually perverted husband. Such was the case of a well-educated woman, a psychologist by profession, who 'for love of her husband', consented to the divorce he wanted, and of which she disapproved, and who afterwards suffered a serious breakdown, due to her deep feeling of having betrayed her principles. And such, too, was the case of a woman who admitted to me that she had asked her parents' forgiveness for sins she had never committed, in order to win their favour, without after all obtaining it.

And then there was the case of a young girl, a Catholic, whose Protestant fiancé wished to compel her to give up the idea of having a religious wedding ceremony in her Church, as required by that Church. In the course of our conversation, she recognized that though she must respect her fiancé's religious belief, she could not hope to build a blessed home on a denial of her own.

There are, therefore, for every man, certain convictions over which he may not give way to any pressure whatsoever, whether from family, husband or wife, State, or Church, without himself destroying the inner harmony and the healthy vitality of his own person. Concessions of this sort, once made, inevitably lead to others. As a result of abdicating at one point after another, a man ends up by losing all confidence in himself. To every question his answer is 'Perhaps'. He has so often adopted other people's opinions that he no longer knows what his own are. Once on this slippery slope, instead of developing his personality, he falls ill.

When people abdicate their legitimate right of self-defence, their self-respect breaks down. They neglect themselves, and blacken their own characters. Sometimes they abandon themselves to vice, as if driven by an overpowering need to degrade themselves in their own eyes. They hate themselves, and speak roughly and offensively to themselves, in terms to which they would be quick to take exception were they used of them by someone else.

It is not easy to rid oneself of this habit of self-depreciation. Those who have caught it are ashamed to take care of themselves, to spend money on themselves, to use up other people's time, and to speak for themselves.

They tell us: 'Give your time to patients that are more interesting or more worthy of your attention than I am.' If we were to listen to them, our consultations would cease just when they are keenest for them to go on. Great patience is needed if we are to restore their self-respect, without which no man can assert himself.

And the fact is that nothing does this more effectually than the biblical concept of man which confers on him an indefeasible value as a person, and the assurance that God loves all men equally and totally, his own death on the Cross being the ineffaceable guarantee of his love.

Then weak men can become strong, with a strength quite different from the automatic strength of strong reactions. It is not a mechanical, natural strength—with that they are not endowed; it is a supernatural strength, the serene self-assertion which is forged when we are in touch with God, when he awakens firm convictions within us and calls us to defend them in loyalty to him.

Psychoanalysts, as is well known, hold that there is a close relationship between the sex instinct and what they call aggressiveness. The Freudians consider the latter as being merely a projection of the sex instinct. According to Jung, the sex instinct is only a particular expression of the libido, the instinct of life and of the expansion of the person. At all events, it will be readily understood that the three attitudes I defined earlier also involve three distinct concepts of sexual behaviour. The doctrine of systematic, self-abnegation implies a negative, disdainful, and repressive view of the instinct of sex. The psychoanalysts' doctrine of aggressiveness implies the assertion of the individual's right to allow free rein to his sexuality. Finally, the Christian attitude involves the concept of the sex life as being directed by God. The God of the Bible does not condemn sex, since he created it and gave it to mankind; but he reveals to men how they ought to use it.

'Following the period of prejudiced struggle against the sexual instinct,' writes Dr Maeder, 'the opposite reaction sets in. We must now strive towards a middle position which could be characterized as judicious self-discipline.'[1]

It is true that in the case of a man who suffers from unhealthy psychological dependence on his mother, the experience of sex, even outside marriage, may represent a beneficial manifestation of liberation. But it is not true liberty. It is only a reaction. It is a strong reaction taking the place of a weak reaction, and to that extent it is a step towards a more normal life—a therapeutic act.

But true liberty is not to be found at the level of psychological reaction. It is to be found in obedience to God. It is to be found when a man turns to prayer, seeking to know God's will and governing his behaviour in accordance with it. At that point the determinism of mere biological reactions is broken, giving way to a creative and independent attitude. Remember William Penn's words: 'Men must be ruled by God, or they will be led by tyrants.'

In order to be free as regards men, we must depend on God alone. Liberty is not to be found in the imitation of another man —even an outstanding and much-admired man—any more than in systematically taking the opposite view to that of a man we dislike.

A young wife adores her husband and admires her mother-in-law. The latter is an accomplished housewife, and although she is very kind to her daughter-in-law, the younger woman is always filled with anxiety when she has to entertain her mother-in-law, feeling that she is going to criticize the way she runs her home. On one such occasion her mother-in-law brings a hare for her to cook for supper, but so great is the wife's anxiety that it makes her ill, and she cannot accompany her husband to a concert to which he has asked her to go with him. Really she is afraid that her mother-in-law may think that these modern young wives

[1] Op. cit., p. 160.

are more suited to going to concerts than to cooking! My advice to her is to let her mother-in-law practise her talents on the hare, and herself to cultivate those which God has given to her. 'No doubt your husband chose you because he appreciates your artistic taste,' I tell her. 'He will get more pleasure out of going to the concert with you than seeing you weeping in the kitchen over a miserable hare.'

A deeply religious young man consults me because he has come to depend far too much on his spiritual director. He sees that he is constantly trying to imitate him and win his approval. He has come to pray with me that he may be enabled to abandon this false attitude.

But to defend oneself against the influence of another person does not make one any more free. A woman admits to me that a constant fear of becoming too attached to me has for a long time held up her cure. This, however, did not stop her being afraid that I should lose interest in her if she were cured. The frank discussion of all this does far more to liberate her than all the precautions she took in her secret anxiety.

There are people who constantly defend themselves against those they most admire, for fear of their own personality being swamped. And this very attitude of perpetually being on the defensive is what prevents the free development of their personality. One can make a clean break with everything without being any more oneself as a result.

The same happens when we are afraid of being deceived, of being criticized or judged. A young woman realizes that she is in the wrong job. She dare not tell her parents, because they are constantly criticizing her for being undecided and changeable in her ideas of what she wants to do. In fact it is precisely this criticism that has upset her and not allowed her the peace of mind indispensable to the making of mature decisions. Another is the only woman in the firm for which she works, and she lives in constant fear of the vulgar pleasantries of her male colleagues. Her fear disturbs her emotionally, and this provokes further pleasantries from her comrades.

I do not need to insist on the fear of 'what people will say', which makes prisoners of so many people and prompts them either to servile conformity, or to mocking nonconformity. 'The pedant', writes Alain, 'acts in his own way and thinks the same as other people. The wise man, on the contrary, acts like everyone else, but thinks on his own.' And Dr Tzanck adds: 'To think on one's own is truly to think.'[1]

A dependent attitude gradually becomes a second nature, so that a person no longer knows what his true nature and beliefs are. What proves that strong and weak reactions are not so different as we suppose is the fact that we so often pass from one to the other, just as Maître Jacques de Molière used to change from one to the other of his two costumes. It is like a game which is played now one way, now another—but it is still the same game.

One woman told me that as a child she used to play two special games of pretence. She played them turn and turn about, really living them, as children do in their play. One was the 'conscience game', and the other the 'don't-care game'. When she chose the first, she had to be terribly good and obedient, doing exactly as she was told. But when she tired of this irksome perfection she would decide to play the 'don't-care' game, and this meant that she had to be as difficult as possible. She went on to tell me that something of this lasted on into adult life; she still found herself going from one role to the other, from exaggerated scrupulosity to wilful wrong-doing. So we often pass from weak reactions to strong reactions, and *vice versa*, without in either case ceasing to be actors playing a part.

*   *   *

It is not easy to break free from our psychological reactions. The first requisite, of course, is to recognize them. But that is not enough. Their determinism is powerful. It is nourished—as I showed in Chapter 3—by the accumulation of past failures, remorse, and bitterness which we all carry about in our hearts, by the knowledge we have of our inner weakness. That is why

[1] Arnauld Tzanck, *La conscience créatrice*, Charlot, Algiers, 1943.

true liberty is not to be found without the confession of our sins and the experience of divine forgiveness.

This experience leads at once to dedication, to a decision in every circumstance to choose God's will. 'The action of liberty,' writes Charles Secrétan, the philosopher of liberty, 'does not consist in willing without motives, but in choosing between motives, without being completely determined in our choice by our internal or external antecedents as individuals.'[1]

He who comes on to Christ's side can freely collaborate in everything that seems to him to conform with Christ's will, by whatever human party it is advocated—but he can never again give such a party his exclusive allegiance.

A new strength is born in the person thus liberated, a strength that is very different from biological strength: that of true conviction. I am reminded of a young orphan girl who had suffered under a despotic régime in an orphanage, and who kept telling me that she had no purpose in life. She came one day and admitted that this was not true. 'Ever since I can remember,' she said, 'I have wanted to be a nurse, but it is only recently that I have come to realize the fact.' And from that moment she set out with indomitable determination to overcome every obstacle in her way, saving up halfpenny by halfpenny the money necessary for her studies as a nurse.

I am reminded of another young woman who had been crushed by a childhood spent amidst poverty and indignities. When, after certain religious experiences, she began to develop her personality, she told me of a dream she had had. She was in a room; a lion which had been lying asleep at her feet had risen majestically and stretched itself. It was an awe-inspiring beast, *but it was friendly*. Slowly it had made its way out into the world, imposing respect as it went. She was afraid that people would be frightened of it, but she felt that it would do them no harm. That lion was herself, or rather the potent, awe-inspiring yet benign strength which she felt coming to life within her.

[1] Frank Abauzit, *L'énigme du monde et sa solution selon Charles Secrétan*, Delachaux and Niestlé, Neuchâtel, 1938.

This is spiritual strength, which is not a game, but a committal of the self. 'The coward makes himself cowardly,' writes Sartre, 'the hero makes himself heroic; and . . . there is always a possibility for the coward to give up cowardice and for the hero to stop being a hero. What counts is the total commitment.'[1]

As we formulate our convictions, we commit ourselves. A young girl confesses to me that she has carefully avoided letting me know about the resolutions she had secretly made in her heart, so as to protect herself against the risk of being blamed by me if she happened to be unfaithful to them. And of course she had not been able to keep them! Nothing venture, nothing have. We are often like that girl, and our prudence prepares the way for our unfaithfulness.

At the same time as he finds his new strength the weak man is freed from making false claims. It is readily observable that the weak are always complaining about other people, as an excuse for their own weakness. Their inability to assert themselves is blamed on their parents' failure to understand them. But when their parents are no longer there they still do not assert themselves. Now they accuse their husbands or wives, their employers or society at large. I have shown clearly enough in this book how much ground there is for such complaints not to be suspected of failing to do justice to it. But the remarkable thing is that when a weak person becomes strong, after a religious experience, he comes and says to us: 'It was easier to complain about my parents than to stand up to them. I see now how much satisfaction I got out of my role as a misunderstood child, because it gave me a good reason for not doing what I knew I ought to do.'

Thus a man comes to tell me that the reason why he constantly provokes and argues with his mother and accuses her of stifling his personality is that he is afraid of life and is himself taking refuge in his mother's protection. And a woman perceives that her constant complaining against her old father is a way of excusing herself for the malaise she feels at always being too weak in regard to him. She has said that she can no longer have him living with

[1] Op. cit., p. 43.

her, but if she changes inwardly she will be able to put up with him.

A young girl is distressed at not being able to take up the course of study it is her ambition to follow, because of the financial situation of her parents. But when I find means of providing the support necessary for the removal of these difficulties, she gives up the idea of studying. A husband complains that his wife is so jealous that he can never have an evening out by himself. I manage to persuade the wife that it is a good thing for husband and wife to separate sometimes so that each can be free to do as he pleases. It so happens that that very evening she wishes to go to a lecture, so that her husband will be free. He accompanies her to the door of the lecture-hall, and then wanders aimlessly about the town, passing several cinemas without being able to make up his mind to go into any of them. Then he goes back home, where his wife eventually finds him sitting in his usual easy chair!

As La Bruyère wrote, it is those who waste their time who complain of not having enough. A hospital nurse complains that nobody is lending her a hand over her heavy task; but when someone does come and offer help she is offended. A husband is annoyed with his wife for having gone off on a journey when he needed her. 'Why did you not ask her not to go?'—He answers that he did not dare; he would have liked her to guess his wish. His tenacious rancour against her serves as a screen for the rancour he nourishes on account of his own timidity.

A strong, narrow-minded woman complains that her husband amuses himself and deceives her, leaving her to look after his business affairs. Behind her complaints she hides the fact that she blames herself for having exercised over him a domination which left him no alternative but escape. A husband complains of his wife's shortcomings, and when we discuss the matter seriously he admits that he himself feels responsible for them. He has abetted her through the culpable weakness he has shown in regard to her. Another husband complains of his wife's frigidity. He perceives that its real cause is to be found in his own lack of virility, which he has masked under an appearance of virtue. A few days later he writes me a magnificent letter about the marital happiness they have found together again.

So then it is no part of my intention in this book to write an apologia for the weak, as the reader has perhaps at times reproached me for doing. I know that we are often responsible for our misfortunes because of our laziness, our cowardice, and our pusillanimity. I wish only to show how far removed is the spiritual life from the natural faculties of reaction, weak or strong. I have denounced the error of confusing our weak reactions with Christian self-denial. It remains for me to examine also the distinction between spiritual strength and psychological strength.

Faith is a strength, a concrete and practical strength. The Christian life is not abstention. Genuine conversion, far from paralysing the person, makes it dynamic. I can still hear a young man saying to me eagerly, after the prayer in which he had dedicated his life to God: 'I have accepted now the idea that life is a battle.'

But what is that battle, and with what strength do we wage it? It is no longer the battle between the strong and the weak; nor is it waged with the biological strength which the strong have derived from their heredity and which the circumstances of life have developed in them.

8

PSYCHIC STRENGTH AND SPIRITUAL STRENGTH

ALL THE OBSERVATIONS we have collected in this book therefore lead us to distinguish two perspectives in human behaviour, one natural and one supernatural, a biological and psychological perspective and a spiritual perspective. They are not confounded together, but neither are they opposed to each other. It cannot be claimed either that spiritual strength is always translated into victory and success, or that it is only manifested in deprivation and defeat. The New Testament gives examples of weak men becoming strong under the action of the Holy Spirit. There are sick people who are healed, people hurt by life who regain their courage, timid and cowardly people who take on authority and become indomitable. But there is also the Cross, there is Christ trembling in the face of death, and seeming defeated to the point of believing himself forsaken by God; and there is his greatest apostle confessing his weakness.

It is necessary therefore to make a differential diagnosis between natural strength and supernatural strength, between natural weakness and supernatural weakness; by this expression I mean sin, separation from God. This is a complex and subtle undertaking. The supernatural life is lived within the natural life; it manifests itself in the behaviour of human beings. However, while the natural life belongs to the field of scientific study, the supernatural is beyond its purview. The human mind is too small to embrace the scientific perspective at the same time as the metaphysical perspective, and even more inadequate when it comes to comparing the one with the other. So we are incapable of formulating abstractly, inclusively, intellectually, the line of demarcation which we seek to draw between natural strength and spiritual strength. We are reduced to marking out its limits when and where we can, by quoting large numbers of examples and making our differential diagnosis case by case.

What we said in the last chapter about false self-sacrifice might be expressed in the following proposition: natural weakness is not always to be taken as virtue, nor natural strength as sin. This is in fact the mistake made by those who equate Christianity with a false kind of asceticism which systematically exalts sacrifice and renunciation, as if their value resided in themselves. It identifies sanctification with a negative attitude to life, to the body, and to sex. I very often meet this distorted conception of the Christian life—many people thus think that when they want something very much God must necessarily condemn it.

Many weak people use this doctrine to justify their weakness. They are content to follow their natural propensity, flattering themselves that it confers on them a certain moral superiority over those who fight their way to success in life.

The contrary is very often the case, and psychological weakness is an obstacle to the spiritual life. There is, for example, the case of a man who when still quite young has sworn not to indulge in any sexual relations before marriage. That, of course, is a very proper resolve. But—a fact which he now realizes—it was dictated by his psychological weakness, by his fear of sex and of himself, much more than by his religious faith. As a result his life has been set all awry since then by the sexual obsessions which have laid hold on him. His life is a defeat and not a victory; and finally in this distress he has lost his faith. Another case is that of a woman who is haunted by the memory of a guilty kiss which she has, however, confessed. She believes in God's forgiveness for every sin—but not for that one. Thus a psychological disorder— her fear of sex—has disturbed her religious life, to the point of making her believe herself unworthy to pray.

I could quote here all the melancholics who come to pour out on us their load of self-reproach. They accuse themselves of having

Psychic Strength and Spiritual Strength

turned a deaf ear to Christ, and see their disease as a divine punishment. But they are never able to tell us exactly what was this
call from Christ which they have refused to answer. Here is where
the psychologist must make a differential diagnosis: a vague, all-
inclusive and systematic self-accusation is generally pathological.
A concrete feeling of remorse, which relates to a precise act or
attitude, is generally genuine. The importance of the distinction
is clear. A melancholic of this pathological type happens to meet
a believer, a pastor, or a priest, who suggests that he should go
down on his knees, repent and pray. 'I cannot pray,' answers the
patient. In such a case all efforts at cure through pastoral care will
be vain, because misdirected, and will only deepen the patient's
depression, for the problem is not a religious but a psychological
one. The patient's sense of guilt and his inability to pray are merely
the projection into the religious sphere of his psychological
depression. Whereas for a healthy man to humble himself means
that he finds liberation through the experience of forgiveness to
which it leads, in a sick man it aggravates his depression, his self-
disparagement and despair. As if driven by a need to make martyrs
of themselves, these patients try one religious approach after
another; they go from one church or sect to another, they submit
to the laying-on-of-hands, to baptism by total immersion and to
various forms of mortification of the flesh, and see the failure of
all these methods of spiritual healing as the proof of God's displeasure towards them.

On the other hand, intelligence, health, self-mastery, all the
qualities which bring success to the strong, may often be the
expression of divine strength. While I have shown in Chapter 5
that strong reactions are sometimes only a deceptive mask behind
which we hide our weaknesses and faults, it is only right that I
should now do justice to the strong. The energy which is natural
to them, their effortless authority, their undeviatingly calm
courage, they may consider as being gifts from God, as talents
which they can develop in his service, using them not to ride
rough-shod over others, but in the defence of the weak, in support
of justice and truth.

205

One of my closest friends is a Catholic colleague who leads a quite simple, straightforward and fruitful life. His childhood was happy, his development harmonious, his career brilliant. He never knew the feelings of inferiority and the tragic failures through which it was my lot painfully to forge my faith. In him obedience to God, victory over self, and benign authority over others seem to be easy and natural. He serves God and men with his strength as I try to serve them in spite of my weakness.

Here again the differential diagnosis is important. Of two naturally strong men, one is strong through the harmony and the intensity of his communion with God, the other through a defensive screwing up of his courage, under which depth psychology will discover his secret distress. We saw just now that systematic self-disparagement betrays psychological disorder and not a true conviction of sin. Similarly a constant concern to show one's strength, and persistent self-justification where one is at fault, reveal false strength—psychological, not spiritual.

But the natural strength of the strong may also be a genuine sign of spiritual strength.

This is even more striking when it is a case of a weak man who becomes strong through the strength he finds in his communion with God. In the history of the Church the martyrs were of this type. They indeed were not, in the main, 'strong' by nature, and yet they faced persecution and death with indomitable courage. Such were the Apostles after Pentecost, who a few weeks before had all fled from the Garden of Gethsemane.

The weak man bears powerful witness to the faith when after a religious experience he shows himself all at once freed from fear, from despair, and from inhibitions of various kinds. I once heard of a nice remark made by a child. One evening as he was telling his mother that he was afraid of ghosts, she suggested that he should say his prayers. A few moments later the child said: 'I'm not frightened any more now. Jesus has told me that he'll see to the ghosts.' And one of my patients once expressed her experience of the Christian life as being like flying in a glider—you have to find the rising currents.

Faith is indeed a powerful force, a rising current capable of bearing up our sailplane even though it is heavier than air. 'I was obsessed by fear of the future, of disease, ruin, and death—but God has liberated me from it.' 'I was timid, but God has given me the victory over my timidity.' 'I was in a mess, and too weak to keep the resolutions I made to put things right; all is changed now that I have abandoned my disorderliness to God in faith.' 'I was too cowardly ever to dare to speak of my convictions to my husband. After praying about it I was able to do so quite simply and without effort.' 'When I came to see you I was in an awful state, because I did not think I should be able to confess the fault that I have just confessed to you. It is God who has given me strength to do it—I should never have been able to do it on my own.'

There are some who criticize concrete witness of this kind. They are afraid that people will come to mistake the Christian faith for a recipe for success in life. But Christ gave the cures he worked as proofs of his spiritual authority—quite concrete and visible proofs. We cannot directly grasp the supernatural, unless it be by introspection, but we can objectively observe its effects in the natural order. Christ did not at all despise this material demonstration. It was the real wretchedness of men, physical and psychic as well as spiritual, that he healed: the maladies of their bodies and their weaknesses of character as well as their religious distress.

Several times patients have said to me: 'I have hesitated before coming to you. What I have come to you for is God's help; but I'm a little ashamed to come looking for it only when this trouble has fallen upon me. I should have preferred to get that sorted out first on my own, and then to have turned to God when I felt strong again.' My answer to this has always been to point to the figure of Christ as he is shown to us in the Gospels. It was indeed because they were suffering that the sick cried out to him on his way and tried to come near him. He never repulsed them; he never accused them of being selfish in their approach. I am reminded too of one of my patients who told me that she had doubts about the rightness of praying to God to help her in her work. This feeling is also due to the idea that the world of the spirit is opposed to that of material things. This is a false impression which Christianity, above all, can remove.

Ours is the religion of incarnation. I am writing these lines in the midst of the festival of Christmas. The good news of the Gospel is not only a spiritual message; nor is it only good news for the Beyond. It does indeed concern our eternal destiny, but it also concerns our life here and now.

Into a world which witnessed the triumph of strength—at the time of the Roman Empire—and in which the weak were despised Christ brought an incredible reversal of values, that which is expressed in the Beatitudes. He held out his hand to the weak, the sick, the poor, sinners—to all those upon whom society passed censure. But it was not only a revolution in concepts and ideas that Christ brought. At his touch, the sick were healed, the weak became strong, men who until then had been the slaves of their natural propensities were liberated from them. It was not only the rehabilitation of the weak, but their liberation; and not only the liberation of the weak, but also of the strong.

We may still see today men delivered from the chain of their natural reactions after experiencing the grace of God. We see sick people regain physical vitality; we see neurotics delivered from psychological inhibitions on which sometimes even the best treatment has had no effect. But we also see the strong becoming gentle; we see them throwing off the armour-plating which imprisons them, their armour of health, insensitiveness, and self-confidence.

That is why concrete witness has always made a great impression on me. Nevertheless we must not exaggerate its significance. The fact that a shy person has won a victory over his shyness does not mean that he is saved for all eternity. These victories in the order of earthly things are, as St Paul says, but an earnest of the great deliverance which we shall know only in heaven. Though the drunkard gives up drinking, he remains for all that a sinner. But the freeing of a man from a particular sin is a demonstration of the incomparable power of the Spirit.

* * *

Let us look even more deeply into the problem. A man given to drink, gambling and debauchery was suddenly delivered from these vices upon being converted. In his joy he set about telling others of his experience and proclaiming that the Gospel does not bring only forgiveness of sins, but also decisive victory over sin, a victory so complete that it even frees men from temptation: our preacher no longer wanted to drink, gamble, or engage in debauchery. In face of the theologians, who, with St Paul, maintain that we are saved only in hope, he proclaimed a bold and simple message: the Christian has no more sin. And he added that the reason so many Christians remained in subjection to their natural proclivities was that they did not really believe in the salvation they proclaimed, or at least they did not believe it to have any concrete bearing on their material life. The preaching of this message had a considerable effect. It brought about a large number of conversions, all marked by a manifest moral amendment in the lives of the converts, who banded themselves together in a living community, its rules austere and its doctrine clear: the true Christian has no more sin.

I have quoted this example in order to throw light on the subject we are discussing. But to a less degree we constantly find the two tendencies in Christianity: that of the subtle, complex mind, careful for the truth, which asserts that we remain irremediably and totally sinful to the end of our days, in spite of all our efforts and even of all the grace we may be granted; which maintains that if we gain some success now and then, it is as nothing compared with the immensity of our faults, and that in proclaiming our success we fall into even greater sin, that of spiritual pride. On the other hand there is the optimistic tendency represented by the evangelist of whom I have just spoken. Drawing its inspiration also from certain passages in the New Testament it proclaims that salvation is not only metaphysical, but finds quite concrete expression on this earth in the healing of disease and in decisive moral victories.

I must remark here that those who have helped me most to experience the power of Jesus Christ have been Christians of the second tendency. Men are not likely to be influenced by a very subtle message, but rather by one that is simple and straight-forward. That is why so often hearing someone witnessing categorically and sincerely out of his own experience has sent me also to my knees to beseech God's almighty aid in which up to then I had been struggling in vain. And when in their turn men come to lay before me the private difficulties which hold them prisoner, I know well that I do not help them most by long theological discussions, but by telling them quite simply of my own experiences of God's mercy towards me. We all stand con-stantly in need of the sort of witness that will keep our faith alive. When with our own eyes we see deliverance granted where it is least expected, there is borne in upon us too the conviction that the face of the world could be transformed by a few truly inspired and obedient men.

It is therefore legitimate to proclaim what we have seen and experienced. Much more it is a witness that we ought to bear to the power of God. But I must also confess to the reader the con-sternation with which I have sometimes realized that, carried away by my zeal and enthusiasm, I have been distorting the truth in the accounts I have given, omitting some less favourable detail here, or adding there some embellishment of my own invention. And even when our witness is strictly true it may be misleading owing to the fact that it bears only upon one particular event: we talk about a victory won at one point but remain silent about a defeat suffered at another—a defeat which perhaps we have suffered just a few moments before!

Thus the evangelist of whom we were thinking just now was sincere when he told of how God had delivered him from drink, gambling, and debauchery. But to go on from there to say that the true Christian has no sin, is to make an unwarranted general-ization. Doubtless, in his community there are no drunkards, gamblers, or debauchees. But men lust after many other things than alcohol, gaming, and women. No doubt there are in that community, as in the hearts of all men, jealousies, hurt feelings, and pride.

I have thought long over this problem, which seems to me to be of some importance. Are the two tendencies we have outlined really irreconcilable? Does not each contain a part of the truth of the Gospel? If, for fear of not being sufficiently truthful, we keep silent concerning the victories won by Jesus Christ, are we not betraying him? And if we talk about them, is there not a risk of our discouraging the weak who, in their scrupulous frankness, then compare themselves disadvantageously with us, contrasting their failures with our successes?

I think we may see the answer to these questions if we picture sin as a plant, which has roots and bears fruit. Alcoholism, a passion for gambling, and debauchery are fruits. Men may be suddenly delivered—and for good—from a sin-fruit. It is as if Jesus Christ plucked away the fruit, which can never again be organically attached to the plant. But the root of sin is still there, and we shall be delivered from it only beyond death. And the plant goes on endlessly bearing new fruit. In this way we can explain how it is that there can be at one and the same time definitive deliverances and also a permanent state of sin.

Thus a man will be able—and ought—to tell to the glory of God how he has been liberated for good from masturbation. But that was a fruit, and its roots are in the impurity of his heart, which will soon manifest itself in other and more subtle temptations. Another man will be able—and ought—to tell to the glory of God of how he has been liberated from shyness. But that too was a fruit, whose roots are in his preoccupation with himself, and later on there will be further manifestations of that preoccupation for him to combat.

Those who concentrate on the root lose sight of the concrete application of the Gospel to our earthly life. They dare not say to men that the power of Jesus Christ really is able to deliver them from even the bitterest fruits; that it can give the weakest a strength greater than that of the strong; that it can break down the stoutest walls and straighten out the most tangled personal and social problems. Those who see only the fruit are deceived into an optimism which is not that of the Gospel. They underestimate the power of sin and spread before men the dangerously glittering illusion of a complete individual and social regeneration, which will come only with the triumphant return of Christ.

The first, by identifying the experience of faith with the conviction of sin, enclose man in a perspective of despair; whatever his efforts, he will always remain wicked, and society corrupt. And sure enough, under the impact of such a message a man will lose hope of ever being able to win a decisive victory over his irremediable weakness. Resigning himself to all the corruption amidst which he lives he will allow himself to be caught in the vicious circle of his natural reactions. He despairs of the world and takes refuge in an unincarnate, other-worldly, intellectual or sentimental religion. 'What I am looking for,' a young woman once said to me, 'is a God who is neither sentimental nor intellectual.'

The second, on the other hand, present man with a salutary challenge under the influence of which he achieves unexpected amendments whose consequences are incalculable both for his own life and for society. There indeed is the concrete action of a God who is neither sentimental nor intellectual solely. But through identifying the experience of faith with earthly success, they reduce religion to the dimensions of this world and fondly imagine that they are ushering in the golden age. And I have known men who on the morrow of some victory have found themselves more despairing than before, when they discover that they are still subject to temptations which they thought they had finally overcome.

The message of the first is that of Good Friday, while the message of the second is that of Easter. The Gospel includes both, and to leave out either of them is to distort it; but how difficult it is to embrace both at once! According to whether our natural temperament is strong or weak we incline to an optimistic or a pessimistic view of the Christian life. In this way our psychological reactions affect our faith.

But we must recognize that in general the traditional Christian Churches are more inclined in our day to the defeatist view; and it is for this reason that they have so little influence on a world which scarcely looks any longer to religion for an answer to the ills that beset it, for a remedy for its psychological weakness and its social disorder. Many Christians, of course, have an ardent faith; but they seem to keep it like a precious treasure under glass, rather than to put it to the test in the concrete reality of life. 'Religious faith,' wrote Dr Dubois—a doctor who called himself an unbeliever, 'could be the best preservative against the maladies of the mind . . . if it were strong enough. . . . In such a state of mind, unfortunately rare among right-thinking people, man becomes invulnerable. Feeling himself upheld by God, he fears neither sickness nor death.'[1]

Spiritual strength does in fact become incarnate; it can quicken our physical resistance and our psychological strength. I have quoted elsewhere Dr Ponsoye's thesis, *L'esprit, force biologique fondamentale*.[2] In this study he reveals quite concretely how the spiritual strength we receive from God exerts a vivifying and harmonizing influence on the whole organism.

We must therefore beware, as I was saying at the beginning of this chapter, of seeing in the working of our weak reactions, producing a sort of resignation, the sign of a genuine Christian attitude. Faith, far from making us desert the earthly battle, throws us forcibly into it: we must not always look upon weakness as a virtue and strength as a sin.

But neither must we always look upon strength as a virtue and weakness as a sin. That would be to make the opposite mistake, which we are going to study now.

*   *   *

There are, as we have said, two orders of phenomena: the natural and the supernatural, those which constitute our physiological and psychological reactions and those which arise from our spiritual life, from the action of God in us. These two orders or phenomena have constant mutual repercussions, but never merge. To fail to recognize wherein their difference lies is to lend

[1] Op. cit.   [2] Op. cit.

ourselves to the worst illusions about human nature, our own included. It is to take our natural self-confidence, if we are strong, for faith; it is to take the victories won for us by our natural qualities for spiritual victories. When we are weak, it is to take our fits of depression for lack of faith; and to take defeats due to psychological inhibitions for sins—as a sign that we are under a divine curse.

It is no less dangerous, however, to underestimate the constant mutual influence of the two orders of phenomena. That would be to condemn oneself to a complete misunderstanding of the nature of man, to looking upon him either as an animal or as an angel; it would be to miss the meaning of incarnation and to forget that our supernatural destiny is constantly involved in our natural life.

Take love, for instance. It has its natural and its supernatural aspects. But where is the dividing line? To oppose spiritual love to natural love is to render love unincarnate; it is to make the false antithesis between the spirit and the flesh which has done so much harm among religious people, to fail to recognize what there is of the divine in the 'libido'. But how many people are there who have deluded themselves by taking for a spiritual communion what is no more than an amorous transport, by imagining themselves to be possessed by a spiritual love when in fact they are actuated only by a more or less conscious natural lust?

The differential diagnosis, which we have proposed should be made between psychological and spiritual phenomena, is therefore as subtle and difficult as it is important. One cannot draw any theoretical dividing line. All one can do at any given moment is sincerely to seek to discern under God what comes from him and what from ourselves, in our feelings, ideas, and desires. It is in order to force ourselves constantly to make this self-examination that we make this confrontation of the two domains, the spiritual and the psychological.

We have seen earlier that weak reactions can be an obstacle to faith. We all know that strong reactions can also turn us away from God. I am reminded of a patient who once said to me: 'I am afraid of being cured of my depression, for fear of turning away from God when things are going well again, as I used to do.' To mistake one's natural strength for spiritual strength very often leads to pride, and then it is not long before we imagine we can do without God. When we find it easy to influence others, when we feel stronger than they are, more self-reliant, more able to resist temptations to which they succumb, we are in grave danger of succumbing ourselves, without realizing it, to that other more subtle and serious temptation of thinking ourselves to be better than they are, of believing ourselves to be in closer contact with God, of setting ourselves up as an example, and shutting our eyes to our own failures in other spheres.

Thus, in a meeting for witness, I once heard a number of Christians assert, one after another: 'Now that I have dedicated my life to God, I am no longer afraid of anything.' They were certainly moved by a laudable desire to persuade their hearers that faith is the answer to fear. And that is true. They had experienced it themselves. But their zeal had led them into a generalization which went beyond the truth. In fact, when one of those present, also a Christian with a deep and rich experience of the faith, dared to break into the optimistic chorus by frankly confessing the fears that haunted him, they all, when they prayed about it, also recognized their own.

As I have said, my friends have often helped me by telling me of the concrete victories they have won by their faith, but their witness is always more telling when they are frank enough to talk to me about their failures, their difficulties, and their sins.

It is hard to be perfectly truthful. We see our religious experiences through the rose-tinted or dark glasses of our natural temperament, according to whether it is strong or weak. So when a strong personality presents his experiences in more glowing colours than they in fact possess, the effect is to discourage the weak person instead of helping him. He goes sadly away, saying: 'I shall never be capable of an experience like that.'

I have seen, too, temperamentally strong people complacently making a display of their flattering religious experiences, so long as everything is going well with them, and then when some misfortune has really put them to the test they have crumpled up.

In the self-assurance of the strong there may well be a measure of genuine faith, which will stand up to difficulties and failures; but psychology may be able to show that their strength also consists in part of strong reactions. In this way, in every Church, in every religious movement, just as in secular life, those who find it easy to express themselves, to whom it comes naturally to influence others, who have an uncomplicated mind and a spirit of determination, soon begin to play a leading part. And the mass of the weak, because of the admiration they have for them, put them in great danger of hiding their weaknesses and relying upon their natural gifts, so as to be able to act their part as leaders without faltering.

I do not wish to be misunderstood. I am not criticizing the strong. It is right that they should use in his service the natural gifts entrusted to them by God. But the authentic mark of the Spirit is just this sincerity by which the strong may recognize how much of their action is only too human, and admit that they are not as strong as they are reckoned to be by the mass of their followers who have set them up as leaders. The greatest witness the weak can bear—as we have just seen—is in the victories they can win over their own natures in the strength of the Spirit. The contrary is the case with the strong. The strong man witnesses best not by showing off his strength or his power to dominate others with his mind or his words, but in his victory over himself in becoming humble, tolerant, and gentle. This is the more difficult because he has a part to play that is more in the public eye, and because it is no longer a question of influencing others, which he finds easy, but of mastering himself.

Here depth psychology can be of great assistance to the spiritual life, by revealing to a man to what extent the virtues he has boasted of are in reality no more than a deceptive façade. Dr Maeder shows this vividly in one of the cases he reports. 'Important above all,' he comments, 'is honesty with oneself. This is particularly difficult for an overly idealistic person and is for that reason all the more necessary.'[1]

The fact is that true faith is as difficult for the strong as for the weak.

Another danger lies in wait for the strong. It is that of using the cause they serve as a justification for their strong reactions. If they become authoritarian and intransigent, and try to use force on men's souls, if—as may well happen—their zeal betrays them into claiming that they are more reliable interpreters of God's will than those who disagree with them, they run the risk of forgetting how much of their attitude is due to their individual make-up, and persuading themselves that it is inspired only by their desire to serve God better. The pressure they exert on men's souls is aimed at saving them, and in order to break their resistance they increase the pressure accordingly. I remember one woman who fell victim to a sudden attack of acute mental disease as a result of this type of violence.

Here again I do not wish to be misunderstood. I am not advocating individualism or the total liberty of the Christian. I recognize that Protestantism, not indeed in the mind of the Reformers, but later on, has tended to lose sight of the meaning of the community and of the Church. God himself commands me to submit myself loyally to my Church, particularly in matters of faith, in which as a simple layman it is for me to learn and not to teach. What as a psychologist I wish to show here is that there is a world of difference between the divinely-inspired obedience of the faithful to their Church, and an obedience imposed upon them by a dictatorial leader. The first is fruitful because it is spiritual. The second is dangerous because it is only the operation of the mechanism of domination of the weak by the strong.

The wonderful thing, the thing that makes the spiritual adventure something quite different from any secular adventure, is that God uses our weaknesses. In this way the weak can be as sure as the strong of having a place in his purpose.

I have given many lectures; and sometimes I have been

[1] Op. cit., pp. 36-7.

heartily applauded and yet my message has not borne fruit. But once, when I had been asked to speak at a university, I felt right from the start that I was failing to make contact with my audience. A growing nervousness took hold of me, and I came out in a cold sweat. I clung to my notes, which I could scarcely read, and laboriously recited what I had to say. As the audience left I could see my friends slipping hurriedly away to spare my having to meet them. On the way home in my car with my wife, I burst into tears like a child.

But the next day I had a telephone call from one of the university professors. 'I have heard many first-class lectures in my life,' he said, 'and I have always come away from them arguing mentally with the speaker. I have never heard one as bad as yours last night; but I could not get to sleep afterwards. It has raised a question in my mind—one that cannot be resolved by intellectual argument. Can I come and see you?' Several weeks later that old professor underwent a religious conversion which has made us close friends.

Too often we concern ourselves with the apparent success of a meeting. We choose the best and most authoritative speakers—in a word, the 'strong'. The result is that the latter are overworked, and less gifted believers—the 'weak'—doubt their ability also to be of service to Jesus Christ. This aggravates their feeling of inferiority. In actual fact it is often on hearing one timid man awkwardly stammering out his faith that another is emboldened to believe that he too can bear witness. I vividly remember a certain day when I saw one of the strongest men I know, intelligent, knowledgeable, self-assured, and authoritative, dedicate his life to Christ after God had spoken to him through the modest witness of a humble woman to whom words did not come easily.

I remember too the lively emotion with which I once listened to a young foreigner, whose words, in very halting French, completely lacked oratorical skill. That day I realized all at once that when my services were called upon in the Church, it was much more because of my natural than my supernatural gifts. That evening I was with some friends and told them what God had shown me, and I knelt down with them to pray that thenceforward he would build my service to him more on what came from him, and less on what came from me.

Let us therefore be careful not to confuse natural strength with that of the Spirit. Let us be careful similarly not to identify health with faith, and sickness with lack of it. That also is a mistake which, alas, is too often made! A neurotic, the victim of his heredity and the accidents of his childhood, is ashamed of his disease, because a healthy person whose life has always been easy has said to him: 'If you had faith, like me, you would not be ill.' Faith can, it is true, help the neurotic, but his disease can also prevent him making the step of faith. It is like shouting to a drowning man to whom one has thrown a life-belt, but who because of cramp in his arms cannot grasp it: 'Come on, man, get hold of it!'

It is hard for the healthy to understand the sick, and for the strong to understand the weak.

Imagine now that the emotion of terror in the drowning man is aggravating the cramp in his arms. That is exactly what happens in the neurotic. Feeling himself thus misunderstood and unfairly criticized, he finds it more difficult to take the step of faith, a step which requires an atmosphere of brotherly confidence. Consequently we see many neurotics themselves coming to believe that their psychological difficulties are a sign of God's displeasure, and to think themselves damned because they are anxious, have obsessions, and lack the strength to resist temptation. A woman, for example, who is depressed as the result of being crossed in love confesses to me that she sees her psychic crisis as a punishment sent by God. One feels that this erroneous interpretation is hardly likely to restore her self-confidence.

One does not need to read far in the Gospels, however, to see the particular care that Jesus Christ had for the weak and the sick.

Clearly, we are brought always to the same distinction, which is not amenable to logic, but is grasped only by the heart: faith can fortify a weak man and free him from a psychological trouble; but this does not mean, however, that the weak and the sick are further away from God than the strong and healthy, or that they have less faith.

I owe it to the truth to point out, too, that a religious experience may sometimes exacerbate a person's psychic and physical condition. A friend confided his trouble to me: he had found that his health had deteriorated since his conversion—did this mean that it was not a genuine conversion? I was obliged to remind him that he had not been converted in order to improve his health, but in order to do what God was calling him to do, and that it is better to be sick and to believe, than to be healthy and an unbeliever. This thought in fact helped him to regain his peace of mind, and as a result his health at once improved.

Here we have a subtle and tragic phenomenon, namely that the believer is often more ashamed of his weak reactions than the unbeliever, because he fears that this impairs the value of his witness to the faith; and the added emotional disturbance that results from this increases his tendency to weak reactions.

*   *   *

With this false shame for weakness and disease, we are touching upon one of the gravest problems in religious psychology: that of the pathological feeling of guilt.

A man whose mother died in bringing him into the world reveals himself to us as perpetually burdened with an undefinable sense of guilt, which he projects on to all he does, constantly accusing himself of imaginary sins. He is the 'over-scrupulous' type. He appears to suffer from a groundless and unconscious feeling of responsibility for the death of his mother, and it seems that this remorse must be expressed in endless self-accusations, which never succeed in effacing it.

We find the same in the case of those who have been the victims of the negative upbringing we described in Chapter 2. We find it again in those who have suffered the domination of a possessive mother whom they never succeeded in satisfying, even when they sacrificed themselves completely to her. We find it, finally, wherever there exists the false moral code which psychoanalysts call the super-ego, and which we studied in Chapter 3.

All these have the appearance of cases of conscience, since the subject accuses himself of having sinned. Nevertheless they are amenable, not to religious soul-healing, but to psychological healing. The answer to their anxiety is psychological, not religious; it ought to be exoneration rather than forgiveness. The anxiety is due, in fact, not to a fault or a sin for which they ought to be blamed, but to an injury of which they have been the victims. Forgiveness is needed only where guilt can be attributed. This is why they do not succeed in experiencing a sense of forgiveness; and they see this as further proof of the divine displeasure. It is from this obsessive yearning for pointless forgiveness that they must be delivered, by being helped to discover the true cause of their anxiety. I described the torments they can suffer when I spoke above of the victims of depression and melancholia who never stop accusing themselves. I pointed out at the same time that this vague, systematic and persistent character of their self-accusation is the surest sign of its pathological nature.

But it is very far from being always as manifest as in these extreme cases. I think it most important that theological colleges should include in their courses instruction in the differential diagnosis of true and false guilt.

True and false guilt are dangerously alike in appearance, and to treat a pathological guilt-feeling as if it were a genuine conviction of sin can only result in making it worse. The teaching of pastoral theology is defective in this respect, and the available literature is scanty. Depth psychology has thrown so much new light on the subject that it behoves professors of pastoral theology to recast their courses completely. But doctors in general are scarcely better informed. It is important that this state of affairs be remedied, so that doctors may be able to decide whether to direct their patients to the psychiatrist or to the minister of religion.

No one that I know of has written more discerningly than Dr Charles Odier[1] on the subject of this differential diagnosis

[1] Op. cit.

between a true and a false sense of guilt. Rightly he alludes to Bergson,[1] for these two kinds of guilt-feeling are closely tied up with 'the two sources of morality and religion', that is to say the psychological constraint exercised upon the passive subject by his environment, and on the other hand the inner call of the Spirit, awakening in him an active movement of the true moral conscience.

In the first case, as Dr Odier clearly shows, the patient is put at the mercy of the psychological automatism of his weak reactions; in the second, on the contrary, the mind attains the supreme liberty that comes from obedience to God. In the first case the anguish is primarily provoked by an unconscious conflict, but a mechanism of rationalization comes into play, and the patient attributes it to—and feels it as—a bad conscience, which he tries vainly to quieten through self-punitive impulses. In the second, on the contrary, it is remorse because of a real fault, the conviction that he has betrayed his ideals and disobeyed God, which arouses moral anguish.

The feeling of anguish, however, is the same in each case, and this prevents the subject making the differential diagnosis for himself. I read the Bible or some book on religion or morality; I listen to a preacher or some other person denouncing an injustice; or, what is more, I hear a man confessing his own sin; or else I listen in prayer to the voice of God. Suddenly the humiliating memory of a blameworthy thought, feeling, or action comes into my conscious mind. I know that I was at fault, and a feeling of anguish overcomes me. This anguish is exactly similar to that of a person suffering from depression. But if I confess my fault, make amends for it, repent it, and receive God's forgiveness, I am liberated, whereas the depressed person is not—a fact which he expresses to me in these words: 'I never succeed in feeling that God has forgiven me.'

For the two different kinds of guilt, therefore, there are two different remedies: for true guilt there is grace, and grace alone; for the false, there is only psychoanalytical or psychiatric treatment. The layman has a certain intuitive feeling that this is so.

[1] *The Two Sources of Morality and Religion.*

Take the case of a woman sufferer from depression who stubbornly persists in self-accusation. Her husband says to her: 'You worry too much; you take Christianity too seriously.' There is some truth in these remarks, though it is badly expressed. Furthermore, exhortations of this sort do nothing to reassure a person suffering from depression. Can one really make a sensitive person admit that in order to be happy he ought not to take Christianity seriously? Do not our great spiritual deliverances begin only when we begin to take the demands of the Gospel seriously? Therefore such remarks imply a complete misunderstanding of the moral conscience, whose voice no-one can stifle.

I said, however, that there is a certain amount of truth in the husband's criticism. He realizes well enough that even though there are moments when the Gospel overwhelms us with an anguished flood of remorse and repentance, this is only an acute and passing crisis, very different from the chronic torment suffered by his wife. Therefore, if instead of finding the Gospel a source of peace, she derives from it only endless torture, it must be that something is distorting it for her.

For the sake of clarity I have contrasted true and false guilt as if they were met with in different persons. In reality they intermingle, and this further complicates the problem. Driven by his self-accusatory impulse, the sufferer from depression often reproaches himself for things that are really sinful—a lie, for example. It is quite hopeless in such a case to try to reassure him by playing down the importance of his fault, telling him not to take Christianity too seriously, and attempting to persuade him that his feeling of remorse is the result of an unconscious complex. While only the exploration of his psychic mechanisms can liberate him from the obsessive impulse which makes him accuse himself so also only God's forgiveness can liberate him from the remorse left behind by a real sin.

I have often had to sort out in detail in this way all the various self-accusations made by a patient in order to point out the fallacies of his false guilt-feelings, and to resolve the true ones through God's forgiveness.

I often think that these patients are like a forest in which some wicked gnome has planted false trees among the real ones, in order to discourage the woodcutter and make him give up cutting down the real ones. I am reminded, for example, of a colleague who in childhood had been the victim of a neurotic father, and who wrongly accused himself of having behaved badly towards him. This self-accusation was only the deflected expression of the legitimate defence which he had repressed in the past. It cost him a tremendous effort to relive the unspeakable emotions of his childhood and the unheard-of cruelties his father had inflicted on him. In this father-son relationship it was the father who was at fault, and not the conscience-stricken son. But as soon as he was liberated this patient began to confess to me real faults, and they demanded a religious answer. The memory of them had been, as it were, eclipsed behind the false sense of guilt which overlay his consciousness.

Moreover, theologians have often quite properly stressed the fact that the over-scrupulous person accuses himself of a host of subtle and imaginary sins, while remaining blind to the real errors of his life, engrossed as he is in the detailed examination of the imaginary ones. One may accuse him of taking refuge from a true conviction of sin in the jungle of his scruples. But one can also admit that this mass of false feelings of guilt prevents him making an honest self-examination.

A remarkable chapter in Dr Maeder's book[1] analyses the guilt-feelings connected with masturbation. It is a striking example of the point we are making. As the psychoanalysts have shown, these feelings are principally an expression of the false shame attached by society to sex, and their obsessive character is incontestably derived from this fact. But I say 'principally', because no theory can extirpate from the human conscience the conviction that to give in to masturbation is to disobey God—or nature, or the law of true love, if one does not believe in God.

In the domain of sex we are constantly coming across this double factor in guilt-feelings, the false and the true. In a woman

[1] Op. cit.

who is involved in an amorous liaison with a married man there is perhaps 90 per cent. false shame due to social prejudice, but there remains 10 per cent. of true remorse of conscience. Faced with severe condemnation by a minister of religion she bridles up in protest; she considers herself unjustly condemned, for she feels that he misunderstands the psychological mechanisms which have brought her into her present difficulty—for example, a healthy reaction against the conventionalism of her environment, or a sincere and generous pity for a man who has told her how unhappy he is in his married life. When, however, she goes to the psychologist, who sees nothing but these mechanisms, she is left undelivered from her genuine remorse.

Then there is the case of a girl who, at the age of two or three, used to go out naked into the street. She remembers quite well the sense of guilt she felt, and to some extent even enjoyed. Of course in this feeling too, social suggestion played a large part. It is because of all they know of life, which is as yet unknown to a young child, that adults scold a child who indulges in a naïve exhibition of this sort. Nevertheless, young as she was at the time, this girl had no hesitation in recognizing that there was also something genuine in her sense of guilt. There was a real consciousness of having violated a divine law, that of modesty, which no psychologist will ever be able to reduce exclusively to a social convention.

For these two distinct kinds of guilt-feeling, then, there are two distinct remedies, but as they are closely intermingled, it is necessary also to combine the two types of treatment. A Christian psychoanalyst like Dr Maeder is well qualified to provide the necessary religious answer when analysis has brought to light a genuine remorse of conscience.

Finally, the problem is still further complicated by the fact that however distinct the two kinds of guilt-feeling, there is a connection between them. They interact. It is the same connection as that described in Chapter 3 between the mass of unhealthy fears and the inner kernel of vague but ineradicable fear which haunts the heart of every man, however courageous or strong. As we have seen, this irreducible residue of anxiety is the fear which a man has, not of others, but of himself, of the guilty impulses he feels within himself.

A young woman is assailed by psychological disturbances on the approach of her marriage. Together we analyse the mechanisms at work. Her anxiety is false—'functional', to use Dr Odier's term. It is the expression of inner conflicts whose nature is strictly psychological and not moral. Certain events in her past life have left harmful traces on her mind, and these have been reactivated by the prospect of her approaching marriage. This marriage represents the fulfilment of her dearest wish, and yet a mysterious inner inhibition stands in the way. The patient is intelligent. She readily understands all that is going on inside her, and courageously co-operates in the analysis. But there is still something unreal in our work together; a certain fear subsists.

Then one day she gives me an urgent call. A keen anxiety grips her. But this time she has remembered a sinful act that she herself once committed, and she confesses it in front of me. This time the answer is religious, and not psychological, because this time we are not concerned with an act of which she was the victim, but with an act for which she was to blame. There lies the whole difference between the two kinds of guilt-feeling. Nevertheless, the religious response to her confession—God's forgiveness—does not only allay the genuine anxiety of her remorse. It is reflected on to the false anxiety, the mechanism of which has been revealed in our previous interviews, though they did not succeed in banishing it completely.

One can see here the link between the two anxieties, between the false and the true feelings of guilt. It is a sort of sympathetic resonance, as happens when a crystal vase vibrates to a certain note on the piano. We all have within us a vague anxiety due to our true faults, which sensitizes our minds and makes them prone to the accidents originating from psychological conflicts, and giving rise to a false sense of guilt. And in their turn these false psychological anxieties can re-awaken in the conscious mind the true anxiety, which then takes on the character of a concrete and genuine conviction of sin.

This link may be described by means of another image. The patient suffering from anxiety is stopped by a wall. Up to a certain height, the courses of the wall are made up of his true guilt, part of it being, moreover, buried in the ground and invisible. But the false guilt, due to the incidents of which he has been the victim, have raised the height of the wall of anxiety and made it impossible for him to get over it. In his desire to jump over the wall he fixes his eyes only on the top—the obsessive false sense of guilt. But if he attacks the foundations, and they are blasted away by the action of God's grace in him, the whole wall will come down.

Dr Maeder reports the case of a girl who had suffered a sexual shock in childhood which had implanted in her an unhealthy fear of men. So far the problem was purely psychological. But at his next interview with her, helped by the easing of tension already achieved by what she had been able to admit to him previously, the girl was quick to see that the offence perpetrated on her, in spite of the lively defence she had put up against it, had also encountered the complicity of her own desire. 'At bottom,' adds Dr Maeder, 'without her having realized it until now, she is afraid of her own sex instinct; it is not only men she distrusts, but also herself.'

Where fear, anxiety, and a sense of guilt are concerned, there are therefore two levels: the profound moral and spiritual level, and the superficial, psychological level. I have endeavoured to show how distinct they are, and yet they do interact upon each other. At the level of the psychological reactions the subject is ashamed of his fears, regarding them as a weakness from which stronger people are exempt. This shame is harmful, since he is not responsible for the weakness for which he blames himself, and because this feeling of being weak cuts him off from other people. On the moral and spiritual level the subject is even more ashamed of himself because he feels and knows himself to be fully responsible. But this shame is salutary, because it is common to all men, since all are sinners. This weakness which the subject discovers within himself is the universal weakness of human nature, and his experience of it gives him a firm feeling of his solidarity with the rest of the human race.

The two levels are thus distinct but too closely bound up together for it to be possible to treat our patients fully without providing a twofold answer to their twofold anguish. Another of my colleagues had been the victim of tragic circumstances in his childhood and youth: his father died; abandoned by his mother he was brought up by a sick and possessive aunt; depersonalization resulted—these were the least serious of his misfortunes. Together we went in detail over all these confidences, but up to this point we were still on the psychological level, where the subject is the victim, and there is no question of his moral responsibility. My colleague did indeed find some relief in examining all these matters with me. We were able to establish a mutual bond of confidence; but in spite of this the atmosphere remained heavy. And then suddenly, instead of the improvement I had expected, I saw my patient enter into a truly paroxysmal crisis of anguish. That same evening I received a letter: 'I must go through with this thing to the end now,' he wrote. 'There are also some things in my past for which I am to blame; I intend to make you a full confession of them tomorrow.'

Then came real liberation, a prodigious liberation which opened the door on a quite new and fruitful life.

In this way a thorough clearing of the ground on the psychological level often opens the spiritual channels through which God's grace may flow. Another of my patients was a young woman suffering from a serious inferiority complex. We analysed its causes: she had been dominated by a sister who still treated her as a child. She had been too weak, had allowed herself to be dominated, and had been unable to establish her adulthood. All this she understood, but still it was not enough to 'release adulthood' in her. As it happened, she lived with a Christian friend, and on the evening of our interview this friend spoke to her about her own experiences and about the sins from which she had been freed by her Christian faith. Our session on the following day moved suddenly from the psychological to the moral and spiritual level. My patient had hardly slept at all. What she had heard had awakened in her memories quite different from those of her sister's persecution; and what ensued was a veritable confession. All at once she grew up! Now she was an adult at last, because she had experienced the full power of Christ. Her new spiritual strength was thereafter to be reflected also on the psychological level, and lead her to victory over her weak reactions.

9

TRUE STRENGTH

WE HAVE REACHED the end of our confrontation of the two levels on which our human life is simultaneously lived. 'Confrontation', however, is not the right word, since these two levels constantly encroach one upon another, and since they are not of the same order. This is what makes so complex a problem which in theory is so simple.

In theory, each of our thoughts, feelings, and actions may be the expression of the automatic determinism of our physiological, psychological animal reactions, as well as the effect of a spiritual inspiration, free and creative. But often we think we are acting on inspiration when we are the puppets of our automatic mechanisms. And often, too, the particular style which our natural temperament gives to our behaviour hides its spiritual source. It is easier still to be mistaken about other people! We must therefore abstain from judging others, that is to say we must renounce the claim to be able to make, from outside, a diagnosis of how much of their behaviour derives from the Spirit and how much from nature. Even where we are ourselves concerned, we never know ourselves completely. We can go on indefinitely making this examination of conscience, constantly making unexpected discoveries. At one moment we find that there is something God-given in what seem the most natural of our reactions, and at the next we discover something still human in what we have thought to be our most genuinely spiritual experiences. And these discoveries are made sometimes by psychological means, by the revealing analysis of a dream or of a slip of the tongue, and sometimes through the illumination that bursts upon us when we are at prayer.

Let us consider two men, both fighting for a generous ideal—for example, for liberty of conscience and tolerance. They may put forward identical arguments with equal ardour, and yet both are not actuated by the same force. In the same way a radio station may draw its power from the grid or from its own generators, and yet broadcast the same programme. Without realizing it, one of these men in crusading for tolerance is really seeking vengeance on his father, who in the past has exercised an improper moral constraint upon him. The other has a genuine vocation. The strength of each is derived from a different source: the one is psychological, the other spiritual.

In some respects the automatic, inevitable, and determined character of psychological strength endows it with a greater, more stubborn and indomitable dynamism, at least at first sight.

In international politics, for example, take the case of the nation which inspires fear in its neighbours. It is, of course, its own fear which makes it so formidable. It is dangerous simply because a psychological mechanism is so rigorous, so impulsive and so powerful that reason and sentiment are utterly incapable of arresting it. The stronger such a nation is, the more afraid it is; and the greater its fear, the stronger it tries to make itself, to the extent of sacrificing everything in the mad race for strength, until it unleashes the most terrible catastrophes, in which it will itself be engulfed; and the anguish it feels as disaster approaches only drives it more surely towards its inevitable destruction.

Does this mean that the operation of weak reactions presents a more favourable prospect? By no means. In politics, the tactics born of weakness, all the compromises and deals that are inspired by fear, also precipitate the very calamity they are designed to avoid. So both kinds of natural reactions, strong as well as weak, lead to war and destruction. On the level of these reactions we have no choice but to show our teeth in order to intimidate others, or to make unjust concessions in order to appease them, until the day comes when we can get our own back; or else we must pass alternately from one policy to the other. Neither will lead to true peace.

At a time of international crisis, like the Munich Conference, for instance, men are divided according to their natural temperaments into two camps. Each advocates one or the other of these two policies—that of force and intimidation, or that of concessions at any price. Each can with justice point to the dangers of the other's methods, since both increase the grave risk of war.

Spiritual strength is quite different. It is identified neither with the politics of strength nor with those of weakness. Whether the conflict is one between husband and wife, between two competitors, or between nations, spiritual strength provides a way of escape from the tragic dilemma I have just described. It introduces a new element, a new dimension, into human affairs. It acts on a different level: no longer upon men's power-relationships, but on their very nature. And by changing their nature it changes the premises of the problem.

I am not inferring that in politics—even conjugal politics—all methods are of equal value. In each given set of circumstances we must seek a line of conduct, either strong or weak, which is both appropriate and feasible. But it must be recognized that this is a policy of expediency, and not a true solution that will bring true peace. So long as human nature remains unchanged, our solutions, however prudent, will be precarious. Whether we seek them in a show of strength or in compromise, the most we can hope for is a cease-fire. 'God alone can change human nature,' wrote Dr Frank Buchman.[1] This is also the only true solution of the problem of peace and the problem of social justice. The reason why our modern world is finding it so difficult to solve these problems is precisely because it is trying to do so without God.

I am not preaching utopianism. I know very well that the return of the nations of the world to God will not cut at one blow through the complicated net of their political, economic, and social difficulties. But the premises of those difficulties will nevertheless gradually begin to change. This is the only road along which we can expect to come to a renewal of human

[1] F. N. D. Buchman, *Remaking the World*, Blandford Press, London, 1953, p. 46.

relationships. At all events it must be agreed that there is a tragic disproportion between the technical efforts at solving our political and economic problems by committees of experts and diplomatic conferences, and those which are undertaken to change the spiritual climate of the nations.

When the world is really convinced that the deep roots of its ills are in human nature, in the natural reactions of fear and aggressiveness, at the mercy of which it is put the moment it turns away from God, when the world once more seeks divine inspiration, not only in theology but also in politics, then there will be a real hope of peace.

Spiritual strength changes the premises of our problems bit by bit. That is what the experts never realize, thinking always that the premises are immutable.

As I said just now, spiritual strength seems at first to be less impulsive, less powerful, and less brutal than that of the natural instincts. In reality it is far stronger, if we measure it by the fruit it bears. This is the strength, in fact, which breaks the vicious circles of our natural reactions; it is the strength which gives victory over self and over fear; and thus it is the strength which smashes the strongest thing there is in the world.

It may present itself in the guise of weakness. 'I myself am by no means the heroic type . . .' writes Dr Maeder. 'Without the certainty and support of faith I cannot carry on.'[1]

As we compared just now two doughty fighters, so also we can compare two men who give way—one by a natural reaction of timidity and cowardice; while the other, a man who would be quite capable of resisting or hitting back, controls himself and puts an end to the struggle through his mastery of himself and his charity. The second man is, in reality, strong, but strong in the spiritual sense of the term.

We can go further. A man is involved in a marital conflict. His wife is obdurate and domineering; she dominates him from the psychological point of view. He gives way to her, but against his will; and his wife feels that it is against his will, and this

[1] Op. cit., p. 183.

provokes her to persecute him still more. Then suddenly the pot boils over: all his long-repressed reactions explode in a violent 'scene'. This strong reaction, however, is no more successful than the grudging concessions he has made before. It over-excites his wife quite as much, and she soon gets the better of him again. This man thus goes from weak reactions to strong, but both are the expression of a deep-seated weakness.

The answer, in fact, must be sought on a deeper level. I had listened for a long time to this man's descriptions of all the misery of his married life. He expected advice; I had none to give, for advice is always on the psychological level. I spoke to him about several of my religious experiences, about the fears I had discovered within myself. We spent a long time in prayerful meditation together.

And then, in God's presence, he began to tell me of wrongs he had committed, and for which he thought he ought to ask his wife's forgiveness, and then he spoke of the fear she inspired in him, which he thought he ought to lay before God in prayer. There was at bottom a link between these two points, a link which neither of us saw at first: fear prevents us confessing our sins, and a bad conscience quickens our fear.

The result was splendid. For the first time he was able to approach his wife without being afraid, inwardly prepared and calm, because he was doing so in the knowledge that he was obeying God and acting in fellowship with him. In appearance he was performing an act of weakness, coming to his wife to eat humble pie like this. In reality he was being strong; for the first time he was truly stronger than she—much stronger than before, when he had insulted her in fits of bad temper.

Real marital happiness returned to their home. Naturally he still had to make concessions to his wife, but they were no longer of the same colour, if I may use that term. They were strong concessions, and no longer weak ones, spiritual concessions, no longer psychological ones.

Clearly, spiritual strength can take on at one moment the appearance of strength, and at the next that of weakness. It is really stronger than natural strength, even when it seems to be defeated. It is free of all the inner tension which is the mark of natural strength. It actually gives us strength to confess our weaknesses, whereas natural strength impels us to hide them, without delivering us from the fear of having them discovered.

The act of confessing one's weakness is a stronger one than that of covering it up with noisy exhibitions of strength. Abraham Lincoln provided an example of this when, strong as he was, he said to one of his generals: 'You were right. I was wrong. I'm sorry.' An attitude like that does not come naturally to any man. No one can mistake it for a weak reaction. It is an intervention of the Spirit, turning the order of nature upside-down.

Such gestures are rare, but they always bear fruit. They are as difficult for the strong as for the weak, for the religious person as for the atheist. In 1939 two of the most important leaders of the Norwegian Church, Bishop Berggrav and Professor Hallesby, were in conflict, divided by their differing churchmanship and by personal animosity. In the diary of his private prayers the Bishop wrote: 'There is a war in Europe. There is also war between you and Hallesby. Go and see him and make peace for Norway's sake.' Peter Howard, who tells the story,[1] adds: 'The Bishop was a big enough man to pocket his pride and obey. From that simple action . . . sprang the fighting and unbreakable unity of the Norwegian churches . . . against the Nazi invaders.' 'True freedom,' writes Edward Howell, 'is a decision more than a state of affairs. It is the decision to serve God. When a man makes that decision and acts on it, miracles occur and he escapes to live. . . . No problem is too great and no obstacle too severe for the miracle to overcome. When men make that decision they are free.'[2]

One of my friends has just been telling me of two operations at which he was present, both on the same morning. The first patient was weak—a highly-strung, emotionally unstable woman. But she had faith, and faith helps us to be honest with ourselves. Before God she had been able to confess her fear of the

[1] Op. cit., pp. 170-1.   [2] Op. cit., p. 227.

operation and to pray to be set free from it. The second was strong. He came jauntily into the anaesthetizing room with a quip: 'Well, it's me for the slab today!'

Things were quite different under the anaesthetic. The first was calm and silent; the second as restless and theatrical as a confirmed alcoholic! This patient, who acted the strong man with his jokes, was really repressing under that mask a thorough-going complex dating from his childhood. His father, it appeared, had left his wife and children and gone off with another woman. The bantering attitude which the patient had adopted since that time, and which gave him an air of strength, had distorted his whole life. It had given him the habit of hiding his fears both from himself and from others. Under the narcotic, however, all this artificial edifice crumbled away.

If then we want to understand men—and it is a passionately interesting study—and especially if we want to help them (and that is more thrilling still), we must learn to distinguish between the appearance and the reality. We always find that their true weakness is that which operates on the religious, not on the psychological level; and that the strength they draw from contact with God is the only strength that is truly creative.

There are two motive powers at work in the mind: instinct and the Holy Spirit. Psychology seeks to liberate natural strength, the libido, instinct; and that is legitimate and salutary. But we who are believers seek, over and above that, to tap a new source of power for man, the supernatural strength which comes from the Holy Spirit; it is a different strength, which does not go against that of instinct, but which goes beyond it, controlling and directing it, so that man may pass from mere animal life into the life of the person.

It happens, however, that some psychologists endeavour to fortify the weak and free their blocked instinctive forces by giving them advice which runs counter to the demands of the Spirit. Thus, in order to provide them with one kind of strength, they deprive them of an infinitely more fertile kind. Only through obedience to the Spirit can we receive his power. On the supposition that what is blocking the forces of instinct in their patients is a fear of committing sin that has been artificially suggested by society, these psychologists try to free them by denying morality. They may make them strong in the psychological sense, but it will be at the cost of the repression of the conscience. It is a surface strength, which covers up the great unresolved human problem.

The great human problem is not that of weakness, but that of strength. It is, in fact, that man feels in himself the mysterious power which God gave him when he gave him his dominion over nature. It is that he feels himself free to use it and to abuse it. It is of that strength and that liberty that man is afraid. That is why his fear grows with his strength. This is clearly seen in the case of the atomic bomb. It is evident, therefore, that the psychological salvation which consists in becoming as strong and as free as possible, contains in itself a dangerous weakness. There lies the vast difference between the Freudian doctrine of aggressiveness and Christian doctrine.

The condition on which man receives the supernatural power of the Holy Spirit is his submission to the will of God. And it is quite clear that insofar as a man allows himself to be ruled by God in the use he makes of his strength, he can also deploy it without himself being afraid of it. Christianity does not, therefore, teach a doctrine of weakness. But the strength it gives a man is quite different from his natural strength. It is a God-directed strength, doing what God wills. It wins great victories, but they are only over evil and self, not the destructive victories that are won over others.

Compare the man possessed of great natural psychological strength, with the man who posssesses spiritual strength. The strength of the first is built on his social successes—that is to say, very often on the defeat and humiliation of others. The stronger and cleverer he is, the more he crushes others, the more he undermines human fellowship and weakens those he tramples upon. The strength of the second grows from the strength he imparts to others, and in this way he builds up human fellowship. In what does the value of a journalist consist, for instance? Is it in the success he can derive from conducting violent campaigns and capitalizing on human weaknesses? Or is it in dedicating himself to raising the moral level of public opinion? Which man is the more virile, the one who thinks he is showing his virility by tyrannizing over his wife, or the one who helps her to develop her own talents under the powerful protection he provides?

Only religious faith can supply the calm, creative strength which, far from strengthening one man at another's expense, is propagated from one to the other. 'It is many years now,' writes one of my brother doctors, 'since I acquired the "technique" of our profession, . . . but long ago I learnt that it does not work without faith . . . the whole of psychology is useless if men are not rooted in a sound conception of life.'

*   *   *

The men whom we see in the Gospels coming to Jesus Christ were mostly weak, sick, tormented, the outcasts of society. He afforded them, and in abundance, healing, assurance, and rehabilitation. He withdrew from them when they wanted to make him a strong man of this world, a king. And in order to raise them up to an understanding of the mysteries of faith, he abased himself and washed their feet.

But he brought them much more. The strength which comes from God can heal, it can give strength to the weak, but that is only one aspect of its power. It does much more; it saves and quickens. Salvation and healing do not coincide. Healing may be a sign of salvation, but salvation goes far beyond healing, because it is needed by the healthy and the strong as much as by the weak and the sick.

In so far as weakness derives from an inner conflict, faith meets it by re-establishing the harmony of the person. But that is not the only weakness. That same Jesus, who had healed so many of the sick, and raised men from the dead, allowed himself to be put to death on the Cross, without defending himself. And we are right to see in his supreme acceptance of suffering, in his weakness, in his human defeat, a higher expression of his spiritual strength than in his most striking miracles.

We remember the experience of St Paul, who thrice besought God that a certain disease should depart from him, only to receive the reply: 'My grace is sufficient for thee' (II Cor. 12.9). Yes, sometimes the strength which comes from God—his grace—heals; sometimes it lifts us out of our weakness; but sometimes, too, it leaves our weakness with us, and gives us a quite different strength—the strength to accept it. Psychology cannot do that. Often, in patients who are most sorely tried, but yet are filled with the serenity of faith, I have contemplated the power of God and seen it to be more wonderful than if that tortured body or mind had been healed.

The true believer draws from his faith the strength to persevere despite every obstacle. I am reminded of a young woman who had been obliged by serious functional digestive troubles to abandon all activity and give up her career. The slightest effort caused such a painful recurrence of the trouble that she was compelled immediately to desist. I followed her progress over a number of years. Every form of medical and psychological treatment that I tried failed to give relief: the pains persisted. I was often near despair. But at such moments, when I was ashamed at feeling myself so useless to her, it was she who restored my courage. She would always reply: 'I believe that God has a purpose for me, and that you can help me to find it.'

One day she told me of a vocation she had received while at prayer—a particularly hard and difficult one from the human point of view. First I persuaded the head of an educational establishment, a very understanding woman, to take her on with a part-time curriculum: my patient could work for only a few hours a day, and even that cost her unutterable pain. But, sustained by her conviction, she successfully completed this stage in her progress. Now she must envisage a course of study as an internal student. How would she be able to endure the dietary régime imposed on all the students? How could she work regularly enough to pass her examinations?

Of course it required God's help, and the perseverance that comes with faith. The pains still persisted, but the patient would not let anything stop her. It is now two years since she entered upon the career at which she had been aiming. 'Two years of happiness,' she writes to me today, 'in a task given by God and performed without physical hindrance . . . Since I have been here I have been completely free of my nervous troubles. . . . It is in accomplishing a freely accepted task that a sick person rediscovers the harmony of the body, and hence spiritual harmony.'

Faith does not deliver us from all our ills. It does not liberate us in this world from our natural temperament. It allows us temporarily to overcome it, which is quite a different matter. Those who turn to Christianity as a universal recipe for success will inevitably be disappointed. I have seen many such. A man who had been liberated from an inveterate vice after being converted came to see me in a state of deep despair because after years of almost easy victory he had slipped back into it again. He had, so to speak, identified his experience of Christ's power with this particular deliverance, which was only a reflection of it. I had to persuade him to accept the fact that in spite of all the grace he had received he was still a weak mortal, always in danger of backsliding just when he thought himself to be strong. A woman has been cured by her conversion of her fits of bad temper. But now she is prone to impatience with her other failings, and cannot bear not to be perfect, or not to have her prayers always answered. Impatience like this closes the road to all further spiritual growth.

The first step towards conquering one's weakness is the acceptance of it. In Chapter 4 I described the tragic mechanism which so often aggravates the condition of sufferers from nervous complaints: that it is the tense eagerness with which they strive to hide their weakness which drives them further into it. It is this vicious circle which destroys faith. However, nothing but disappointment, and finally rebellion and doubt, awaits the attempt to find in faith what it cannot bring, namely deliverance from our human nature, from the fundamental weakness which remains our lot in this life, or from the weakness which is peculiar to a particular individual because he has been born with it.

Faith does not completely deliver an over-emotional person from his essential liability to emotion. It delivers him from the fear of his emotion which has been making him still more emotional. Faith does not deliver a sensitive person from his essential sensitiveness; it delivers him from his fear of suffering, which made him still more sensitive.

Faith does help us to accept our nature, to carry its burdens like a cross, to offer it to God to be used in his service, to derive some good from it and not merely suffering.

In this way the emotional person, instead of rebelling against his emotivity, may, to use Bergson's terms,[1] convert it from its harmful form of 'agitation at the surface' into its creative form of 'sensibility in the depths'.

Faith leads us to the acceptance of ourselves, and of others, just as God accepts us all as we are.

Furthermore, there are physical and psychic infirmities from which no medical or psychological treatment can free us. Instead of allowing them to become an obsession with us, we can in the perspective of faith derive benefits from them. A colleague of mine suffers from a sexual abnormality which debars him from marriage. Perhaps there is some psychoanalyst who might undertake the attempt to treat it, though I doubt it, since the most distinguished psychoanalysts are wise enough to realize the limitations of their methods in certain cases. And then they have nothing more they can do, for they have no other answer to give. The answer to this particular case is not psychological, but spiritual, and my colleague has already found it. It is that the goal of life is not health, but to bring forth fruit. Deprived of the natural equilibrium which the satisfaction of the sex instinct in marriage affords, he has attained through faith a different equilibrium—the sublimation of his instinct in a marriage with science, and he sees his celibacy as fitting into the purpose of God for him, so that he may devote himself to scientific researches in a way in which he could not if he were married.

[1] *The Two Sources of Religion and Morality*, pp. 32 and 33.

This is also the answer for unmarried women. To suggest that they should indulge in 'free love' is to plunge them, apart from any moral considerations, into psychological difficulties in which the woman is always the chief sufferer. To suggest that they should stoically accept their lot is to condemn them to the moral and psychological tension inseparable from the stoic attitude—a thorough-going strong reaction. To advise fatalistic resignation, on the other hand, is to open the door to weak reactions. But from the moment they are able to see their celibacy not as a grievous blow of fate, but as a vocation from God, in which he is calling them to a life of service, a ministry such as St Paul describes in his own case, their lives are transfigured. Doubtless it is only very few who succeed in doing this. Doubtless too, in the sense in which I have spoken in this book of our human condition, they can never be certain of having solved the problem permanently. Nevertheless this is the only solution which brings true victory.

But there are crosses that are even heavier to bear: those of unrequited love, of a vocation missed, of a tragic family secret, of an irreparable wrong. How often has a man said to me after a painful confession: 'You understand now why I keep myself to myself. I can never have a close friendship with anyone: if they knew what I have done!' One does however come across some who are able to rise above this feeling, and achieve a deep enough sense of God's forgiveness to enable them once again to make contact freely with their fellows.

In these great moral struggles, not only is psychological strength too weak, but so also is the 'strength of religion' as it is sometimes called. What is needed is the living strength that comes from personal fellowship with Jesus Christ. The reader will no doubt grasp the distinction I am making here. 'Religion' has still something intellectual, sentimental, or impersonal about it; even, at times, something stifling, because of everything that has been said or written about it. To satisfy the burning thirst of tormented souls nothing will do but to take them to the well of living waters, to true fellowship with Christ.

That is what a woman who is racked with serious anxieties means when she writes in a letter to me: 'It is not Christianity in general that I long to possess, but God himself, in a quite personal way.' The personal God—God with us—is Jesus Christ. That is precisely the meaning of the Gospel: the incarnation of God himself in a human person, with all the anxieties, fatigues, and tears that human flesh is heir to. He is the strong God whom we dare approach even when we are very weak.

Open the Bible, and this is what you see: he was severe and implacable with the strong, the powerful, the virtuous, the rich, and the great ones of this world. Not, indeed, in any spirit of animosity, but in order to smash that confidence in themselves which closed to them the road to humility. But with the weak, with those whom society condemned and crushed, with the poor, with those whom sickness or sin had thrown into despair, he had only words of tenderness, gestures of encouragement, and a way of looking upon them which banished all their distress.

It is impossible to write about the strong and the weak without underlining, in all its fullness, the way Jesus Christ completely upset the scale of human values. However close our fellowship with him, we never succeed in being as free as he was from the social prejudices which make us revere the strong and despise the weak. Again and again in my daily meditation God has shown me that a certain attitude of condescension has once more insinuated itself into my words of encouragement, sincere and friendly though they were, to one of life's outcasts.

*   *   *

Some of my readers were perhaps disappointed just now, when I wrote that faith does not deliver us from our natural temperament. Others no doubt protested in their hearts. How does this assertion tie up with the witness of numerous Christians who have declared their lives to have been completely changed since they dedicated them to Jesus Christ?

True, the power of God does not only touch our states of mind; it is incarnated in us, transforming much of our actual behaviour. The first time this was demonstrated to me was when I met an old comrade of my student days. He had not played an important part in our student activities, being shy, retiring, and infirm of purpose. He had gone abroad, and I had heard nothing more of him beyond a rumour that he had undergone conversion. But when I saw him again I was staggered. He radiated such an air of fearless authority that I hardly recognized him as the same person. And one of my friends whispered in my ear: 'Now I believe in the Holy Ghost!'

Since then I have seen many lives profoundly changed, and at times very swiftly. And yet I must add here what I also believe to be true: however decisive the change that faith makes in our lives, each of us lives his new life in his own natural style. Little by little the dominant features of our temperament assert themselves once more, in one form or another. Except in the case of spiritual backsliding, our lives do indeed remain different from what they were before the change took place, but they retain a certain personal stamp. At any moment some inspiration may break in upon our natural reactions, but not so as to suppress them entirely. The shy person has overcome his shyness, has stood up and spoken with authority before large audiences. In the joy of his liberation he has perhaps thrown himself zealously into public life. But one day we shall find him engaged once more in some humble form of Christian service. This is no longer shyness: he could easily take the limelight again. But his temperament has not changed, and is still giving his work its particular stamp. It is no longer seen as a hindrance, however, but as a natural talent which predisposes him to serve God in his own particular way.

A strong man, similarly, undergoes a profound spiritual experience, and as a result gives up the excessive and ostentatious activity in which he had been engaging. He realizes the extent to which he has been using the giddy whirl of this feverish activity in order not to have to face his problems; and now he feels that what he needs is to withdraw and be quiet in order to seek their solution. But the cast of his mind will not allow him to remain in contemplation for long. From the new convictions formed in the course of his meditations there spring new plans, and he will soon be throwing himself once more into the realization of them.

His activity will not be the same as it was. It will be more relaxed, calmer, and more fruitful. Nevertheless he will have come back to the natural dominance of his temperament. There is something more here than interaction between his natural life and the new inspired life. What has happened is that his natural gifts have been put at the service of his new life, and are being 'directed' to that end. In a sense, his temperament has been sanctified.

It would not be right, however, for me to present this process only in this favourable light. What Pascal said is still true: 'Banish what is natural, and it comes running back.' There is a certain permanence in our innate tendencies, in spite of all the upheavals that faith brings.

So then, if we observe with care the lives of those on whom Jesus Christ has laid hold, we find in them a mixture of the liberty of the Spirit and the determinism of nature; a combination of the new elements their conversion has brought into their lives, and the old elements that went to make up their inborn temperament.

Most men are averse to the consideration of the full and subtle complexity of reality. They prefer dogmatic systems. Thus we find that in general they over-simplify things, denying the existence of one or the other of these groups of elements. Or else they affect complete scepticism as regards the Spirit. Against all the evidence they deny that conversion brings any real change in a man's life. They see it as no more than a fleeting subjective feeling, an illusion due to suggestion. They accord an absolute character to Pascal's remark: they see what reappears of the natural temperament, and not what remains of the spiritual transformation.

Others, on the contrary, in the enthusiasm born of their experience of conversion, believe themselves to be more completely changed than in fact they are. They are upset if we suspect them still of acting to a certain extent in obedience to their original natures. Unhappily this refusal to recognize the fact puts them in danger of depriving themselves of further liberating experiences.

When I consider my own life and those of the Christians I know, I always find the same balance and interaction between the spiritual and the natural factors which jointly control our thoughts, feelings, and actions. Would the reader prefer a fairy-story, in which the strong became weak and the weak strong? Or one in which everyone became unfailingly strong? In particular, am I going to discourage the weak by telling them that despite frequent and genuine victories over their weakness, they will always have to reckon with it in this life; that they will always have the innate disposition which we were discussing at the beginning of this book? Illusions can be more discouraging than anything else.

If our lives are directed by the Spirit, we may count upon real particular victories over our natures, but we can never expect a total, final victory. It is quite as wrong to deny the partial victories as to exaggerate their importance. Our nature may be transformed in part; but there remains a part of it that we must simply accept as it is. To prefer the fairy-story is in fact to rebel against our human condition, to refuse to carry our cross, to seek to know in this life the complete liberation which will be ours only in the life hereafter.

I have shown similarly, in *Technique et foi*, that the most genuine faith is not one which claims to be exempt from doubt, but that which feels its way through many a hesitation, many an error, many a discouragement and false start. In his book *Escape to Live*, Edward Howell tells of how when he was a prisoner-of-war in Greece he patiently sought God's guidance in planning his escape. No sooner did he think he had seen it than doubts and objections came crowding into his mind. He had to return to his prayers, recognize his faults, quell his impatience, and overcome his hesitations. All this bears the mark of the humble and difficult struggle of faith, whereas men would always prefer the easy magic of an infallible oracle. And yet, in spite of all the perplexity, God's purpose is unfolded, its lines gradually become clearer, and success comes to crown the fidelity which stubbornly refuses to give in.

Another recent book, that of Mlle Madeleine du Fresne,[1] bears no less impressive testimony to this fact. Hunted by the Gestapo in occupied France for having helped a Jewish friend to escape, subjected to the attentions of cunning interrogators, imprisoned in a concentration-camp, we see her seeking day by day to be guided by God. We see both the power of fear, never far from her mind, always threatening disaster, and the power of the Spirit always enabling her to overcome it. Side by side we see the contagion of fear and cowardice, and the contagion of faith with the sovereign serenity it brings. We see also the miraculous experiences which the believer may enjoy, alternating with heart-breaking failures; the times of illumination when we are led by God, and the dark hours in which we try to cling to the memory of past experiences; 'the adventure lost', and then 'the adventure refound'.

Such indeed is our life, an odd mixture of unhoped-for victories and unexpected defeats. We never know the security of a spiritual discipline without backsliding. Inspiration is fleeting, but it is always springing up anew. Scarcely have we lost our way when God brings us back. Constantly losing sight of the road and finding it again, we are constantly reminded of our weakness and of the power of faith.

It is this paradoxical situation in which the Christian finds himself that Roger Mehl describes in philosophical terms;[2] the situation of the Christian who is born into a new life which is already real on this side of the grave, but which will be full and unblemished only beyond his death and resurrection. Mehl notes that in the Bible 'some of the passages which speak of this new life are eschatological, while others relate to the present time. The Scriptures speak of the grandeur of the new man both

[1] Madeleine F. du Fresne, *De l'enfer des hommes à la cité de Dieu*, Spes, Paris, 1947.
[2] Roger Mehl, *La condition du philosophe chrétien*, Delachaux and Niestlé, Neuchâtel, 1947.

247

as something that is to come and as something already realized.' There lies 'the mystery of the new man, real and hidden, real but not yet made manifest . . . The new man is an objective reality apprehended by faith. . . . His newness will be made manifest only at the last day. But, though hidden, it is already at work in men: it bears its fruits, without our ever being able to accord to its empirical manifestations a normative or probative value.'

So then, the true meaning of a religious experience does not lie in the transformation it effects in our lives, but in the fact that in it we have known God. That is what is lasting, even if our life remains a mixture of the divine and the human. That is what helps us to accept the drama of human life, which results from the very fact of the unending conflict in us between the divine and the human. It is indeed to the extent to which our experience has borne real fruit, to the extent to which our lives and our natures have undergone palpable, manifest change, that we can witness to the power of God. But that power goes far beyond our puny witness. What matters is not our experiences, but the fact that in them we have known the power of God's grace. That is a thing we do not forget, even if the day must come when the weaknesses, temptations, and sins from which we had thought ourselves finally delivered reappear on the horizon; even if we must tirelessly battle on against our nature.

That is our task, to battle on, to hold our own against our inborn tendencies to strong or weak reactions, which we were given when we were given life itself, and which will be with us as long as we live. But the battle will not be the same as it was before. The faith born in us as the result of a concrete religious experience, survives even if we backslide. What is radically changed is the climate of our lives. Though our innate tendencies will remain with us, we shall on the other hand find it possible to break out of the vicious circles I have described, which constantly exacerbate those tendencies. Then if we still discover in ourselves, to our dismay, strong or weak natural reactions, far from being discouraged, we shall see them as opportunities for new deliverances.

It is on this note that I should like to end my book. The Christian life is not a decisive and radical experience undergone once and for all. It is an uninterrupted series of experiences in which by God's grace even defeat and backsliding generate new victories.

Now let us consider once more the situation I described, in which people having at first asserted that 'everything is changed', then find that the old natural man is still very much alive, when they had thought him defeated. Actually, in so far as they are frank enough with themselves to recognize the fact, we shall see them changed again—and more changed. It is this progression from change to change which constitutes Christian experience.

As we travel this road, we find that grace constantly increases. At first it was God's forgiveness washing away one particular sin, a limited victory over a specific natural inclination. But with this first experience of grace we learn to know ourselves better; we discover many more sins, and are better able to measure the tenacity of our natural propensities. And the grace given increases.

I am reminded of one of my patients, who had been brought up in that atmosphere of pious but over-simplified faith which I have already described—an atmosphere in which sin means drink, gambling, and women, and to be saved from them is grace. Following upon a course of psychotherapeutical treatment, my patient had discovered a great number of other sins in herself, and was shocked at the discovery. 'I feel that the grace I was brought up to believe in,' she said to me, 'was a tiny box, much too small to contain all these sins that I am learning to recognize now!'

Grace is infinitely bigger than we imagine. All has already been accomplished in Jesus Christ. In proportion as we recognize the evil in our own hearts, we appreciate more fully what he has done for us. In proportion as we become aware of our wretchedness, we see that he has already answered it in advance by his sacrifice.

And so the sombre journey to the discovery of our distress is transformed into a bright journey to the discovery of grace. The 'tiny box' of grace grows in proportion to what it has to contain.

Many weak people come to see me. My experience of helping them with patience and perseverance has taught me two apparently contradictory truths: the incomparable power of the spiritual life to overcome the weakness of the natural temperament, and the formidable tenacity of this natural temperament which reasserts itself continually, even immediately after the most splendid victories. One learns in the process to distinguish between faith and optimism. It is a hard struggle, in which ground is frequently lost as soon as it is gained. Often one is near to despair. But in spite of all our back-sliding the upward march always begins again so long as we go back faithfully each time to ask on our knees for the assistance of God's grace. At last the day comes when we can see the fruits of this unremitting perseverance. Grace has grown. The climate of our lives has gradually changed, in spite of the alternation of defeat and victory. And in this new climate victories are more easily won. Our natural propensity towards disorder, flight, and discouragement are indeed stubborn; but for that very reason we shall, through the months and the years, have multiplied our experiences of liberation. In the end of the day that is what counts: the need to cling always to God, the habit, if I may call it that, of coming back to him, of familiarity with him, which is in a sense imposed on us by the very difficulty of the enterprise.

The Bible in its realism does not present us with an idyllic picture of an élite stripped of all natural weakness; it shows us men like you and me who carry the whole weight of their inborn temperaments. There are strong men like Elijah, hotly pursuing the priests of Baal. There are weak men like Jeremiah, beset by the temptation to remain silent. There are men full of contradictions like Jacob, like David, or like St Peter, who alternate between sublime impulses and treachery.

And if we suffer the continuing slavery of our natures, the Bible shows us that we do not necessarily have to be freed from it in order to experience the power of God. God takes hold of these men just as they are. He comforts Elijah when the prophet is in despair at the failure of his miracles. He strengthens Jeremiah and draws him out of his silence. To St Peter he announces both his denial and his vocation to be the leader of the Church.

Furthermore, in each of these lives, as well as throughout the long period of history which it covers, the Bible reveals a movement from one experience to another towards the discovery of God, in spite of all that each man retains of his human nature.

Only Jesus Christ, God incarnate, is seen to be at once completely human and completely exempt from the reflexes which we have described under the name of strong or weak reactions. He is always free, because he is always led by the Spirit. Nevertheless he shares our weaknesses and our strengths: our weariness, disappointments and despair; our enthusiasm, joys and ardour. He remained silent before Pilate, but took a whip in the court of the Temple. He had compassion on the weak, but violently attacked the strong. He cried out in anguish on the Cross, but proclaimed his divinity with authority. And yet his words and actions never have the automatic character of psychological reactions. He is neither strong nor weak, in the human and natural meaning of these words.

He is alive. If we open our hearts to him, he fills them with his presence. In so far as he thus lives in us we are delivered from our weak reactions, while at the same time becoming more aware than ever of our weakness. We are delivered also from our strong reactions, while at the same time receiving from him a strength that is beyond compare.

For he alone answers the deep-rooted anguish which we hide under our apparent reactions. Through him we can both accept our weakness and overcome it. Then from within society we can help to break the tragic vicious circles which throw it into disorder and drive it into war, suffering, and oppression. And we can point it to the true remedy for its ills: faith in Jesus Christ.

INDEX